CHURCHILL AND ROOSEVELT AT WAR

Also by Keith Sainsbury

BRITISH FOREIGN SECRETARIES SINCE 1945 (*with A. Shlaim and P. M. Jones*)
THE NORTH AFRICAN LANDINGS: A Strategic Decision
THE TURNING POINT: The Moscow, Cairo and Teheran Conferences

Churchill and Roosevelt at War

The War They Fought and the Peace They Hoped to Make

Keith Sainsbury

'I've come here to try to find a way to be
a catalytic agent between two prima donnas'
Harry Hopkins, 1941

MACMILLAN

First published 1994 by
MACMILLAN PRESS LTD
Houndmills, Basingstoke, Hampshire RG21 6XS
and London
Companies and representatives
throughout the world

Reprinted (with alterations) 1996

ISBN 0–333–48042–2 hardcover
ISBN 0–333–48043–0 paperback

A catalogue record for this book is available
from the British Library.

10 9 8 7 6 5 4 3 2 1
05 04 03 02 01 00 99 98 97 96

Printed in Great Britain by
Antony Rowe Ltd
Chippenham, Wiltshire

To
Maurice and Dorothy Shock
Robert and Margaret Ladkin

Haec olim meminisse iuvabit

Contents

Preface to the 1996 Reprint

I have taken advantage of this reprint to make a few necessary corrections. Otherwise, the book remains as I wrote it. I take the opportunity of adding to paragraph 1 of the Introduction, the point that no one except Joseph Lash (to my knowledge) has written a book which focuses specifically on the Churchill – Roosevelt relationship as the *core theme* of the book. I thought it was time someone made the attempt.

K. S.
1996

Introduction

It is hardly necessary to justify another book about Churchill or Roosevelt, even though there has been a sudden surge of such books in recent years. When the canvas is so broad there are always areas which repay closer examination and the possibility of finding new perspectives. Since the British as well as other archives have now been open for some time there has not, naturally enough, been much new information in recent years. But available information and known facts can always be interpreted in an entirely fresh way, as at least one recent book on Churchill has shown. Indeed, if I may be permitted a slightly heretical observation, it is possible to attach even too much importance to new or unpublished facts and original documents. A source is none the less valid because it is widely available, and the worth of a document is dependent on many factors – the knowledge, accuracy and truthfulness of the writer for example. A minute, a contemporary letter or an entry in a diary are the product of partial and fallible human beings, just as much as subsequent memoirs are. Official minutes of meetings are often sanitized to obscure or soften differences of view, and sometimes omit remarks regarded as either damaging or inessential. Subsequent accounts by the participants often give a different picture from the official record. Memoranda and diary entries, too, are sometimes composed with half an eye on the future historian, as one suspects a number of Churchill's celebrated memoranda were. All this is not to say that documentary evidence is not extremely valuable, but that, like all other sources, it is not infallible evidence. Moreover, on the Second World War, so much has been divulged over the years by the participants that reading the documents is often more valuable for the purposes of checking and comparing the various accounts than for the discovery of totally new facts.

The book that follows does not attempt to be a biographical study, still less a history of the Second World War. At least one pioneer study of the two men, that of Joseph Lash, seemed to hover somewhat between the two, and consequently became bogged down in a welter of detail so that the relationship itself was obscured rather than illuminated, and after five hundred pages the author had only reached the year 1941! I have tried to avoid that pitfall. An attempt has been made here to focus on the relationship itself, and the contribution that relationship made to a number of key areas of wartime and post-war policy. It examines, that is to say, the contribution each man made, the degree to which they were able to forge a common policy, and the extent to which they were able to achieve their joint or separate aims. It seemed to the author that this was an area that would repay further study, and no doubt there will be much still to be added to it.

It has not been necessary in a work of this character to ask for assistance from the various bodies which generously provide it, but I have to thank Sir Maurice Shock, Dr Anne Deighton and Professor Geoffrey Warner for valuable comments and suggestions, and my daughter, Frances Seward, for improving the English in places. They are not, of course, responsible for any errors or imperfections in what follows. I should perhaps add that I deliberately refrained from reading the most recent studies until my text was finished: partly because I wanted to avoid being influenced by the conclusions of others, and also because I wished to avoid being sidetracked into commenting on, or controverting, recently expressed opinions. It may, of course, be thought that I am to some extent, like Dr Charmley, modifying the Churchill legend, though I did not set out to do so. A good friend of mine, in a review of a previous book, gently questioned my claim to 'let the records take me in the direction they seem to lead'. I can only say that one always tries to allow the facts to shape one's conclusions, rather than the other way round, as I suppose do all historians. Certainly, in some cases, the conclusions I have drawn are not entirely what I expected. I have been led in fact, in some areas, to be rather more critical of Churchill than I had foreseen. But I fancy that, where Dr Charmley has perhaps wielded a pick-axe, it will be conceded that I have only employed a chisel.

As one who lived through the Second World War, and was old enough to take a reasonably intelligent, though not very well-informed interest in events, I would not of course agree that one is thereby debarred from taking an objective view of Churchill, as has recently been suggested. The Churchill

legend is a powerful one, and has been lovingly tended by
Churchill himself in his memoirs. But it is not as potent as all
that. One advantage of first-hand knowledge and recollection
is, indeed, that one can remember how people felt at the time,
and the author's recollection is that the admiration felt by the
British people for Churchill as wartime leader fell well short of
idolatry. A substantial section of the British working people
still retained the image of Churchill in peacetime as a class
enemy. Many Conservatives still distrusted him as an
unreliable party man. These critical attitudes were reflected in
the Commons by Labour and Conservative 'independents',
such as Bevan, Shinwell, Hore-Belisha and Winterton. If one
wishes for further proof, although a 'party truce' was in
operation, various independent candidates won by-elections
against official government candidates during the war, and
Churchill himself and his party were massively defeated in
1945 (it is an error to suppose the vote was solely against the
Conservative Party, not against Churchill). Moreover, not too
long after the war, various eminent authorities, notably Lord
Alanbrooke, started to chip pieces off the statue, and no one
who has encountered any of the official British war historians
could imagine that their critical instincts suddenly ceased to
function when they encountered the Churchill legend.

A word on methodology is appropriate. I have adopted the
conventional method of identifying end-notes by numerals,
but I would hope readers will read straight through each
chapter, without stopping to look up each note. In a book of
this kind, which is essentially a work of discussion rather than
detailed scholarship, I have not thought it necessary to
include documentary references, though the book is based on
a fairly considerable acquaintance with British and US
documents. The books I have given as references are likely to
be more accessible to most readers than the documents in the
Public Record Office, and many of them do, of course, give
the documentary references, for those who are interested. I
have naturally made full use of Professor Warren Kimball's
comprehensive edition of the Churchill–Roosevelt correspondence, and its accompanying commentary. I disagree
with Professor Kimball on a few points, but he is always
instructive, and all historians of World War II are much
indebted to him.

I cannot end this Introduction without expressing my thanks to Bruce Hunter, of David Higham Associates, for his unvarying encouragement; to Macmillan for their extreme patience when illness held up this work; and above all to my wife, Mary, who typed painstakingly every word of the manuscript, and helped to improve it in the process.

Keith Sainsbury
Emmer Green, 1988–92.

1 Uneasy Partners:
The Roosevelt–Churchill Relationship

The wartime friendship between Franklin Roosevelt and Winston Churchill was not precisely all it seemed to be; nor was it totally a myth. It was one of those half-truths which played a valuable part in the conduct of the Second World War. From the point of view of usefulness to the allied cause it had some disadvantages, but more advantages. On the whole it was, as Eleanor Roosevelt described it, 'a fortunate friendship'.

One of the advantages was that each of the two men appealed to an important part of the other's constituency, which might otherwise have been disaffected. For each of the two leaders was deeply disliked by an important section of his own people. Roosevelt was regarded by the more reactionary members of the American industrial and financial community as a socialist and a traitor to his class; Churchill by most British trade unionists as an enemy of the workers. In both cases this was a misrepresentation and distortion of the truth, but once established such images are difficult to shake off. Ideas which people find comforting or convenient are clung to, as children cling to a favourite toy. Thus it was useful to the allied cause that Churchill's reputation as a staunch Conservative and foe of the trade unions appealed to Roosevelt's enemies, and Roosevelt's record as a radical and social reformer was attractive to Churchill's enemies. Between them, they spanned very nearly the whole range of political views.[1]

They were men of diverse attributes, but each of them had gone through the fire of testing experiences and been toughened by adversity. Churchill had experienced both great success and abysmal failure during a long political career – and was to know both again. Roosevelt for his part had been forced to struggle with the physical and psychological problems imposed by a crippling illness. Whether such an experience genuinely transforms character, or merely develops characteristics which were always latent, is of no great importance. It is the testimony of those who knew him both before and after his illness that Roosevelt was in many respects a different man afterwards – tougher, more determined, more patient, altogether more formidable, both personally and politically.[2]

Nearly 50 years after their partnership began, it is no new idea to say that Roosevelt and Churchill were in many respects an ill-assorted pair. The picture of Roosevelt, the liberal internationalist, trying to find common ground and create a common policy with the dyed-in-the-wool Tory imperialist, is a familiar one. Yet it is possible to exaggerate the difference in outlook, certainly in social philosophy. Churchill's 'liberal' period tends to be obscured and almost obliterated by the image of the wartime prime minister. It is easy to forget that for ten years (1905–15) he was a member of a great Liberal government, which laid the foundations of the Welfare State in Britain. Churchill himself was directly responsible for a number of progressive measures, personally supported a policy which sharply increased direct taxation and property taxes, and even advocated public ownership of the railways. In this phase of his career he had talked of 'the cause of the left-out millions', a phrase reminiscent of Roosevelt's 'forgotten man', and had said, 'I would give my life to see [the poor] placed on a right footing in regard to their means of living'.[3]

Subsequently the Russian Revolution had turned him sharply to the right and driven him back to the Conservative party. But even so, he was not unsympathetic to Roosevelt's New Deal, and as wartime prime minister supported a progressive measure on state education and encouraged new thinking on the problems of unemployment and social insurance. Later, as peacetime prime minister, he was to accept the consensual approach to politics advocated by men like R.A. Butler, a world away from the confrontational stance and reversal of long-standing British social policies adopted by Margaret Thatcher.

Unfortunately, it was not on domestic issues that he had to deal with Roosevelt, but imperial and world issues, and here they differed on almost every point. Whatever his views on British social policy, internationally Churchill was a convinced imperialist, a dedicated anti-Bolshevik and, towards the end of the war, profoundly fearful of the growing power of the Soviet Union. Roosevelt, however, pinned his hopes for the future on a Soviet–American entente, and looked to a world order in which Russia, and eventually China, would be as important – perhaps more important – than a British Empire which he foresaw would be in decline. Churchill thought the sole hope for the future lay in the continuance of a close Anglo-American alliance, buttressed by a rehabilitated France, and a Central European order in which a reconstructed Germany could play a respectable and necessary role. Roosevelt, on the other hand, doubted that France could ever again become a 'great power', and was, for most of the war, more intent on destroying Germany's war-making capacity for ever than rebuilding its economy.[4]

For Churchill, the British Empire, and to a lesser extent the French Empire, were forces for stability, order and, on the whole, justice over wide areas of the globe. In the nineteen-thirties he had resisted even a modest measure of self-government for India. It was not only that the British role as a world power depended on its control of a world empire: he also feared that instability and disorder might replace European rule in Africa and Asia, if it were withdrawn. He was not wholly wrong.

Roosevelt, *au contraire*, was by temperament and association a lifelong anti-imperialist, who equated the colonial peoples with the poor and exploited at home. In his early, formative years he had been unfavourably impressed by that aspect of British imperialism manifested in the Boer war. His Dutch name and ancestry – though truth to tell the latter was much diluted with French and Anglo-Saxon admixtures – probably made him the more sympathetic to the Boers. The liberal wing of the Democratic party, to which he had attached himself from his earliest beginnings in politics, regarded the European colonial empires as an instrument of oppression, contrary to all the principles of democracy, and as a part of the system of 'power politics' which was an important cause of war. These empires also constituted, as his subordinates Cordell Hull and Henry Morgenthau often reminded him, a means of economic exploitation. Further, they distorted the natural and more beneficial flow of commerce which international free trade would have promoted.

Just as the two men differed over France and Germany in Europe, so in Asia they differed over the wartime contribution and future role of China. Roosevelt attached great importance to the latter, and for a much of the war to the former also. Churchill and his Foreign Secretary, Eden, thought the President's estimate of China grossly exaggerated. Neither man, of course, foresaw that Chinese progress would be held back for the next half-century by the rigid grasp of Maoist Communism – like Stalinist Communism a particularly virulent form of what most people in the West, including many democratic socialists, regard as a disease, and many Marxist theorists as a perversion of the true doctrine.

In character and personality the two men had some points of similarity, but more differences. Both were combative, and loved a fight. Both had great vitality, confidence and determination, though Churchill's stamina was the greater. Roosevelt needed occasional intervals of rest and relaxation, when tiredness and staleness could be overcome by his remarkable powers of resilience. Churchill seldom felt the need for a holiday, though it has to be remembered that Roosevelt had already experienced seven gruelling years in office when the war began, during which Churchill, out of office, had fretted on the political sidelines. Roosevelt was an unquenchable optimist, confident that no problem was insoluble, and that he, Roosevelt, could provide the solutions. Churchill, however, had a vein of pessimism and a depressive streak which could only be kept in check by constant activity. Both men had a sense of history and of their own place in it, both had been involved in naval affairs and loved the sea – and both inherited certain standards of Victorian behaviour and manners.

Paradoxically, however, though Churchill was of aristocratic descent, Roosevelt was in some respects more the upper-class, public school, English gentleman. The Churchills, deriving as they did from a supreme adventurer and social climber – John Churchill, first Duke of Marlborough – were always liable to throw up a type best described by that old-fashioned but expressive term 'bounder'. Churchill's father, Lord Randolph, was such a type. Mixed with the aggressive Irish-American vitality of the Jeromes, this heredity produced in Winston Churchill 'a sport', a man who had little in common with other upper-class Englishmen. He cared little for the field sports beloved by his class, but greatly for literature and painting, for history and military affairs. Like that other 'bounder', General Montgomery, he had few social graces, took no pains to disguise his ambition and confidence in his own abilities, and had the professional's rather than the amateur's approach to his chosen profession. In a word he ignored most of the shibboleths of the English upper class.[5]

Roosevelt by contrast was the product of Groton, which had been modelled on an English public school. He had been brought up on a country estate by an elderly father and a possessive mother. He was descended from an old colonial family, had many of the traits of the upper-class Englishman, and clear ideas of how a gentleman should behave. He once said to his eldest son, on the subject of drink, 'a gentleman knows his capacity, and does not exceed it. I presume you are a gentleman'. Churchill, whose capacity was almost limitless, would not have thought of speaking to his son in these slightly pious terms. Essentially Roosevelt was the child of privilege. What Groton had begun, Harvard at the turn of the century had finished. It is revealing that Eleanor Roosevelt once said that her husband was more at ease in his off-duty moments with people 'of his own social class' than with hard-nosed political bosses like Jim Farley. Churchill for his part had all his life a predilection for rumbustious and slightly vulgar self-made men – the Birkenheads, Brackens, Beaverbrooks – and indeed David Lloyd George, whose lifelong friendship for Churchill may be contrasted with Roosevelt's uneasy relationship with Al Smith.[6]

As applied to government, their methods again had some points in common, but more differences. Churchill's experience of administration at the highest level was far wider than Roosevelt's. He had held almost every major office of state before becoming prime minister, including the navy, army and air-force ministries. Roosevelt's experience of central government, before his presidency, had been confined to the Navy Department. However his four years as Governor of New York had provided a respectable apprenticeship in administration, and the presidency had widened and deepened this experience and added foreign affairs and world strategy to the curriculum. In practice he was as well prepared as Churchill to deal with the gigantic problems of waging global warfare. Neither man was by conventional definition a good administrator. Churchill, however, preferred an orderly and structured administrative environment (though one adapted to his own peculiar hours of work), with clear lines of authority and responsibility. Roosevelt was noted for his preference for fluid and rather chaotic organizational patterns, which tended to preserve his freedom of action and, by creating conflict, ensured that the final decision on major matters would often have to be referred to him. In terms of ideas, Churchill was the more fertile. Roosevelt's intelligence was not, perhaps, primarily a creative one, but to compensate for this he was extremely receptive to new ideas and would take them from as wide a range of sources as possible – hence the celebrated 'Brains Trust'. Churchill, however, was inordinately fertile in ideas, which flowed from him in a steady stream, but less sure in judgement. His early mentor, Lloyd George, had remarked of him, 'there's Winston, now. He has ten ideas a day, but he does not know which is the right one'. In military matters, Churchill needed men like Generals Brooke and Ismay, and in political affairs the experience of Eden, Attlee, Anderson, to suppress the bad ideas, and tell him which was 'the right one'. Fortunately Churchill loved argument, and did not feel the need to surround himself with yes-men.[7]

A word must be said here about their relationships with their service advisers and their conduct of the war. Roosevelt began the war with a military adviser whom he trusted and respected, and who had the strength of character to tell him unpalatable truths: General George Marshall. Churchill, too, found, at the outset of the Anglo-American alliance, another such man in General Alan Brooke. It was very seldom that Roosevelt ignored Marshall's advice, or overruled it – though one such occasion, which will be examined later, was crucial. Similarly Churchill rarely ignored or overruled Brooke's considered opinion, however much he might goad, argue and prevaricate before giving way. In this they were alike, but not in their attitudes to the day-to-day running of the war. Roosevelt confined himself for the most part to matters of high policy, and rarely interfered in matters of detail. Churchill, on the other hand, sat constantly with the Chiefs of Staff, communicated directly with commanders in the field, and kept a firm hand through the Defence Committee on the running of the war. As Harry Hopkins put it, 'wherever Churchill is, you feel you are at the command post'.[8]

Whatever their merits as administrators, there is no doubt whatever that Roosevelt excelled Churchill in the arts of management. Roosevelt was warm, friendly, persuasive, had great charm, and seems to have been genuinely interested in people and what made them tick. Without that latter quality it is difficult to excel in man-management, and Churchill rather lacked it, except in relation to his family and a few close friends. He was interested in ideas, policies, events and actions rather than people. He was convinced that the closely reasoned argument, in speech or on paper, must eventually prevail; that the weight of evidence would in the end beat down opposition. To appeal to people's prejudices and peculiarities would have been difficult for him, since he could not be bothered to study them closely. On the contrary he could be, and often was, insensitive, tactless and inconsiderate, as well as arrogant and petulant. If those who worked with him came to respect and even to love him, it was in spite of these defects, and because he had other more endearing qualities – generosity of spirit, magnanimity, humour and at times an unexpected streak of humility. At bottom he was a simple and uncomplicated man, whose qualities could be assessed and then regarded as more or less predictable. But it is not at all surprising that many people, including many Americans, at first overawed and overwhelmed by his prestige and his oratory, eventually developed an immunity to his eloquence, and even began to find the interminable flow tedious and irritating.

Roosevelt, in fact, was a much more complicated man. Some of his associates, notably Dean Acheson, concluded that there was nothing to be found under that mercurial façade, no deeper personality beneath the surface: that he was, in short, a hollow man. In reality, he was infinitely various. There were many different Roosevelts, some less appealing than others. But to be multi-faceted is not necessarily to be shallow. Certainly he could be devious, though less often than is sometimes imagined. Anyone who seeks political skills, who wishes to manage men, must sometimes feel driven to courses which are not absolutely frank and open. It is only when it becomes a habit that censure is really merited. Part of his reputation for deviousness, indeed, derived from other facets of his character, not all of them blameworthy. He hated to sack people, hence sometimes found circuitous means of getting rid of them or diminishing their power. Particularly in the last years of his presidency, he could not always be bothered to argue with some proselytizing visitor, preferring to conserve his failing energies. Churchill loved argument and opposition; Roosevelt did not. Thus people sometimes left his office believing, wrongly, that they had converted him to their point of view. When the President subsequently took the opposite course they felt betrayed. Also he liked to try out notions, throw out ideas simply to 'test the water', to see their effect on others, then often discard them. This, too, led to accusations of inconsistency, if not deviousness.

Roosevelt certainly played his cards close to his chest, and was cautious, ever aware that politics is the art of the possible. His management of Congress and American public opinion between the fall of France and Pearl Harbor is often cited as a pre-eminent example of this caution and sensitivity to the nuances of public sentiment. When it is remembered that a key measure – the extension of Selective Service (conscription) – only passed the House of Representatives by one vote, it is difficult to blame him for this caution, this desire to appear to be following public opinion rather than leading it. Roosevelt had learned from bitter experience. In the mid-thirties he had burnt his fingers over an unsuccessful attempt to purge the Democratic party of recalcitrant senators, and the failure of his proposed Bill to 'pack' the Supreme Court with more amenable judges. Now, with great world issues hanging on the outcome, he was not going to make the same mistake.[9]

It is perhaps not surprising that it was Roosevelt's conduct of this very delicate and supremely important piece of political management that led to the most strident accusations of deviousness. Roosevelt had said that 'he would never send American boys to die in foreign wars'. This pledge had been given during the 1940 election, his critics argued, with the sole purpose of safeguarding himself against the dangerous charge of warmongering, at a time when public opinion was strongly opposed to US intervention. Yet the President had known full well at the time, it was said, that the US would have to become involved eventually – that this indeed was his object. Therefore he had deceived the American people for electoral advantage.

Yet this charge was not wholly fair. Roosevelt could not know for certain, in the autumn of 1940, that the US would have to become involved, however much he may have suspected it. At that time the European situation was still fluid. The part that Russia would ultimately play was still uncertain – and in fact Russia eventually became an ally, and not one that would go down like a ninepin before the German juggernaut, as so many predicted. There was also the distinct possibility that the whole of the French colonial empire might revert to the control of the Allies. Balkan possibilities still seemed more promising than they turned out to be. British military capacities had not been fully mobilized or fully tested, and in fact Wavell was about to launch two highly successful campaigns in Africa, one of which was to make the vast area of East Africa secure for the Allied cause. It yet remained to be seen how far British capacity could be increased by the generous supplies of material from a more fully mobilized US industry plus 'all aid short of war' in the Atlantic. Above all, no one could know for certain that Britain would be assailed by another opponent in the Pacific.

Later, of course, as 1941 wore on, it became increasingly evident to Roosevelt and others in his administration that ultimate US involvement was more likely than not, and might be inevitable. The very measures that were necessary to help Britain – especially the extension of US patrols further into the Atlantic – might eventually provoke Germany into a declaration of war. Yet Roosevelt could still argue that, faced already with two major opponents, Hitler might choose to ignore the provocation, and this in fact proved to be the case. In the end it was the Japanese who responded to provocation by attacking the US, dragging Germany into war with the US at its heels; and it is fair to remember that the purely economic measures directed at Japanese aggression had been, on the whole, supported by public opinion, and were not expected to provoke an attack. To sum up on the charge of 'deviousness': Roosevelt was probably not being deceptive when he told the American electorate in 1940 that he still hoped to keep the United States out of war. But, if he had been completely frank, he would have added that this could be no more than a hope, and he could not guarantee it. As it was, he gave, in his biographer's words, 'enormous hostages to the isolationists'. He did not exactly tell lies. But, as the novelist Jane Austen puts it, 'there might be some truths that were not told'.[10]

Churchill, more fortunate in this, never had to 'manage' public opinion, or the House of Commons, to any great extent. It was as well that this was so, since, as has been noted, this was not his forte. But when Churchill became prime minister, Britain was already at war.[11]

One should not make too much of it, but it was not unimportant in their relationship that Roosevelt, as head of state as well as government, outranked Churchill. The latter never forgot this, and preserved a certain deference in their public relations. In practical terms the greater degree of power which a British prime minister has over the legislature compensated for any formal difference in status. In the wartime political situation, in which the Labour and Liberal opposition parties formed part of the government, Churchill could always count on the overwhelming support of the House of Commons, even in the darkest moments of the war. The nature of the British political system also meant that a general election could be postponed until the end of the war, whereas Roosevelt had to fight one fiercely contested election under the shadow of war and another as it drew to a close. Again, too much should not be made of these differences. Roosevelt could still say that, in contrast with Churchill and Stalin, he alone was guaranteed by the constitution four years of supreme power. Equally there was a grain of truth in the remark once made by Roosevelt's friend and associate, Harry Hopkins, that the unwritten nature of the British Constitution enabled Churchill in practice to do or to get pretty well everything he wanted. Nor, for Roosevelt, was Congress the obstacle in wartime that it had been in peacetime. During his second term of office, Congress had certainly required a great deal of managing, had often been obstreperous and had more than once thwarted his most cherished plans. Once hostilities had begun, however, most senators and congressmen felt it unpatriotic to deny the President anything that he certified as necessary for the conduct of the war, especially when this certificate was supported by the much-respected Army Chief of Staff, General Marshall.

More important in the end, for the relationship between the two men, was the plain but unpalatable fact of British dependence on the United States, in the first instance for economic assistance, and more and more in the last phase of the war for the manpower and resources that only the United States could provide. Britain alone could not have defeated Germany, let alone Germany and Japan combined. So far as the economic picture was concerned, even before Pearl Harbor British overseas assets had largely been disposed of and her international financial reserves exhausted. There were no more dollars to purchase indispensable munitions from America. It is pointless to argue whether Lend-Lease was, as Churchill emotionally called it, an 'unsordid act', or whether, being in the long-term interests of US defence and security, it was ultimately self-interested. The more important truth is that without it Britain could not have continued the war. Similarly the manpower resources of Britain, even with the Empire, were not inexhaustible, and by 1944 were under great strain. For many reasons, the vast African and Asian manpower of the Empire could not be mobilized to more than a small extent (and many would now argue it would have been wrong to attempt more than this). The white population of the Empire, however, amounted to less than half that of the United States, and again, so far as Australasia, Canada and South Africa were concerned, could not be fully mobilized. For all these reasons, Churchill was aware, from the beginning of their relationship, how important it was for Britain that he should cultivate and conciliate Roosevelt. As far as in him lay, he disciplined himself to show uncharacteristic patience and restraint in his dealings with the President; but he lacked the personal sensitivity that would have enabled him in any real sense to 'manage' Roosevelt. In particular he never, it seems, sensed that his sustained assaults could weary and irritate the latter, especially in the last years of increasing frailty on Roosevelt's part. In so far as Churchill and his British associate were able to 'persuade' the President, it was essentially by providing the facts and figures, the weight of evidence, which convinced Roosevelt and his associates of certain necessities, rather than through Churchill's inherent persuasiveness. One who was, in fact, much more capable in these arts was Sir John Dill, the British military representative in Washington, whose tact, integrity and personal warmth enabled him to establish a genuine friendship with General Marshall. Dill could and sometimes did convince Marshall, and through Marshall the President, that the there was something in the British case, in matters where the overwhelming weight of evidence, and the necessities of the Alliance were not unequivocally on the British side of the argument. Hopkins, too, provided a valuable link. He got on well with Churchill, and shared certain characteristics with him – a love of good living, and a propensity to 'needle' associates in order to provoke them into fully justifying their case. Hopkins would never give an inch in presenting Roosevelt's case to Churchill; but he might subsequently, at the right moment, nudge the President into considering some of the points on the other side of the argument.[12]

Roosevelt, of course, for his part recognized that Britain was indispensable to the Allied war effort, and therefore it behoved him to establish a good relationship with Churchill. As with Stalin later, every such situation was a challenge to Roosevelt. Could he win over this curmudgeonly, died-in-the-wool old Tory? He set out to do so, and on the whole succeeded.

Roosevelt's idealism was genuine. His firm grasp of practical politics and the realities and limitations of international affairs, his occasional deviousness, did not affect the reality and sincerity of his ideals. He genuinely wanted an international order based on law and justice, which would provide peace and stability for the future. He wanted, too, to create an international economic order which would work better than the unstable system which had collapsed in ruins in the early 1930s. Certainly he had a firm understanding of the realities of power politics, and the need to make compromises over objectives, and even matters of principle, to gain the larger end. He was aware, too, of the need to preserve and increase American power, and to buttress it with a network of agreements and bases in areas vital to US security, such as the Pacific. He could not always see that this concern for US national interests was not so very different from the pursuit of national interests by Britain and other countries, which he and men like Cordell Hull were apt to condemn in lofty terms. But all this, he would have argued, was a matter of means rather than ends, and did not affect the fundamental long-term objective. It is right to call him an idealist, an idealist even a little naive in his optimism – for example about the prospects of long-term cooperation with Stalin's Russia. His critics in years to come had a point when they argued that there was an element of wishful thinking here. But it is always easy to be wise after the event, and it could equally be argued that, in seeing the USSR as the only possible partner in a future bi-polar partnership of two 'superpowers', Roosevelt was a supreme realist.[13]

Roosevelt, of course, was well aware that Churchill did not fully share his ideals and hopes, or in some cases was simply sceptical about the possibility of attaining them. It would be necessary therefore to nudge him along, using a judicious mixture of persuasion, inducement and pressure. In the last resort it might be advisable to lean on Churchill and the British, making use of the fact that Britain was dependent on the US in so many ways. Roosevelt did not shrink from this, if all else failed. Towards the end of the war, when Britain was almost at the end of its resources, and Churchill was very conscious of the need for American aid for post-war reconstruction, this became easier to do, as Roosevelt fully recognized. It is perhaps a slightly uncomfortable truth, but one that has to be acknowledged, that the United States emerged from the war if anything more prosperous, Britain less prosperous, and that Roosevelt was prepared to make use of this fact.

What kind of relationship then was it that emerged from this complex of personal characteristics and attitudes, of mutual needs and obligations? Certainly they admired and appreciated each other's qualities, recognizing that each was in many ways a supreme professional in his own field. Churchill's liking for Roosevelt was probably greater and more unreserved than Roosevelt's for Churchill. Certainly Churchill was more generous in his comments on his partner. A roman-tic by nature, he tended to romanticize the relationship. In his post-war memoirs he continued to present a somewhat rosy view, softening the harder outlines of the partnership; though here there was an element of policy in the picture presented. In the early years of the cold war, during which most of the volumes appeared, it was important that nothing he said should 'rock the boat' of Anglo-American relations. He was grateful, too, to Roosevelt, recognizing that the latter had steeled himself to undertake an enormously difficult task of

political management during 1939–41, and that the very
survival of Britain had depended on this. Much could be
forgiven to one who had done so much. At times he was
irritated, it is true, by Roosevelt's brash self-confidence,
especially about European or imperial issues where he felt the
President was often not specially well-informed. He was hurt,
too, when on occasion, especially towards the end of the war,
Roosevelt seemed to slight or snub him – and he did not
appreciate the latter's high-school teasing. There were notable
occasions before the Teheran and Yalta conferences when
Roosevelt deliberately avoided a meeting with Churchill in
advance of the proposed meeting with Stalin. This was hurtful.
At the Quebec Conference of 1944 Roosevelt seemed to keep
Churchill in suspense over his plans for post-war economic
assistance, which Churchill found humiliating. But these were
pinpricks, and overall Churchill seems to have felt to the end
that Roosevelt was a friend. He was in general frank and
unreserved in his dealings with the President, and expected
similar frankness from Roosevelt, though he did not always get
it. He would have been shocked, one feels, if he had known at
the time the suspicions of his actions, sometimes quite
unjustified, which Roosevelt was confiding to his advisers.

Roosevelt's attitudes to his partner were more mixed.
Admiration of his courage and abilities, yes, appreciation of his
humour, his erudition and his quirks and foibles certainly, but
there were reservations. The President was always worried by
what he saw as Churchill's rigid and out-dated imperialism and
uncompromising anti-communism, with the impact these views
might have on relations with Russia and China (where Chiang
Kai-shek was notably suspicious of British imperial intentions).
Whatever Churchill proposed, Roosevelt suspected him of
pursuing British interests – and worse, British imperial interests
– as much as the speedy winning of the war. This suspicion
poisoned the debate over both cross-Channel versus Mediterranean strategy, and over Far-Eastern strategy: and influenced
Roosevelt's judgement on political issues as well. If Britain
proposed a pact forbidding 'spheres of influences' in the
Balkans this was somehow a ploy to ensure the primacy of
British influence in that area. If the British preferred the US to
have an occupation zone in southern Germany rather than
northern Germany, that was somehow designed to involve the

United States more deeply in the problems of France and Central Europe. Roosevelt too could be irritated, like others, by Churchill's obstinacy and pertinacity in argument; and annoyed by what sometimes seemed the wearisome necessity of dragging him every step of the way. In an unusual outburst, he once complained, 'Yes, I'm tired – and so would you be if you'd spent five years pushing Winston uphill in a wheelbarrow!' It has even been suggested that there was an element of jealousy of Churchill's achievements and oratorical powers in Roosevelt's attitude, though this would seem strange in view of the latter's own achievements, not to mention the fact that as president of the richest and most powerful country in the world, he wielded incomparably the greater clout. But both, of course, were prima donnas.

For many reasons the partnership was at its best in the earlier years of the war, and deteriorated towards the end. In the early years the threat of irretrievable catastrophe and the pressing need for unity drove them together. Churchill's urgent need for American assistance was matched by Roosevelt's perception of the equally urgent need to keep Britain fighting. They could not afford to quarrel. Then, too, before American resources were fully mobilized (which was not until the end of 1942) Britain could claim to be matching the US contribution to the war effort, and could fairly be conceded the rights of an equal partner. After 1943, as the British resources more and more came under strain, and post-war problems loomed, it seemed to Roosevelt and the Americans more important to cultivate and conciliate Stalin and Russia than to satisfy Churchill and the British. Britain, it was felt, was now definitely the junior partner and should agree to American proposals without too much argument. There was a revealing moment at the Teheran Conference, when Roosevelt called for the figures of the US manpower contribution to the war effort – a move clearly designed to spell out the brute facts of the matter to Churchill. And when Churchill suggested that landing-craft might be diverted from the Pacific to other operations which he favoured, Roosevelt sharply replied that none were available. Landing-craft were, of course, largely US produced and under US control.

Over and above the shifting balance of power between the two, and the rise of formidable rival for Roosevelt's attentions, there was the simple fact that both men were increasingly worn down by the years of gruelling effort and endeavour. Increasingly they were ailing, and their patience and tempers were on a shorter fuse. It is not surprising that they found it more difficult to refrain from bickering.

There is a case for the view that Churchill, for all his great qualities, was possibly not the ideal person to work with Roosevelt or to represent Britain to America. His ultra-conservative views on imperial and international issues gave Americans a slightly distorted view of majority British opinion, which was sometimes to Britain's disadvantage: and his pertinacity and obstinacy in argument were sometimes ill-judged, so that even close colleagues and friends regarded it as counterproductive. Yet it must be questioned whether any other British politician would have had the prestige, force and stature to make the impression Churchill did on US leaders and the US public alike, especially in the crucial early days of the Alliance.

How this complex and shifting relationship influenced allied dealings on a number of key wartime issues is the theme of the remaining chapters of this book. But perhaps in the end the old adage 'there is no friendship at the top', must be held to apply to the Roosevelt–Churchill partnership: or maybe the truth lies somewhere between this bleak judgement and Mrs Roosevelt's 'it was a fortunate friendship'.

2 Grand Strategy I: The Second Front – Where, When and How?

The 'High Noon' of the Roosevelt–Churchill relationship was undoubtedly the period between Pearl Harbor, in December 1941, and the summer of 1943. Nowhere is this more evident than in the discussions and decisions reached on Grand Strategy. During this period the strategic ideas of the two men coincided. This is probably a more accurate statement of the case than to say that Churchill was able to persuade Roosevelt to see things his way. Much though many Americans feared Churchill's persuasive powers where Roosevelt was concerned, these fears were probably misplaced. No one could question Churchill's eloquence, on strategic as on other matters, but eloquence is not necessarily persuasiveness. Probably it had less effect on Roosevelt's strategic decision-making than is commonly supposed. In the early stages of the Alliance, however, whatever the reason, Churchill's views largely seemed to prevail. From December 1941 until the Quebec Conference in the summer of 1943, Anglo-American strategy in Europe was in effect British strategy. But it was also, in the last resort, Roosevelt's strategy – though not that of his advisers. Churchill (and the British Chiefs of Staff) therefore got what they wanted. It was to prove in some ways a Pyrrhic victory, which was to exact a certain price from Britain and the British people.

The British view of Grand Strategy in 1941–2 boiled down to two fairly simple principles. Firstly, Germany should be regarded as the prime enemy, and allied efforts be concentrated on Europe first, leaving the defeat of Japan to be accomplished subsequently. The defeat of Germany, it was argued – quite validly – would mean the inevitable defeat of Japan. The converse was not true. Secondly, the British argued that while the continent of Europe would have to be assaulted eventually, the approach to this objective should be a cautious one. First of all North Africa should be cleared, the Middle

17

East safeguarded, the Mediterranean reopened to allied
convoys. This would not only be valuable in itself, but would
also expose Axis-controlled Europe to attack from the south as
well as the west, and therefore make it easier to keep the
enemy guessing as to where the blow would fall. It would have
the additional advantage of 'blooding' inexperienced allied
troops and allied generals in the most favourable
circumstances, before they tackled the formidable German
army behind its array of prepared defences – the 'Atlantic
Wall'. There is no doubt that Roosevelt could see the force of
these arguments.[1]

On the first grand principle – 'Germany First' – there was in
fact no need for persuasion, either of Roosevelt, or of the US
Chiefs of Staff, consisting in this early period of General
Marshall and Admiral Stark. Long before Pearl Harbor, US
strategic thinking had accepted this principle, and embodied
it in the appreciations code-named Rainbow 5 and Plan Dog.
These appreciations had been discussed with the British
military representatives in secret talks as early as January 1941;
the principle was restated in discussions at the first
Washington Conference between the British and Americans,
just after Pearl Harbor.[2]

The fact that military talks had taken place at all while the
US was still neutral, though these talks were necessarily secret
and informal, is an indication of how far Anglo-American
cooperation had already progressed before December 1941.
The Roosevelt-Churchill correspondence, of course, began
even earlier. From the moment Churchill went to the
Admiralty at the outbreak of war, Roosevelt had encouraged
him to correspond directly, recalling the fact that both men
had been associated with the conduct of naval affairs during
the First World War. When Churchill became Prime Minister,
in May 1940, the correspondence became much more
frequent and intimate. During the next eighteen months, if
the United States was theoretically neutral, it was neutrality of
a very positive kind, as Roosevelt edged, by successive stages,
closer and closer to active involvement in the war. How far was
this in response to Churchill's persuasive appeals? Certainly
from May 1940 onwards, Churchill increasingly bombarded
the President with requests, importunities, demands – for
destroyers, for munitions, for economic assistance as British

currency reserves ran out, for US naval patrols to be extended, US participation in convoy escorts and above all for US entry into the war. In so far as these requests were ultimately met with action, it could be argued Churchill's persuasions were successful. Yet it might be doubted if Roosevelt needed to be persuaded on the central point – that it was in the vital interests of the United States that Britain should be enabled to continue fighting, and therefore that the US should take whatever steps were necessary – to the extent that Congress and US public opinion permitted – to this end. Churchill's contribution then – an important one – was to supply some of the arguments which Roosevelt could use with his own Cabinet, with selected members of Congress, and in the broader task of educating US public opinion. With each request, Roosevelt considered the urgency of the situation, weighed the possibilities of action, and, in his own time, responded with some positive step: and so, successively, 50 destroyers were handed over in exchange for US bases in the West Indies, the Lend-Lease Bill was put through against considerable opposition, US troops sent to Iceland, Atlantic patrols extended, and the US Navy encouraged to adopt a more aggressive attitude towards German submarine warfare. Military cooperation went a good deal further than simply the supply of equipment. When Catalina aircraft were sent to assist the British naval-air effort, selected US pilots went with them to train British pilots. So it came about that in May 1941 the co-pilot of the Catalina which sighted the *Bismarck* after it had been lost was an American naval officer.

In accordance, therefore, with the accepted thinking that all efforts should be concentrated on the defeat of Germany, the most overtly provocative American acts were in the Atlantic. Yet paradoxically US economic pressure on Japan was in the end to prove more provocative, and to constitute the catalyst which precipitated the US into World War II. After Pearl Harbor, however, the sense of outrage felt by the US public would, the British feared, constitute an immediate threat to the principle of 'Germany First'. It was therefore with a sense of relief that the British representatives arriving for the First Washington Conference in December 1942, discovered that the US Chiefs of Staff were still firmly committed to giving priority to Atlantic and European operations. The principle was reaffirmed and, in theory at least, held the field for the rest of the war. Two threats to this principle were soon to present themselves, however. One took tangible form in the shape of the formidable Admiral Ernest King, soon to become US Chief of Naval Operations, and hence director of US Naval strategy. The other, less apparent, but in the end equally insidious, was Churchill's and the British Chiefs' very success in gaining the victory, in the strategic argument, for North Africa and Mediterranean operations.[3]

STRATEGIC CROSS PURPOSES

On the North African question, Roosevelt had early given signs of sympathy with Churchill. It is probably not unimportant that Roosevelt at the outset of the war clearly felt a greater rapport with the US naval Chief of Staff and with the thinking of the US Navy Department, than he did with the Army Chief of Staff and the War Department. For this, no doubt, Roosevelt's naval background was partly responsible. Also he found the Chief of Naval Operations, Admiral Stark, more approachable than the austere General Marshall, one of the few people Roosevelt did not venture to address by his first name.

Whatever the reason, the US Navy Department's concern after the fall of France about the possible danger of German air, naval and submarine bases in north-west Africa, and the importance of the Mediterranean in the allied war effort, found an echo in Roosevelt's thinking. In October and November of 1940 there had been considerable discussion of the danger of US security resulting from a possible handover of the French bases at Dakar, Oran and Bizerta to Axis control. Churchill had raised the subject in his correspondence. The US Navy Secretary, Colonel Frank Knox, had floated the possibility, in the extreme case, of a possible US occupation of Dakar. A little earlier a US Army-Navy memorandum had stressed the Mediterranean as well as the Atlantic as part of the European theatre; and North Africa as an alternative theatre of action to Europe. This clearly reflected US naval thinking. It was no accident that a little later Roosevelt, during a conversation with the British Deputy Premier, Attlee, placed his finger on Algiers and said 'this is where I would like to have US troops'. Later, in May 1941, there was some discussion of an American or joint Anglo-American descent on the Portugese Atlantic island group, the Azores, and at the same time Roosevelt expressed an interest in Tangier.

If Roosevelt and the Navy Department, however, had ideas about North Africa, one man did not share these opinions. General Marshall, while fully supporting the principle of 'Germany First', had from the beginning believed in the strategy of the single direct thrust, with overwhelming force, against the heart of Germany – in other words, across the Channel, through France and the Low Countries, into the Ruhr. Indeed, noting that dangerous ideas about North Africa and the Mediterranean had crept into appreciations such as Plan Dog, Marshall had early sounded a note of warning about the danger of dispersing US strength in a multiplicity of operations. It was this latter approach to the problem of defeating Germany that US War Department thinking was to categorize as the 'peripheral' or 'dispersionist' approach, an approach that Marshall and the US War Secretary Henry Stimson most wished to avoid. Thus the United States Chiefs approached the first Anglo-American war conference in Washington with divided counsels. It was partly for this reason, and partly because of Roosevelt's innate sympathy with the idea of North African operations, that British ideas on strategy were to prevail at that conference. The consequence, however, was to be a period of strategic disagreements and misunderstandings which was to last until August 1942, and not to be fully resolved even then. The disagreement over the question of North Africa versus north-west Europe was further compounded by a difference of viewpoint. The US – that is to say primarily the US Navy – looked at North Africa with an Atlantic perspective, conscious of the threat to US sea communications with Europe and Latin America. The British, on the other hand, were equally alive to the importance of Mediterranean communications with the Middle East and India. This difference of approach, reinforced by Marshall's desire not to be drawn into committing large number of US troops to Mediterranean operations, was to surface later on in disagreements over precisely where in North Africa Allied landings were to take place – an argument Roosevelt himself was obliged to settle in the end.[4]

At the Washington Conference Marshall was preoccupied with the question of organizing the Allied war machine at the highest level, through the creation of Combined (British-American) Chiefs of Staff; and also with the establishment of the principle of one Supreme Allied Commander, over all arms and all nationalities, for every Anglo-American operation. Because of this he allowed Churchill's strategy – with Roosevelt's agreement – to prevail. At the conclusion of the conference the US chiefs accepted a joint agreement to the effect that 'in 1942 the main object will be to strengthen the ring (round Germany) by sustaining the Russian front, by arming and supporting Turkey, by increasing our strength in the Middle East, and by gaining possession of the whole North African coast... *It does not seem likely that in 1942 any large-scale land offensive against Germany...will be possible.* In 1943 the way *may* be clear for a return to the Continent, across the Mediterranean, from Turkey into the Balkans, or by landings in Western Europe'(Author's italics).

There could hardly have been a clearer commitment to Gymnast (the putative code-name for the North African operation) as having priority in 1942 over European operations. Even for 1943, operations 'across the Mediterranean' were put ahead of 'landings in Western Europe'. Roosevelt, at least, was clearly 'sold' on Gymnast. It was otherwise with Marshall and Stimson, when they turned their minds fully to the implications of what had been agreed. The point is worth making, because some valid criticism has been made of the apparent acceptance by the British, three months later, of Marshall's counter-proposal for a limited (and possibly suicidal) landing in France in 1942 (Sledgehammer), followed by a major offensive in Europe in 1943 (Round-Up). There is some justice in the criticism that the British, including Churchill, appeared to agree to the US Sledgehammer/ Round-Up programme, while in fact having grave reservations about it, and that they later went back on this agreement. But the point is sometimes overlooked that Marshall and the US chiefs were likewise reneging in April, on a commitment to Gymnast made only three months earlier.[5]

One can readily see how the American volte-face came about. Apart from the fact that Marshall had been preoccupied with other matters at the January conference, he no doubt assumed that all strategic decisions made at that early stage would necessarily be provisional, and liable to be swept away by the urgent necessities of stemming the Japanese tide in the Pacific, and propping up the Russian front with generous supplies of munitions. So it proved. By 4 March 1942 Churchill was already cabling to Roosevelt that Gymnast was 'out of the question' for several months. Roosevelt could not but agree. Taking advantage of the favourable moment, Marshall and Stimson persuaded Roosevelt to put to Churchill a fresh proposal for a 'new front' in 1942, in the shape of a landing in north-west France – even if it took the form only of a temporary lodgement. US public opinion, they pointed out, was clamouring for an operation in Europe which would effectively aid Russia. Otherwise, the pressure to give the Pacific priority might prove overwhelming. Churchill's first reactions were, not surprisingly, ambiguous. On 12 April he cabled Roosevelt that, 'while agreeing in principle with all you propose, we must of course meet day to day emergencies in the east and far east (i.e. hold the Middle East, and prevent a junction between Japan and Germany through a successful Japanese invasion of India'). Later, after apparently accepting the US proposals for Sledgehammer and Round-Up at a London conference with Marshall and Harry Hopkins, Churchill wrote to FDR on 17 April reiterating that a proportion of our combined resources must, for the moment, be set aside to halt the Japanese advance'. He stressed, too, that Sledgehammer was 'fraught with grave risks'. The truth is, of course, that Churchill and the British Chiefs had very considerable reservations about Sledgehammer, and Churchill at least had doubts also about Round-Up; but they hesitated to express these openly, lest the American Chiefs, denied the European strategy they wanted, should decide to concentrate on the Pacific. Churchill and his advisers therefore preferred to wait until the inexorable logic of a rigorous examination of Sledgehammer should demonstrate (as they fully expected it would) that the operation was not feasible. It was not until 28 May that Churchill felt able to suggest to Roosevelt that he should send Admiral Mountbatten to Washington to prepare the ground for a further Anglo-American conference, adding significantly 'Dickie will explain to you the difficulties of 1942' (i.e. Sledgehammer). At this moment, however, Roosevelt had just committed himself unequivocally to a Second Front in 1942, in discussions with Soviet Foreign Minister Molotov. Molotov was on a visit to Washington, having previously visited London. He had not hesitated to stress the desperate nature of the Soviet position on the Eastern Front, and to make the Americans' flesh creep with the possibility of a total Russian collapse. Notwithstanding Roosevelt's knowledge that the British had been much more cautious in their assurances to Molotov, the President had felt bound to promise a 'Second Front in 1942', in language more explicit than even Marshall had wished. Not surprisingly, Roosevelt's first reaction to the proposed Mountbatten visit, and to Churchill's rider 'we must keep "Gymnast" in mind', was to cable Churchill on 31 May that he was 'anxious for Sledgehammer to proceed to definite action in 1942'. Nevertheless he was influenced by the obvious evidence that the British were lukewarm on Sledgehammer but clearly still keen on Gymnast. Churchill, in fact, had chosen his emissary well. Mountbatten was the one British military leader whom the Americans did not suspect of being over-infected with caution, as a result of Britain's repeated military reverses. By this stage of the war his reputation for daring, one might say recklessness, was well-established. It was not for nothing that a naval colleague had said of him, 'there is no one I would rather have with me in a tight corner than Dickie Mountbatten – and no one who would get me into one sooner'. Marshall and his colleagues respected Mountbatten. They could not dismiss him, as they might have dismissed another British service chief as 'over-cautious'.

Roosevelt for his past was disposed to be receptive to Mountbatten, whom he insisted on seeing alone, without the US Chiefs' presence, much to the latter's annoyance. Mountbatten presented Churchill's and the British Chiefs' case forcefully. Neither the troops nor the landing-craft were available to make a landing on the French coast in 1942 powerful enough to draw off German troops from the Russian front. The US contribution, he pointed out, would at this stage be minimal – at most three and half divisions; the British quota perhaps seven to ten divisions. German forces already in France could contain such a landing and probably destroy it. If that argument were accepted, and Sledgehammer ruled out, there remained for 1942 only the options of (1) continuing the build-up of US troops in Britain for Round-Up in 1943; (2) reinforcing Britain in the Middle East with US troops; or (3) some operation elsewhere than in Europe – i.e. Gymnast, or possibly Jupiter (an attack on Norway also favoured by Churchill). The first was ruled out by Roosevelt's promise to Molotov of 'a Second Front in 1942'. The second was open to the same objection and, since it would have meant placing the few US divisions which were combat-ready under British command, was anathema to Marshall. If that seems ungenerous, it must be remembered that the record of British generalship during the first two and a half years of the war had not been exactly a successful one. That left Gymnast (or perhaps Jupiter).[6]

Marshall and Stimson were therefore disgusted to find, during the second Washington conference with the British in June 1942, that the President was already wavering. They had bulldozed Roosevelt into supporting Sledgehammer in April, but that had not altered his long-held attraction to the idea of North African and Mediterranean operations. Even during the March–April discussions, Stimson had been worried by the President's hankering after Mediterranean operations – the wildest kind of 'dispersion debauch' according to Stimson's (and Marshall's) way of thinking. It should not have surprised them, therefore, when Roosevelt, in discussions with his advisers immediately before Churchill's arrival for the conference, suddenly reverted to the case for Gymnast as an alternative way of taking the pressure off Russia. Nor that in the discussions with the British, the President again mentioned the possibility of sending US troops to the Middle East. Indeed, if the British Chiefs had pressed the case for Gymnast wholeheartedly, the conference might have resulted in a firm decision for Gymnast rather than Sledgehammer. But the British chiefs were not totally at one with Churchill at this point. Shocked by yet another massive British defeat at Tobruk while the conference was actually in progress, General Brooke was inclined to backtrack from the idea of *any* fresh operation in 1942. Roosevelt, therefore, allowed the conference to end inconclusively, contenting himself with reiterating that US troops *must* engage German troops in 1942. But one important point had been made. The two other US Chiefs of Staff, Admiral King and General Arnold, had conceded that from the air and naval point of view Gymnast was feasible. Marshall was, then, increasingly isolated from his colleagues. No doubt King was influenced by the thought that Gymnast would present less of a threat to the Pacific operations on which he had set his heart than Sledgehammer/Round-Up. It would be easier to argue that Gymnast was a British operation, so let the British get on with it. If that was Admiral King's thinking, it was percipient.[7]

THE DEMISE OF SLEDGEHAMMER: GYMNAST REVIVED

Once back in Britain, Churchill continued to keep up the pressure. Finally, on 8 July and again on the 14th, he told Roosevelt that the British Chiefs, after months of discussion, could find no feasible plan of operations for a successful Sledgehammer. Roosevelt's reaction – hardly a surprised reaction, one would imagine – was to send Marshall yet again to London, with Admiral King, to reach a final agreement with the British on the 1942 programme. His instructions were quite clear. American troops *must* be brought into action against the Germans somewhere in 1942. The options amounted to one of three things. Marshall could despatch US troops to the Middle East, accept Churchill's other suggestion of an attack on Norway, or agree to Gymnast. Marshall agreed with the British Chiefs that the Norwegian idea had little to recommend it. Taking into account the British attitude to Sledgehammer, Marshall's determination not to put US troops under British command and Roosevelt's clear directive, the result of the talks was a foregone conclusion. On 24 July 1942 the US Chiefs accepted that Gymnast (now renamed Torch) should be undertaken in 1942. Only the day before, Roosevelt had cabled that he definitely favoured the North African operation. The US Chiefs really had no choice. The decision had in fact been inevitable ever since Roosevelt had fobbed off a last attempt by Marshall and Stimson on 15 July to rescue Sledgehammer. With the agreement of his colleagues, Marshall tried to get the President to threaten that, if the British turned down Sledgehammer, the US would concentrate on the Pacific war. Roosevelt, in reply, had simply reiterated his commitment to the strategy of 'Germany First', and in his turn, in effect, threatened Marshall that, if he would not agree to Gymnast, US troops would be dispatched to the Middle East. Marshall accepted defeat – Roosevelt had called his bluff – and capitulated. The President was, after all, his commander-in-chief.

To Marshall it was clearly a disastrous outcome. It was probably not so much the abandonment of Sledgehammer that worried him. Although Marshall maintained to the end of his life that Sledgehammer was a feasible operation of war, and should have been carried out, he tended to forget that the original agreement for the operation had been hedged around with conditions. It was only to be undertaken in the event of two contingencies – either if Germany seemed to be crumbling, or if a Russian collapse seemed imminent. The first contingency never seemed likely in 1942, and by the time Sledgehammer could have been launched the second contingency also seemed to have been averted. A possible outcome, then, of adherence to the Sledgehammer/Round-Up programme would have been that there would have been *no* major Anglo-American operation in 1942, but a steady build-up for a powerful invasion of France in 1943, which would have stood a reasonable chance of success. From a purely military point of view this would probably have seemed not a bad outcome to Marshall. He had always known that it would take eighteen months from Pearl Harbor to muster and train a powerful US army. The fatal thing was not so much that there should be no Sledgehammer, but that there *should* be operations elsewhere, i.e. North Africa. For Marshall feared very much that Torch would not merely rule out a cross-Channel attack in 1942, but also gravely prejudice one in 1943. In this he was proved right, though ironically it was he himself who was to contribute as much as anyone to this result.[8]

As for Roosevelt, it was perhaps reflecting on the Sledgehammer scenario, and its limiting conditions, which in the end led him back to Gymnast as the only likely means of redeeming his pledge to Molotov. Indeed, the more the sequence of events is considered, the more probable it seems that Roosevelt never really abandoned his personal hankering after Gymnast, and was not sorry when the logic of events drove them all back to the North African option. If that be so, it would be wrong to say that the period between April and July 1942 saw the first major strategic disagreement between Roosevelt and Churchill, and that Churchill eventually persuaded Roosevelt to accept his view. The disagreement was in fact between Churchill and the British Chiefs on the one hand, and Marshall, Stimson and the US War Department on the other; and the controversy was resolved, not by any subtle or persuasive Churchillian arguments, but by the British *non possumus*. Effectively, the British vetoed Sledgehammer, and Roosevelt for his part accepted, perhaps without too much reluctance, this veto.

Roosevelt and Churchill, therefore, between them decided on the North African strategy, Churchill by vetoing Sledgehammer, and Roosevelt by insisting on a major Anglo-American operation in 1942. It was one of the few occasions during the war when Roosevelt overruled Marshall. It seemed to the latter a doubly disastrous decision, since it not only threatened to prejudice Round-Up in 1943, but also made it likely that US troops would be drawn into further Mediterranean operations following Torch. Both these fears proved justified. Yet, if Roosevelt and Churchill were principally responsible for these long-term consequences, Marshall himself played a part in making them inevitable. Having been prepared to take great risks with Sledgehammer, an operation in which he believed, he became ultra-cautious when it came to Torch, an operation in which he had little faith. The consequence of this caution was that a disproportionate weight of the attack was directed at the north-west African coast (the Casablanca landings), and too little inside the Mediterranean itself. Furthermore, landings inside the Mediterranean were not made as far east as they should have been, if they were to ensure a rapid advance on Tunis. Churchill, supported usually, though not always, by his Chiefs of Staff, had to fight hard for landings even as far east as Algiers. There were, of course, practical reasons for Marshall's caution – it was not merely due to his prejudice against involving any more US troops than he had to within the Mediterranean. In particular, there was the fear that the Germans might react to a North African operation by entering Spain, taking Gibraltar and threatening, or indeed cutting off, Allied naval communications through the Straits. The prospect of a substantial number of US troops being virtually cut off inside the Mediterranean was naturally worrying to Marshall. The British view, on the other hand, was that Spain would remain neutral, and that the Germans would react, not by undertaking a politically undesirable operation in Spain, but by sending a sufficient force across the narrow channel between Sicily and the African coast, to take Tunis and Bizerta before the Allies could get there. So it proved; but Marshall's fears were not unreasonable.

A DUBIOUS VICTORY

Churchill, arguing that the only worthwhile strategic objective of the operation was control of the entire Mediterranean coast, and a link-up with British forces in the Middle East, got his way in the end – up to a point – partly because Eisenhower, the US commander for the operation, was inclined to support him. The British arguments made strategic sense, and Roosevelt could see the force of them. After Churchill had twice appealed to Roosevelt in August, the latter directed Admiral King to provide additional US transports and escorts, which, with the powerful British naval forces, would make landings possible at Algiers as well as Oran and Casablanca. But two-thirds of the Allied forces were still to be concentrated on the two western ports, hundreds of miles from Tunis; and there were to be no landings east of Algiers, at Philippeville and Bône, as the British had hoped. The effect of this limitation was that the Allied forces immediately available for a push on Tunis and Bizerta, before the Germans could occupy them with sufficient force, were inadequate for the task. Taking considerable risks, Anderson's British First Army came very close to its objective. Three weeks after the landings, in fact, they were between 15 and 20 miles from Tunis and Bizerta. But then a combination of organizational difficulties, winter rains and long, inadequate supply lines, plus the increasing weight of the German forces, compelled a pause. From that moment the Germans, with their shorter supply lines, had the advantage. It was to require a six-month campaign, and the arrival of the Eighth Army from Egypt and Libya, before Tunis and Bizerta could be taken, and the North African coast

cleared of Axis troops. It could be argued, therefore, that it was
Marshall's caution, as much as the original decision for North
Africa, which finally ruled out a cross-Channel attack in 1943.
Perhaps that operation would still have been possible if the
North African campaign had been wound up before Christmas
1942, as Churchill for one may have hoped. By May 1943,
however, it was far too late to relocate the battle-hardened
troops and landing-craft necessary for the first assault, and to
resume the build-up of US troops in the United Kingdom. For
that 'build-up' had been irretrievably weakened between the
autumn of 1942 and the spring of 1943.[9]

That this was so was partly due to the pressure exerted by
Admiral King, but a least as much to Marshall's conclusion
that the decision for Torch committed the Western Allies to a
'defensive, encircling strategy for 1943', and so ruled out
Round-Up in 1943. If the arguments set forth above are
accepted, this was a prophecy which Marshall himself, by his
caution on the eastern landings for Torch, had helped to
make self-fulfilling. Be that as it may, from September 1942
onwards Marshall ceased to fight as vigorously as he had
previously for the concepts of 'Germany First' and priority for
European operations. Admiral King was allowed to siphon off
men and materials, including the lion's share of the vital
landing-craft essential to Round-Up, and to enlarge the
concept of 'strategic defensive' operations against Japan, to
the point were it suspiciously resembled a 'strategic offensive'
strategy. Correspondingly the flow of troops and supplies to
the UK (Bolero) slowed down to a trickle. By the autumn the
US Chiefs of Staff were calculating that even by the spring of
1943 there would still be no more than half-a-dozen combat-
ready US divisions in the UK, compared with the estimated
figure of *twenty-seven* required for Round-Up. Marshall's
attitude in this matter was in marked contrast to the vigour
with which he and Stimson had earlier resisted pressure from
General MacArthur for further troops to be allocated to his
South-West Pacific Command; and by it, no less than by his
attitude on the Torch landings, Marshall was helping to make
his prophecy of 'no cross-Channel attack in 1943' come true.
Yet Marshall was not wholly consistent. In December, after the
Torch landings had taken place, he was still saying to his
friend General Dill that he preferred even a small-scale

Round-Up to further Mediterranean operations in 1943. But one is inclined to wonder whether this was prompted more by a desperate desire to stave off further Mediterranean operations, than by a genuine belief that an effective cross-Channel operation was still possible in 1943.[10]

Churchill, for his part, was at first unwilling to accept that there could be no Round-Up in 1943, though he was, as always, quite ready to substitute some other operation if necessary. On the one hand he was saying to the British Chiefs in November '42. 'I am still aiming at Round-Up in August'; but he had already written to Roosevelt in terms that suggested a major operation against Norway or Italy would do just as well. Whether the campaign in North Africa was over by December 1942, as he at first hoped, or dragged on until Spring 1943, as proved to be the case, the important thing was to keep the momentum going. If Round-Up, an operation for which the Allies had envisaged using 48 divisions, was really ruled out, some other operation *on a similar scale* must be undertaken. Minor operations, such as the occupation of Sicily or Sardinia, or both, would not suffice. How could they face Stalin otherwise? Not surprisingly, Churchill protested vigorously to Roosevelt in November when it appeared that the US Chiefs had reduced their 'target' for Bolero by as much as a million men. Roosevelt replied significantly that the US was now 'much more heavily engaged in the Pacific than was expected a few months ago'; but added soothingly that the US would proceed with the Bolero build-up as rapidly as circumstances permitted – 'circumstances' being the conflicting demands on scarce shipping resources of the Pacific, Torch, and supplies to Russia. This was not very consoling to Churchill. He was more encouraged by an earlier cable from Roosevelt which talked of 'possible forward movements against Sardinia, Sicily, Italy, Greece and other Balkan areas', including Turkey in the latter category. Here was Roosevelt as his very worst from Marshall's and Stimson's point of view, apparently prepared to set off on another 'dispersionist debauch'. For Churchill, on the contrary, here was welcome evidence that Roosevelt's mind was still moving along the same track as his, and that the President would be receptive to suggestions for further Mediterranean operations.[11]

So matters stood when the participants assembled for the next Anglo-American conference, at Casablanca in January 1943. The conference almost inevitably turned out to be a replay of what had happened the previous year. It was now clear that the Tunisian campaign would continue for at least another four or five months: at the same time the most optimistic prediction of the number of US divisions which might be available in the UK by *August* 1943 was 21 – six less than the minimum estimate of the necessary figure. The British Chiefs were by this time firmly convinced that Round-Up in 1943 was out of the question and, whatever he may or may not have thought earlier, Churchill now sided with them. Marshall was forced to play a lone hand in his effort simultaneously to stave off the 'Pacific Firsters', contain further Mediterranean operations to the minimum, and preserve the concept of a cross-Channel attack as the goal towards which all Anglo-American operations should ultimately lead. He had little effective support from King, whose heart was in the Pacific, or, as we have seen, from Roosevelt. Moreover he had fatally weakened his own hand by allowing the Bolero build-up to be slowed down during the previous five months. In the circumstances, Marshall could hardly resist the compromise proposed by General Dill. Essentially this involved, like most similar bargains, a 'trade-off'. Marshall accepted that Anglo-American forces could not simply stand idle for the whole of 1943. He agreed therefore that planning should begin for an invasion of Sicily in the summer of 1943. The British Chiefs were wise enough not to demand that this should be accompanied by a definite commitment to follow up the occupation of Sicily with a full-scale invasion of Italy. They were content to wait on the logic of events. In return for Marshall's reluctant consent to a further but theoretically limited Mediterranean programme, the British offered a definite commitment to support a cross-Channel attack in 1944. Furthermore, they agreed that systematic planning for the operation should begin at once under the direction of a chief of staff to the Supreme Commander (Designate): COSSAC, as he would be called. A British officer, General Morgan, was appointed to supervise the initial planning.[12]

For Roosevelt, as so often, the clinching argument was the Anglo-American obligation – and commitment – to take some of the burden off Russia. If Round-Up was impossible, they must do *something*. Even as it was, the combined Anglo-American effort for 1943 would be little enough. They would be putting into the field against the Germans less than a third of the number of troops fighting with the Red Army on the Eastern Front. It is hardly surprising that Stalin's reaction to the Casablanca programme was icy, even when that programme was filled out by a definite commitment to invade Italy, and sweetened by the assurance of a cross-Channel attack in 1944. Relations between Russia and its western allies consequently plummeted in 1943 to their lowest depths since June 1941. For what these decisions meant was that the Red Army would continue to bear the brunt of the German assault for the third successive year.

Had Stalin been privy to the Churchill–Roosevelt correspondence during the next few months he would not have found it reassuring. There was little mention of plans for north-west Europe in 1944, at any rate by Churchill. Repeatedly, however, he pressed the case for further Mediterranean operations – in Italy, on the Dalmatian coast, in the Dodecanese or Greece itself – together with the necessity of bringing Turkey into the war. Meanwhile the principle of 'Europe First' was being further eroded. US troops and materials were now in practice being allocated to the Pacific and Europe virtually on a 50–50 basis. Only 15 000 men out of a promised 80 000 reached Britain between January and March 1943. Alarmed by this, Churchill demanded another meeting with the Americans in May. It was as essential for Mediterranean operations as for the cross-Channel attack that the US should continue to concentrate on Europe and sustain the flow of men and munitions to that theatre. This time, however, Churchill found US resistance to his programme had hardened. Under continuous pressure from Marshall and Stimson, Roosevelt was beginning to shift his ground. With unfamiliar sharpness he told Churchill that nothing must now prejudice the attack on France in 1944. If operations in the Mediterranean were allowed to develop too freely, it might have just that effect, or as Roosevelt put it 'might prejudice "Bolero"'. He did not need to remind Churchill that the effect of his victory over Torch had already, through its effect on Marshall, had precisely that consequence. Marshall had in effect served notice that, while he was prepared to commit 28 US divisions – and ultimately many more – to an invasion of France, he was not prepared to contend as forcefully with Admiral King in order to commit the same number of US divisions to Mediterranean operations. Roosevelt had got the message, and passed it on to Churchill. Before the British could make even slight progress on the Mediterranean, they had to commit themselves unequivocally to the cross-Channel attack in 1944 (Overlord). On 19 May 1943, the British Chiefs did so, in chapter and verse. They agreed to match the initial US contribution to Overlord with 24 British divisions, and accepted May 1944 as the target date to be aimed at. In return they did not even get a firm US commitment to an attack on Italy, even though, if no follow-up to Sicily was agreed, it would mean that British and US troops would not be fighting the Germans *anywhere* between August 1943 and May 1944. The most Roosevelt and Marshall would agree to was that the Sicily invasion should be followed up in some way – the way 'best calculated to eliminate Italy from the war and contain the maximum German forces'. This pointed pretty strongly towards some sort of Italian operation, but left US options open. For the first time, Roosevelt had not in the end come down on Churchill's side of the argument.[13]

It was in many ways a turning-point, not only in Anglo-American strategic decision-making, but in the Roosevelt-Churchill relationship. Churchill would never again enjoy quite the same cosy relationship, or feel confidence that eventually, when all the arguments had been thrashed out, the President would support him. Admittedly, the logic of events, and of decisions already made, would carry Mediterranean operations one stage further. Marshall, no less than Roosevelt, could see the force of the argument that it would not look well, nor make for amicable Soviet–American relations, if US troops stood idle for ten months while the Red Army continued to bear the heat of battle on the Eastern Front. Moreover, soon after the Washington Conference, Mussolini's fall from power (at the end of July) was a clear indication that Italy was on the point of suing for peace – or changing sides. If the Allies acted quickly enough, it might be possible to occupy most of Italy before the Germans could move. In that case, Italy should not make very large demands on Allied troops, or become the kind of 'suction-pump' which Marshall always feared any Mediterranean operation would turn out to be. Even so, Marshall was taking no chances. When the British again came to a meeting with their US allies, at Quebec in August 1943, the conditions were spelt out for US approval of an invasion of Italy. The British must reaffirm their commitment to Overlord in May 1944 and agree that it should have *absolute priority* over Mediterranean operations. As an earnest of their good faith in this matter, the British should also agree *now* that seven divisions and a proportion of the relatively few Mediterranean landing-craft should be transferred back to the UK in November 1943, to take part in Overlord. These experienced troops would, it was expected, provided the nucleus of the spearhead assault on the beaches, which was not expected at that time to be more than five divisions. Stiffened by Marshall's intimation that he would resign if these conditions were not met, Roosevelt had no hesitation in enforcing them as a price for the Italian operation. Churchill had kept up the pressure for Mediterranean operations all through June and July, but even when reinforced by his presence in Quebec it had had little effect. For one last time, certainly, Churchill had got what he wanted – but only on strict conditions, and in return for conceding to Marshall on the main issue. As a British observer later put it, he had 'sold the pass' on Overlord. The climate had indeed changed. Furthermore, in gaining his 'famous victory', in the strategic argument, for Mediterranean operations, Churchill had put in jeopardy the other principle which he had taken to the first Washington Conference – the principle of 'Germany First'.[14]

3 Grand Strategy II: France, Italy and the Balkan 'Spectre'

To Churchill the Balkans and east Mediterranean as an area of strategic interest – and the ancillary concept of Turkish entry into the war – was something of an obsession. It reappears again and again in his strategic appreciations, like a recurring decimal. To the US Chiefs of Staff, however, and particularly to Marshall, it was like a red rag to a bull; and whenever Churchill raised it, they charged. Churchill himself realised after a while – though it took him some time to do so – that this was a dangerous subject to bring up, and not conducive to achieving his general objective of sustaining Mediterranean operations; but he seemed unable to desist. In one form or another – an attack on the Dodecanese, British use of Turkish air-bases, a landing in Greece, on the Dalmatian coast, in Trieste – it continued to occupy his thoughts, and consequently to raise dire suspicions in the minds of Marshall, Stimson and, more and more as time went by, of Roosevelt himself. The reassurances that Churchill felt bound to give, that he did not wish to see a major campaign in the Balkans, were simply not believed. Churchill's pertinacity, a virtue when confronted with Hitler or indeed Stalin, became a weakness in the long-drawn argument with the Americans over Grand Strategy, and ultimately eroded what influence he possessed with Marshall, and increasingly with Roosevelt.[1]

The causes of this near-obsession have been much discussed by both British and US historians. Variously, they have attributed it to (a) a desire to restore and sustain British power and influence in the Middle East and eastern Mediterranean – a popular view with US leaders then, and US historians since; (b) a wish to vindicate his World War I strategy in the Dardenelles, and British strategy in general during that period; and (c) a general prepossession in favour of attacking the 'underbelly' of Axis-controlled Europe from the Mediterranean. In turn, the third of these reasons – the Mediterranean 'bias' – was fuelled, or so many historians believe, by his memories of the long-drawn-out stalemate and consequent carnage on the Western Front in the First World War. It was not simply the possibility of a 'bloodbath on the beaches' which made Churchill wary of a cross-Channel attack and a direct thrust at the heart of Germany. It was also the possibility that the British and Americans might, after a successful lodgement, get bogged down in a prolonged and costly stalemate in France and the Low Countries. The Americans, who had not endured this prolonged carnage in the First World War, and who had not been engaged at all between 1939 and the end of 1941, might be able to contemplate this possibility. The British, who before Pearl Harbor had lost many thousands killed or captured in Norway, France and the Low Countries, Greece, Crete, Syria, Eritrea, Somaliland, Abyssinia, Egypt and Libya, could not. Even taking into account the invaluable contribution from the Empire and Commonwealth, Britain could draw on less than half of American manpower. When Stimson said to his colleagues in 1942, apropos of the cross-Channel–Mediterranean argument, that it was a case of 'a fatigued and defeatist government blocking the help of a young and vigorous nation', there was some truth in the assertion. But the more important point was that at this juncture the US could only contribute three and a half divisions to a cross-Channel attack. By 1944–5 those three and a half divisions had grown to four armies in France, with a fifth in reserve, and a substantial force in Italy. By that time the British were at the end of their manpower resources: including New Zealand, Polish and South African forces, they could just manage to put two armies in the field in Europe, plus a Canadian army. It was a more equitable division of effort, but it took nearly three years to achieve it. The point is made, not to denigrate the US war effort, which included a massive contribution to the air war in Europe, as well, of course, as virtually the sole responsibility for the Pacific Campaign; but to illustrate the contention that the British victory in the strategic argument in 1942–3 had long-term consequences which were not willed by either the British or the Americans, and which were certainly not an unmixed blessing for the British.[2]

Churchill's championship of operations in the eastern Mediterranean and (possibly) the Balkans, particularly the ill-fated Dodecanese campaign which poisoned Anglo-American relations in 1943, can certainly be seen as part and parcel of his general belief in the Mediterranean strategy, but that is not a sufficient explanation. More moderate champions of that strategy – for example General Brooke – saw that the North African campaign, followed by a sustained effort in Italy, met all the most valid arguments for the Mediterranean option and most of its requisites. It could be argued convincingly that sustained pressure in the western and central Mediterranean would draw German troops away from the Eastern Front and the potential front in north-western Europe. In so doing, the Italian campaign would contribute to the gradual erosion of Axis resources, and so facilitate a successful cross-Channel attack. Marshall was too fair-minded not to accept the validity of these arguments, at least in part. The capture of the Dodecanese islands, on the other hand, made far less obvious a contribution to Overlord, was much further removed from the main scene of action, and was necessarily linked to the entry of Turkey into the war, a project of dubious utility to the Allies.

It is unlikely that Churchill's wish to vindicate his First World War strategy and championship of the Dardenelles campaign was a major factor in all this. It would probably be truer to say that the same turn of mind that led Churchill in World War I to the Dardanelles, led him this time to the Dodecanese. Using naval power to take the enemy by surprise in an unexpected quarter was for British strategists a tactic as old as the Napoleonic Wars, indeed much older. Nor was it, as Brooke fancied, pique at not getting his way on Overlord and being pinned down to a definite date, which made Churchill hammer away at this theme. All men can be petty, but Churchill was not as petty as that. But he certainly did wish to see the powerful British Common-wealth forces in Italy and the Middle East fully employed until the end of the war. He wanted Britain, in fact, to have its full share of the glory: a romantic, but not necessarily a wise point of view.

THE 'POLITICAL MOTIVE' AND THE SOVIET THREAT

At this point a ritual obeisance must be made to two long-argued contentions, namely the British contention that no major Balkan campaign was ever planned or intended; and the American contention that Churchill's prepossession for the Balkans and the eastern Mediterranean was motivated by a desire to restore and further British imperial power in this area. Less convincingly, this objective has also been linked to the North African and Italian campaigns, though neither of these two areas had ever been part of Britain's imperial zone of influence, nor necessarily would be after the war. This was the so-called 'political motive' on which so much ink has been spilt. A further ramification of the 'political motive' was the argument that Churchill was concerned to forestall Soviet power in the Balkans and central-eastern Europe. This was more convincing, if applied to the later stages of the strategic argument, though not to the earlier stages. Churchill, indeed, himself supplies a good deal of evidence for this view.[3]

These two arguments – that there was never a plan for a Balkan campaign, and on the other hand that the motive for the Mediterranean (especially east Mediterranean) strategy was political rather than strategic, were put forward by British and American leaders respectively at the time, and have been reiterated by many British and American historians since. They must be considered in any survey of the strategic debate. On the first point, the British official war historians have demonstrated convincingly that the British Chiefs of Staff and their planners never produced any specific plan for a campaign in the Balkans. This might seem to settle the matter. However, it is only fair to say that American fears were prompted ·not only by Churchill's references to the Balkans in his strategic appreciations, but by the possibility that *any* operations other than those directly related to Overlord would act as a 'suction pump', drawing away valuable resources from the main theatre. Once allow such operations to begin, and the pressure to sustain them might prove irresistible. The US Chiefs fought continuously, and largely successfully, to prevent this happening in Italy. They did not wish to have the additional contra-pull of 'Balkan operations' to increase these difficulties. Under the general 'Balkan' heading they tended to lump any Anglo-American operations east of Italy or Germany, whether in the Aegean, the Balkans proper, the Adriatic, or even Central Europe. In American demonology they all amounted to the same thing. Operations in the Aegean, for example, would not, they felt, stop at the occupation of the Dodecanese, or the use of Turkish air-bases. Even if there were no demands for more troops and supplies for the operation than originally envisaged, these operations might lead to Bulgaria being drawn into the war, and the opening of a new front in that quarter. There would be demands also for more supplies to nourish the Yugoslav and Greek Resistance, perhaps for amphibious landings in Greece or on the Adriatic Coast. In short, the risk of 'dispersion' was too great.

As far as the 'political motive' is concerned, the underlying truth is that any war is an acknowledgement that diplomacy has failed; and any war is directed to achieving the same ends by other and more costly means. This is as true of the Second World War as it was when Clausewitz first uttered his celebrated dictum. Politics and Grand Strategy cannot be completely separated from each other. Most strategic decisions are motivated by a compound of factors, of which the political advantages are – and properly – one element. Roosevelt and Churchill both acknowledged this by their advocacy of particular operations. The recovery of North Africa, for example, might stiffen French opposition to German diktats; the occupation of Sicily might encourage wavering Italian politicians to consider the advantages of opting out of the war; Aegean operations might on the other hand stimulate Turkish participation or encourage Balkan resistance. By the same token, when Roosevelt urged on the British a more positive pursuit of operations in Burma or in the Indian Ocean, he had in mind the need to encourage Chiang Kai-shek and the Chinese war effort, as much as the military advantages of these operations. Similarly, the desire to conciliate Stalin, not merely in terms of the advantages of good relations for the war effort, but also to encourage post-war cooperation, entered into Roosevelt's acceptance at Teheran of the proposal to invade Southern France and his subsequent insistence on this operation.[4]

In the broader sense, also, this proposition is true. Any Anglo-American success in the Mediterranean would serve *inter alia* to strengthen British (and US) influence in that area. Equally, each successive American victory in the Pacific restored and extended American power, prestige and influence in that area. To Roosevelt, operations which might help to turn the Pacific into an American lake naturally wore a more attractive aspect than operations in, say, Sumatra, which might help to restore British power and influence in South-East Asia. But the fact that Pacific operations served long-term US interests does not mean that Roosevelt and his advisers were not sincere in believing this to be a sound strategy, or that they were wrong in that belief. Exactly the same may be said of Churchill and his Mediterranean strategy. The strategic merits of parts of that strategy, particularly the east Mediterranean aspect, are certainly more arguable than the Pacific strategy. But the question of strategic merit is in no way dependent on the question whether it had political advantages for Britain or not. One comes back, in considering the question of 'the political motive' in its broadest aspects, to the original point, namely that a war fought simply to defeat or even to destroy totally a given enemy is not usually a rational proceeding. In Rome's Punic Wars, the destruction of Carthage might have seemed a sufficient object to Cato; but control of the then fertile lands of North Africa, and strategic control of the western Mediterranean were equally attractive objects of policy for many Romans.[5]

So much for 'the political motive' in the form that it is usually raised for debate in this context. A word must be said also about the other aspect, as it applies to Churchill, namely the view that his advocacy of certain operations in the latter half of the war was motivated partly by a desire to forestall Soviet power and influence in Central and Eastern Europe. As indicated earlier, there are grounds for this view, especially in relation to his 1944 proposals for an operation eastwards from north Italy into Central Europe. Churchill has perhaps been somewhat overpraised for prescience in this matter by some commentators, just as he has been too much criticized by others for allegedly allowing British interests to dictate strategic policy. He did not foresee the problem of Soviet dominance in Eastern Europe as early as he might have done, and it did not enter into his advocacy of North African operations, for example. Political motives for these operations certainly existed, and applied to Roosevelt as much as Churchill, but they did not include a future Soviet threat. In 1942 both men were more concerned about a possible Soviet collapse than a future danger from that quarter. Churchill indeed was writing to Roosevelt at this period: 'the balance of power [at the end of the war] will favour the Anglo-Americans, and the Russians will require our help more than we theirs'. The 'political motive' for Torch, as far as Churchill was concerned, was that its success would sway French and Italian public opinion in favour of the Allies. For Roosevelt, the 'political motive' was the necessity of some substantial Anglo-American military effort in 1942; to reassure the Russians that they were not being left to fight alone; and, it was hoped, to take some pressure off the hard-pressed Red Army. Later, of course, Churchill came to feel, and increasingly to voice, great anxiety about future Soviet power in Europe. Especially did this apply to Eastern Europe. Soviet military successes on the Eastern Front, and the likelihood of a Soviet thrust into Eastern Europe were one reason for this. Equally important was the fact that the military and strategic decisions forced on Churchill by Roosevelt and Stalin in 1943 meant that there would be no Anglo-American military presence in Eastern Europe. Therefore there would be no obstacle to complete Soviet dominance in that region in 1944–5, or in the post-war world. Furthermore, the Americans resolutely refused to join with the British in their attempts to limit Soviet influence by diplomatic means and by written agreements. Roosevelt and Hull did not wish to offend Stalin by showing distrust and attempting to fetter Soviet policy: nor did they wish to put US power at the service of 'real or fancied British interests', as Roosevelt put it, especially if it involved 'wasting men and material in the Balkan mountains'. Marshall was expressing the same thought when he said, apropos of Aegean operations, that if he had his way, not one US soldier 'should die for Rhodes'. Roosevelt in fact was not worried about Russia becoming stronger in Europe. Churchill increasingly was, and it strengthened his belief in the need for such operations as the Dodecanese, or later on, the strengthening of the Italian campaign so as to make it possible for the Allies to invade central-eastern Europe through the so-called 'Ljubljana Gap', or via amphibious landings in the Adriatic. Though Churchill talked of 'joining hands with the Russians' in the Balkans, or the Dardanelles and Black Sea, it was less the joining of hands than 'hands off Greece or Yugoslavia' that was in his mind. By September 1944, at the Second Quebec Conference, he was openly saying not only to his own chiefs of staff, but also to the Americans, 'we must forestall the Russians in Central Europe ... it is important we retain a stake in Central and Eastern Europe, and do not allow everything to pass into Soviet hands ... [a landing in Istria or Trieste] would have political as well as military advantages, in view of the Russian advance in the Balkans ... I prefer to get into Vienna before the Russians do', and much more in this vein. At times he thought he was converting Roosevelt and the Americans to this view. He was quite wrong.[6]

We may take the case as proved, then, for the view that in the last eighteen months of the war Churchill's strategic views were influenced, though not wholly determined, by the 'political motive' of erecting barriers to the spread of Soviet influence in Central and Eastern Europe. But it is not legitimate to reason back from this fact to the conclusion that the above (or any other 'political motive') was a major influence on Churchill's strategic views in 1942. What is certainly true is that the deterioration of the Churchill–Roosevelt relationship from the summer of 1943 was accelerated by the continuing arguments over Grand Strategy, and the misconceptions both men often had about each other's views, objectives and motives. There are many reasons, of course, why the Anglo-American relationship should have become less close after this period. The United States was becoming more and more the stronger, militarily, of the two: post-war objectives were becoming increasingly important, and these objectives seemed to Roosevelt to require Russian goodwill even more than British goodwill. This would all have been true, even if there had been no arguments about strategy. But certainly these arguments, and the mutual suspicions, irritations and frustrations generated by them, played a part in the deterioration of the personal relationship between the two men.

CHURCHILL'S DELAYING ACTION: BUT OVERLORD
PREVAILS

The ink was hardly dry on the Quebec agreements of August
1943 – including the British acceptance of 1 May 1944 as the
target date for Overlord – when the arguments began. At
Quebec the prospect of fairly 'easy pickings' in the
Mediterranean following an Italian surrender – which was
clearly imminent – had seemed bright. Anglo-American
forces, it was thought, could occupy southern Italy, take Rome
on the run and, who knows, advance well into northern Italy
before the Germans had time to react. Outlying Italian
possessions in the Aegean, such as the Dodecanese, might be
taken with relatively small British forces from the Middle East.
Turkey might enter the war and Yugoslav/Greek resistance be
stimulated to the point where, as Brooke put it in an
uncharacteristically feverish phrase the Balkans were 'set
ablaze'. With the growing pressure from the Red Army, this
might lead to a German withdrawal from the Balkans. In no
time at all, however, these bright prospects dimmed. The
Germans, reacting quickly, held the Allied forces well south of
Rome, and mopped up British forces in the Dodecanese with
almost contemptuous ease. Churchill's appeals for help to
Roosevelt and Marshall fell on deaf ears. The Dodecanese
were a side-issue of no great consequence, and the Americans
were not disposed to throw good money after bad. Even the
Italian campaign was no more than an auxiliary to 'Overlord'
and should absorb no more resources than were strictly
necessary. As for the Balkans, the Yugoslav and Greek
resistance factions seemed to be spending as much time
fighting each other as fighting the Germans, as Roosevelt
pointed out to Churchill.[7]

Churchill then began to regret that he had agreed to a
fixed date for Overlord, and even more to the withdrawal of
troops and landing-craft from Italy *now*, to participate in an
Overlord six months or more distant. To rob Peter to pay
Paul, when Paul would not present his bill for some
considerable time, seemed contrary to common sense. The
Moscow Foreign Ministers' Conference of October 1943
provided the occasion for Churchill's first *démarche* on the
subject. Eden and General Ismay, representing the British,

had just reaffirmed to the Russians the Anglo-American commitment to Overlord in spring 1944. From Churchill's point of view Stalin had to be undeceived – one might almost say 'nobbled' – before it was too late. Churchill cabled Eden instructing him to see Stalin personally and sound him out on the possibility of postponing Overlord for a month or two, so that key troops and landing-craft could be retained in the Mediterranean and employed in amphibious operations. The purpose of such operations was to get the Italian campaign going again; perhaps also to retake the Dodecanese. As it turned out, Stalin received the suggestion amiably at first, but after reflecting on all the implications, soon decided that Soviet interests required him to come down heavily on the American side of the argument. This he did at the Teheran Conference later in the year. Whatever Stalin's reaction, however, the effect on Anglo-American relations was disastrous. Churchill could hardly have chosen a more effective means of inflaming them. Stimson was furious, Marshall angry and Roosevelt extremely vexed by this latest example of Churchill's incorrigibility. You simply could not pin the man down. Relations had already been somewhat embittered by the US refusal to help in the first, abortive, attempt to seize the Dodecanese. Churchill had felt obliged to say, more than once, that he was not arguing for a 'Balkan campaign' or for sending an Allied army into the Balkans. Roosevelt retorted that major Aegean operations only made sense as a prelude to a Balkan campaign. At one point Churchill had talked rhetorically of 'going to the King and laying down the mantle of his high office'. He reminded Roosevelt that the British Commonwealth had put more than twice the number of troops into the field in Tunisia, and twice the number of troops into the Italian campaign as the US had sent. Roosevelt in turn was stung into saying flatly that eastern Mediterranean operations could not be allowed to divert resources from Overlord, and adding, unkindly, that the Balkan resistance movements (which were encouraged and supervised to some degree by the British) were in such a mess that perhaps an American general should take charge and put things right. It was not an edifying episode in the Anglo-American Alliance, and the Roosevelt–Churchill relationship never really recovered from it.[8]

When they had had time to cool down, both Roosevelt and Marshall acknowledged that there was something in the British contention that the Mediterranean campaign had to be kept going, to the extent at least that was required to support a successful Overlord; that the Italian campaign could not be allowed, therefore, to 'wither on the vine'. Between them, Italian operations, Balkan resistance movements and the possible threat in the Aegean were keeping about forty German divisions in those areas, and therefore away from both north-west Europe and the Russian front. Even Stalin acknowledged this. It was worth keeping whatever was required in the way of troops and landing-craft in that area to maintain this state of affairs, even if it did mean postponing the date of Overlord by a month or so.

Therefore, when Churchill and his advisers again met Roosevelt and the American team at the Cairo and Teheran conferences, he was able to get a concession on this point, but only after a great deal of acrimonious discussion, and only in return for the British acceptance of an operation that neither Churchill nor the British Chiefs liked – an amphibious landing in southern France (Operation Anvil) to support Overlord. This latter operation, moreover, would take yet more troops from Alexander's command in Italy. The Cairo meetings in November 1943 were indeed an altogether disagreeable experience for all concerned, possibly the most ill-tempered of all the Anglo-American conferences. Churchill was angry because he wanted to use this occasion to get together with Roosevelt and the Americans to agree on the Overlord-Mediterranean questions and so present a united front to Stalin, whom they were going on to meet at Teheran. Instead he found that the Chinese leader, Chiang Kai-shek, who had been invited to Cairo, had been brought there by Roosevelt on the very first day of the conference, leaving no time for separate Anglo-American talks. Worse than that, Roosevelt not only spent an inordinate amount of time with Chiang (as Churchill thought), but made it clear that he did not want to concert agreements with the British before meeting the Russians. He did not want, he told Churchill, to give Stalin the impression that they were 'ganging up' against him. Brooke and the British Chiefs were equally annoyed that Chiang's presence forced them to engage in long discussions about operations in Burma and the Indian Ocean before they had settled the crucial questions of European strategy on which all else depended. If the principle of 'Europe First' still meant anything at all, this was the wrong way round. Moreover, the US master-plan for Pacific operations was not yet ready, and it might well turn out to be the case than when its implications had been fully studied, the Burma campaign would prove to be unnecessary. Instead, Japanese troops in the area could perhaps be bypassed and starved of supplies by cutting their lines of communication. If the British were frustrated by all this, the Americans for their part were still extremely angry because their Allies were reopening the whole question of the Overlord date, which they thought had been settled at Quebec. It is not surprising that the discussions at Cairo were often acrimonious.

Roosevelt contrived, during the conference, to make things worse. Finding in his talks with Chiang that the Chinese were, not unnaturally, disheartened and weary after nearly ten years of unsuccessful struggle with the Japanese, he sought to encourage them by promising, on behalf of his British allies, that there would soon be a major campaign in Burma, and in addition a large-scale amphibious operation in the Indian Ocean (Operation Buccaneer). He made this promise without consulting Churchill, or for that matter, his own chiefs of staff. Ironically this was an operation that Churchill and his South-East Asian commander, Mountbatten, were not averse to – at the proper time. But Churchill was not prepared to give it priority over Mediterranean operations that he considered more vital. The question of the essential landing-craft, perennially in short supply, was again involved. The same landing-craft could not be used in two places at once. Landing-craft were in short supply, in fact, because Admiral King had monopolized the greater part of them for his Pacific operations. When Churchill ventured to suggest that the Admiral might disgorge a few of them, Roosevelt replied coldly that it was out of the question. In truth the principle of priority for European operations over Pacific operations had long been abandoned. The horse had bolted.[9]

With the additional complication of Buccaneer adding to the problem of reaching agreement, the American and British Chiefs in the end could only agree to differ. The whole linked question of the Overlord date and Mediterranean operations, together with the unresolved question of Buccaneer, was left open until after the Teheran meeting. They would see what Stalin had to say.

That decision, in fact, ensured that the Americans would win the argument. For, although Stalin at Moscow had shown signs of favouring a thrust in the east Mediterranean involving Turkey, at Teheran he came firmly down in favour of the north-west Europe strategy, and against extensive Mediterranean operations. Adopting the US position in full, he said that France offered the shortest way to the heart of Germany. Overlord should have priority, and should be supported by a landing in the South of France. Italy was subsidiary. As for operations further east, they were all very well in their way, but a long way from Berlin. Whatever Stalin's motives – and he had every reason for wanting to keep Anglo-American forces well away from the eastern theatre of operations – this was decisive. Churchill could not hope to prevail against both his allies, particularly as Roosevelt was now adamant for Overlord. As the President jovially remarked to his son Elliott during the Teheran Conference, 'Winston knows that he is beaten'. So he did, though this did not prevent him keeping up the argument to the bitter end. Finally, however, he was forced to accept the Soviet–American programme for 1944. Overlord, that is to say, should have absolute priority over Mediterranean operations, and be supported by the southern France operation. When they returned to Cairo to tidy up the loose ends, it soon became clear that if Overlord and Anvil were both to be allocated sufficient resources for a powerful 'first-wave' assault, this would not leave sufficient landing-craft and troops available for more than *one* major operation in the Mediterranean. Both Churchill and Brooke agreed that it was more important to get the Italian campaign going again than to retake the Dodecanese. So Churchill reluctantly abandoned the latter. The fact that the Turks were proving extremely cautious about committing themselves helped to ratify and justify that decision. In return, however, Roosevelt had to give up the Indian Ocean operation (Buccaneer) for lack of the necessary landing-craft. This decision in turn was fortified by Mountbatten's judgement that far more troops and other resources would be necessary for Buccaneer than the two leaders had expected. The end product of all the argument, then, was that neither of the two leaders were able to secure the go-ahead for the two operations on which they had respectively set their hearts. They were left with Anvil, which Churchill disliked, and an amphibious operation on the Italian coast (Operation Shingle), which the Americans regarded with only moderate enthusiasm. Roosevelt, however, had far more cause for satisfaction than Churchill. He had by this time fully committed himself to supporting Marshall's preferred strategy, – Overlord – and furthermore Overlord with absolute priority *vis-à-vis* all other European operations. There might be occasional backslidings, when his imagination was temporarily stimulated by some proposal of Churchill's – for example at Teheran the idea of a 'right hand turn' from Italy into Yugoslavia or Hungary – but on these occasions he was firmly steered away from the danger area by Marshall. At the end of the conference he could say to Stimson with satisfaction, 'I have brought Overlord back to you safe and in the ways for accomplishment'.

It was otherwise for Churchill. He had lost the battle for east Mediterranean operations completely, and for good, and was forced to accept the shift of emphasis in the Mediterranean from east to west. The one small concession he had been able to extract from the Americans was a month's delay for Overlord – from 1 May 1944 to 1 June. This would enable the precious landing-craft to be retained in the Mediterranean and used for a landing near Rome (Shingle). Shingle in turn, it was hoped, would not only enable the US Fifth Army to take Rome, and advance to the line Pisa–Rimini, but all being well might lead to a 'break-out' into the Po Valley in the summer, and thence to the Ljubljana Gap, and so on to Vienna, Prague and Budapest. Churchill did not confide these more generous hopes to the Americans. An advance to the Pisa–Rimini line was all they had catered for, or approved. But these were Churchill's hopes. In fact they were not to be realised. Indeed it was too much to hope for from Alexander's weary troops, fighting across difficult mountainous country. If there had been top priority for the Mediterranean, yes. But in fact Alexander had already lost some of his best troops to Overlord and was to lose more for Anvil. Moreover, and logically from his point of view, Marshall had also shifted the brightest and

best of his generals from the Mediterranean to Overlord –
Eisenhower, Patton and Bradley. Some of those who were left
to support the experienced Clark were a job lot, including
unfortunately the nominated commander for Shingle. As
a consequence – and also because the Germans, as always,
reacted quickly – the Anzio bridgehead, established in January
1944, was to be surrounded and sealed off for five months.

ANZIO, ANVIL AND THE FIGHT FOR THE ITALIAN
CAMPAIGN: THE DETERIORATION OF THE CHURCHILL–
ROOSEVELT RELATIONSHIP

All this was still in the future. For Churchill, lying ill in
Morocco after Teheran, a more dismal reflection was the
extent to which his relationship with Roosevelt had
deteriorated. It would be an exaggeration to say that Roosevelt
had cold-shouldered him entirely at Cairo and Teheran, but
he had certainly snubbed the British leader on a number of
occasions. He had so arranged matters that there could be no
confidential talks with Churchill and the British Chiefs of Staff
before the meetings with Chiang Kai-shek and Stalin. He had
refused to meet Churchill privately until he had two meetings
with the Soviet leader. At Teheran he had chosen to stay at the
Soviet Embassy rather than at the British Embassy: and he had
publicly needled and teased Churchill in front of Stalin.
Churchill had not relished any of this. It seemed a bad omen
for the future. He may or may not have realized that Roosevelt
had good reasons – or reasons that seemed good to him – for
these actions, reasons which had nothing to do with his
personal feeling towards Churchill. Roosevelt had, after all,
never met Chiang Kai-shek or Stalin before, and he wanted to
get to know them, if possible to win their trust and friendship.
He expected to work with both leaders after the war, and their
cooperation he thought would be necessary to build the new
world order he envisaged. Churchill he knew already – only
too well. Roosevelt's advisers had been warning him for some
time that after the war Russia would be the strongest power in
Europe, while Britain would be exhausted, and British power
would be declining. A world statesman has to be cold-blooded
about these things. Whatever sacrifices Britain had made for

the common cause, one had to deal with facts as they were. Moreover, the British were heavily dependent on US aid and supplies. The US contribution to the global war effort already exceeded the British contribution in most ways, and once Overlord was launched, US ground forces in Europe would increasingly outnumber British forces. Quite simply, at this point in the war it was more expedient to slight Churchill than to thwart Stalin. But it was also true that Roosevelt's attitude to Churchill had changed. He had been angered and wearied by the revival of the Overlord/Mediterranean controversy and the arguments over the Dodecanese. Possibly, also, he felt a twinge or two of regret that it had been thought necessary to leave the British forces to their fate in that area. One never likes to be made to feel guilty, and Roosevelt was not immune to the common human reaction, which is to feel resentment towards the person who makes you feel guilty. Churchill's tactless reminder that the US ground forces' contribution to European (i.e. Mediterranean) operations had so far been pretty small in relation to US resources had also stung. Roosevelt made a point of having the disparity in the *global* contribution of the two countries spelt out publicly when they met again at Cairo and Teheran.[10]

It is noticeable how from this time forward Roosevelt gave increasingly free rein to suspicions of British policy – suspicions which would always have been latent in the mind of an American liberal democrat in regard to British imperial policy and the British pursuit of 'power politics', as Roosevelt saw it. Moreover, he was surrounded by men who in different ways fed these suspicions – Leahy, his Chief of Staff and Chairman of the US Joint Chiefs, Admiral King, Hull, Stimson, and in his more dispassionate way, Marshall. Harry Hopkins, who, perhaps surprisingly, provided something of a counterweight to these men, was soon to be incapacitated by illness, and lose his influence with the President. Whatever the reasons, it is impossible to read the US accounts of Roosevelt's discussions with his chiefs of staff on his way to the Cairo Conference, or his son's account of their conversations during the conference, without being struck by the extent to which Roosevelt harboured dire suspicions of British policy, and the wildness of some, though not all, of these suspicions. Marshall and Stimson and the others had done their work only too well, and from this time onwards, Roosevelt was virtually fireproofed against any suggestions from Churchill on Grand Strategy, and apt to receive Churchill's views on many other matters – France, Italy, the Middle East – with considerable scepticism.

From the viewpoint therefore of the influence of the two men on allied strategy, the period after Teheran merits less attention. Up to this time there had been both a Roosevelt and a Churchill input into allied strategic policy-making, varying in degree, but considerable on both sides. After Teheran, or to put it more accurately, after Quebec, Churchill's influence diminished to the marginal. Roosevelt had committed himself irrevocably to Overlord, and to the proposition that all else in Europe was subsidiary to it. Marshall was firmly in the driver's seat. Churchill could do little more, however hard he tried, than extract a few minor concessions for the Mediterranean. It was clear to Churchill, indeed, after Teheran – and even clearer to Brooke – that for the moment one had to concentrate on Italy and forget about the Aegean and the Balkans. He did not forget them entirely, of course. The political consequences of handing over Eastern Europe to the Red Army became more and more apparent to him throughout 1944, and were in his mind in his advocacy of a 'right turn' rather than a 'left turn' from Italy, his attempts (which were the other side of the coin) to abort the Anvil operation, and also his determination to get British troops at least into Greece before it was too late. But since the Americans regarded only Italy as of consequence in the Mediterranean, and that only in the light of the help it might give to Overlord, it was necessary to concentrate on getting what one could for Italy. The failure to achieve a decisive breakthrough to Rome and beyond immediately after Shingle was a bitter disappointment for Churchill. To the Americans it was fresh cause to question Churchill's military judgement. To Churchill, it was additional proof that the impoverishment of the Italian campaign in the interests of Overlord, which was still months away, was a major strategic error. But there was still hope that Alexander and Clark might capture Rome and break through to the Po Valley in time to launch an operation through the Ljubljana Gap in 1944. To achieve this, however, the Americans had to be persuaded to go back on their unfortunate commitment to Anvil and its accompanying requirement to take further troops from Alexander. During the first half of 1944, Churchill, supported by the British Chiefs, often pressed this view on Roosevelt; but it was a losing battle. Churchill no longer had the clout to wage the same sort of delaying action against Anvil as he had waged against Round-Up/Overlord. A series of rebuttals by Roosevelt followed: sometimes polite, sometimes more forceful. In February, Roosevelt rejected the contention that there would not be sufficient resources to mount an effective Overlord and Anvil, and refused Churchill's request for a further meeting of the Chiefs of Staff to discuss the matter. Although Eisenhower, the nominated commander for Overlord, had begun to have doubts about Anvil, and had agreed with the British (on behalf of the US Chiefs of Staff) that the question should be reviewed in March, Marshall remained adamant on the question, and Roosevelt continued to support Marshall. The most he would agree to was that Anvil should take place two months after Overlord instead of simultaneously, as originally envisaged. On 28 June he finally wound the matter up, cabling to Churchill: 'Anvil, mounted at the earliest possible date is the only operation which will give Overlord material and immediate support: ... I must completely concur with the US Chiefs of Staff ... the use of practically all Mediterranean resources to advance into northern Italy and thence to the northeast [the 'Ljubljana Gap' strategy] is not acceptable to me'. Finally on the 29th he reminded Churchill of their agreement with Stalin to launch Anvil, and again repeated that he could not agree to the employment of US troops against Istria or in 'the Balkans'. The latter cable is an interesting example of the general US tendency to use 'the Balkans' as a 'cover-all' word for all eastward-looking operations. In fact, Churchill was now looking for an advance from Istria north-eastwards and north to Prague, Vienna, perhaps Budapest, not southeast or east into 'the Balkans'.[11]

Be that as it may, Roosevelt had made his point sufficiently clear. Realising Churchill's bitter disappointment that the British-controlled Italian campaign, on which Churchill had pinned such hopes, was being relegated to a second-class operation, Roosevelt added with unusual emotion 'my dear friend, I beg you to let us go ahead with our plan'. Churchill talked of resigning his office, urged that it was a major strategic error to 'ruin the campaign in Italy' for the sake of Anvil, but to no avail. Roosevelt gently countered with the argument that 'a straight line is the shortest distance between two points', i.e. Britain – northern France – the Ruhr – Berlin, rather than Rome – the Po Valley – Istria – Vienna – Berlin. On 15 August the invasion of southern France was launched. The argument was over.[12]

General Brooke wrote the British epitaph on the Anvil controversy. 'All right, if you insist on being damned fools, sooner than fall out with you, we shall be damned fools with you, and we shall see that we perform the role of damned fools damned well'. This was not quite the end of the matter, however. One could say this of Churchill, that he never completely gave up. Against all probability, against all military logic, he still thought it possible that Alexander's weakened forces might break through to the Po Valley before the autumn, and in time to launch an offensive through the Ljubljana Gap. This in spite of the fact that Alexander and Clark had only managed to break out of the Anzio bridgehead in June, and by August were still encountering heavy resistance in the mountains north of Rome. Perhaps in conjunction with an amphibious operation in the Trieste area, Alexander could still get through, and provide some sort of thrust eastwards from Italy before it was too late to forestall Stalin. This, of course, meant another request to keep landing-craft in the Mediterranean. In contrast to their previously unyielding attitude, Roosevelt and the US Chiefs were now disposed to be conciliatory on the matter. The main battle over strategy had been won. Overlord and Anvil had been successfully launched, with all the necessary striking power. If Churchill wanted to keep up his hopes, why not humour him? Roosevelt and his advisers knew full well, as did the British Chiefs, that it was now almost impossible that these hopes could be realised. Roosevelt could therefore write disingenuously to Churchill, on 3 September, that he shared Churchill's confidence that Alexander's forces could still break through the German lines: and was 'open-minded' about whether they eventually moved west or east from the Po Valley. A very different attitude to this question from that he had expressed in June. It was indeed a time of euphoria. The Allied break-out and stunning victory in Normandy, the successful exploitation of the southern France landings and the forward movement in Italy, together with Russian victories on the Eastern Front, encouraged hopes that victory might come in Europe before the end of the year. The participants assembled, therefore, for the next Anglo-American conference at Quebec in September 1944 in a mellow mood, far different from the tense and irritable mood of Cairo and Teheran. In this atmosphere, it was not too difficult to agree that the landing-craft for a possible Trieste landing should remain in the Mediterranean until the result of Alexander's efforts became clear – i.e. until October. If by that time his troops had not broken the German line in the Apennines, wintry conditions would have set in, and there would no longer be any likelihood of a breakthrough before the spring. Brooke for his part could see little point in possibly annoying the Americans by, 'starting the Vienna hare' and exploring Alexander's 'impossible hopes', when the important thing was to get all they could for Italy, so that the Allied forces ultimately would win the total victory their efforts had earned. Roosevelt and Marshall were not perturbed by the 'Vienna hare', however. They knew they were not discussing strategic probabilities. Roosevelt had not even bothered to protest when Churchill, just before the conference, told him that he was preparing to send a small British force into Greece (from which the Germans were clearly about to withdraw), to prevent the powerful Communist section of the Greek resistance from seizing Athens. The President replied that he had no objection to such a move, 'to preserve order' in Greece. Stalin had indicated already that he was prepared to regard Greece as an Anglo-American sphere of influence, so the move would not cause problems with the Russians; and there was no question of involving American troops in these 'Balkan entanglements'. So be it. Cordell Hull and the US State Department felt differently, when they came to hear of it. There was to be considerable friction over what they saw as a blatant attempt to foist an unpopular monarchy and a right-wing government on the Greeks, before they had had a chance to express their views. But Roosevelt was not disposed to make an issue of it. The arguments over European Grand Strategy really ended at this point. There were differences of view later on, about whether Eisenhower's forces should attack on a broad or a narrow front, and over the precise role of General Montgomery and the British–Canadian forces, but those were questions of applied strategy rather than Grand Strategy. The main issues had been decided by the summer of 1944.[13]

What was the upshot of all this? It amounted in the end to a Churchill–Roosevelt agreement to pursue a largely Mediterranean strategy in 1942 and 1943, and a Roosevelt insistence on a mainly north-west European strategy in 1944 and thereafter. It is not proposed here to enter again into the well-worn paths of the argument as to whether things might have turned out better (from the Western point of view) if the US strategy had been pursued consistently from the beginning, or if the Mediterranean strategy had been persevered with to a greater degree in 1943–5. The present writer has said all that he wishes to say on these topics elsewhere. The only thing that might be added is that as one gets further and further away from the events themselves, the case becomes rather clearer for the view that the best and most effective strategy of all – from the point of view of winning the European war as quickly and cheaply as possible – might well have been to have staked everything on a massive build-up in the UK in 1942–3 for a powerful Round-Up in 1943: and not to have attempted *any* major operation in 1942. But this was an option that Roosevelt, and for that matter Churchill, was not prepared to entertain, for reasons that have been stated. Of the options which *were* on offer, whichever was chosen would have disadvantages, which would have to be accepted. To take the argument any further is to enter the field of speculation, and to arrive in the end at conclusions which can never be proved. The historian's main business is to get as close as he or she can to the facts of what happened, why it happened and how it happened, not to get endlessly involved in the might-have-beens of history.[14]

THE POLITICAL CONSEQUENCES OF ANGLO-AMERICAN STRATEGY

The consequences of what was decided and carried out are of course part of the facts of the case. Among the consequences was the fact that the Red Army controlled virtually the whole of Eastern Europe after 1945, with all the consequent political implications. Given the decisions which were actually made, this was probably inevitable. It is easier to accept this, if one reflects that, whatever the military outcome, it would have been difficult to deny the Russians the right to a share in any occupation of Germany. The appalling burden carried by the Russian people in World War II would have ensured this. Therefore Soviet lines of communication would have run across Poland, and Stalin would have had the right to demand that they be secure. There would certainly have been no effective Anglo-American military presence in Poland, and therefore no way of preventing the imposition on the Poles of any political settlement the Russians desired, assuming that diplomacy and persuasion did not have any effect. So far as the rest of Central and Eastern Europe are concerned, much the same must have applied. Even if there had been a substantial Anglo-American military presence in those areas at the end of the war, it is difficult to imagine any US president being prepared to retain that presence indefinitely, and Britain could simply not have afforded to support such a burden. Soviet power and influence must ultimately have been dominant in deciding the political future of Romania and Bulgaria, and probably of Hungary and Czechoslovakia too.

The actual physical and material effects of the Anglo-American strategic pattern were of course considerable, most of all for Russia; to a lesser but significant extent for Britain. For what that pattern meant was that the full weight of American military power was not felt in Europe until the last year of the war. One does not need to understate or devalue the North African or Italian campaigns to justify these conclusions. In Tunisia a quarter of a million Axis troops ultimately surrendered, much the same number as capitulated at Stalingrad: it was a substantial contribution to the war. But the one Army Group employed by the British and Americans in each of the Mediterranean campaigns was still only about a third of the Russians and German forces on the Eastern Front, where each normally had three Army Groups. This was particularly significant in 1943, when the Americans had had time to mobilize and train a substantial part of their manpower. The end result was that the Russians fell and bled and suffered for three years to a very much greater extent than their Western allies. As has been pointed out, this was not something that Roosevelt and Marshall, or even Churchill, really willed. None of them was unwilling to accept the necessary sacrifices which faced their respective peoples. It happened because Marshall, particularly, shrank from expending American lives any more than was absolutely necessary on what he saw as secondary operations in the Mediterranean, just as Churchill shrank from expending British lives on what he saw as a probably suicidal assault on the beaches of north-western France in 1942.

The manpower consequences for Britain were also not inconsiderable. In the end, the British Commonwealth had to provide the bulk of the manpower required for the ground forces fighting the Axis in the European theatre, from Pearl Harbor in December 1941 until D-Day in June 1944: the US contribution being three (later four) divisions in North Africa, and one army (compared with the four US armies committed in 1944) in the Italian campaign. And one must add that this one army, although always described as the 'US Fifth Army' always included a substantial element of non-American forces. British and Commonwealth troops, the Free French, the Italians and ultimately the Brazilians all supplied a 'make-weight' at different times, the US contribution seldom rising above six or seven divisions. Half of the troops that landed at Salerno in 1943 and one third of those that assaulted Anzio in 1944 were from the British Commonwealth. Whatever the reasons for this, which have been sufficiently explored above, one is looking at the manpower effects of five years' warfare on a nation of fifty million, supplemented by the relatively small, though immensely valuable contingents from the Commonwealth plus some of the Allies, notably the Poles. It is not surprising that by the time the Normandy campaign began, the British were scraping the bottom of the manpower barrel. This was the end-product of Churchill's 'victory' in the strategic arguments of 1942–3. In the circumstances, it is reasonable to describe it as a 'Pyrrhic victory'.[15]

4 A Difficult Alliance: Anglo-American Relations with Russia

'Joe is unaccountable', was Eden's summing-up to Churchill on the state of Anglo-Russian relations midway through the war. One might think it odd that both Churchill and Roosevelt, as well as Eden, should have elected to refer to Stalin on occasion as 'Joe', or 'Uncle Joe', as though they were all members of one big happy family. Roosevelt certainly wished it to be so, but it must have been difficult to keep the illusion alive, in the light of the not infrequent brusqueness, and sometimes insulting character of Stalin's messages; though admittedly these qualities were more often visited on Churchill than Roosevelt. But Roosevelt, with his intuitive understanding of the other man's point of view, was in any case more ready than Churchill to make allowances for the burdens and strains on a war leader who was fighting a formidable enemy at his gates, while two powerful allies looked on and apparently did very little – or rather, very little that the USSR wanted. In July 1942 the President cabled Churchill, 'we must understand the psychology of a country which has been invaded', and certainly he made every effort to do so. Roosevelt was consistent, too, in seeking to minimize differences of opinion with Russia, and to seize on any slight indication that the two sides were beginning to understand each other better. As early as May 1942 he was writing hopefully to Churchill of Molotov's recent visit to Washington, 'we have got on as personal a footing of candor and good friendship as can be acquired through an interpreter'. The day before his death, in April 1945, he was to say in his last but one message to Churchill: 'I would minimize the general Soviet problem as much as possible. These problems seem to arise every day, and most of them straighten out ... We must be firm, and our course this far is correct.' Between these two messages lie many attempts on the President's part to achieve a harmonious relationship, and many rebuffs, softened by

59

occasional more jovial interchanges, from the Soviet side. But Roosevelt never gave up. His attitude throughout was based firmly on two clear and incontrovertible positions: first, that it was essential to the allied war effort that the Red Army should continue to fight the Germans (and eventually, it was hoped, the Japanese); second, that no workable international organization could be created after the war without Soviet membership and support, and on a basis of some measure of mutual trust and confidence. Events were to show perhaps that the gap was too wide to be bridged. Certainly there was a yawning gulf between Roosevelt's optimistic vision and the Soviet view of the world, based on a Marxist-Leninist interpretation, which made true friendship with the West impossible. But this is not to say that Roosevelt was to be blamed for trying. The alternative would almost certainly be many years of armed truce, of tension, danger and colossal expense, with the appalling possibility of a third world war as the finale. Roosevelt's efforts to prevent such an outcome, based though they were on mistaken premises, surely cannot be censured, save where he went further than was necessary in appeasing Stalin. But, given the premises, who is to judge how far was necessary?[1]

The difference between Roosevelt and Churchill on the problem of wartime relations with the USSR has sometimes been exaggerated. Though less optimistic than Roosevelt about the possibility of long-term future co-operation – and increasingly so towards the end of the war – Churchill fully agreed with his partner as to the necessities of wartime collaboration and on the first of the two propositions enumerated above, namely that Russia must be kept in the war. Where they differed, on a number of occasions, was in deciding precisely what course of action was necessary to this end. Roosevelt thought that it was all-important to maintain a continuous flow of supplies to Russia, even at the expense of appalling losses of men and ships on the 'Arctic convoy' route: and also to put Anglo-American troops in the field against Germany at the earliest possible moment. Churchill was neither willing to run convoys in which the loss of more than half the cargoes was accompanied by unacceptable losses of warships, nor was he willing to throw British lives and equipment away in rash 'forlorn hopes' like Sledgehammer.

He was more inclined to conciliate Stalin by showing that he recognized and respected Soviet national interests, and by a readiness to make concessions to these interests. This came out clearly in the two men's reaction to the first enunciation of Stalin's territorial demands, during the Eden visit to Moscow in January 1942. Stalin demanded that the West should recognize the 1941 frontiers of Russia, which included the Baltic States and a large slice of inter-war Poland, up the so-called 'Curzon Line'. Roosevelt (and his Secretary of State, Cordell Hull) was at first adamantly opposed to this. It would be, as they thought, a violation of the principles they had inherited from Woodrow Wilson. There must be at least some attention paid, they agreed, to the wishes of the people in those territories. In any case, such issues should wait until the post-war peace conference. There should be no repetition of the secret territorial agreements of the First World War. First Hull, then Harry Hopkins, during his visit to London in April 1942, conveyed this message to Churchill. Better to satisfy the Russians with supplies – and military action. The British Premier's first reaction had also been to oppose Soviet territorial demands, but by the time of Hopkins' visit, he had weakened. A cynical view of this change of front would be that, faced with the choice between territorial concessions and unacceptable military options, Churchill preferred to throw the Russian Bear a juicy morsel or two. Churchill, however, would have defended the policy as a realistic appraisal of what the West could achieve. If Germany knocked Russia out of the war, and the West had to defeat the Germans on their own, then the post-war situation would be as it had been at the end of the First World War. No obligations to the USSR could survive such a catastrophe, and there would be no need to conciliate a defeated Russia. The Western Powers would have a free hand. If, on the other hand, Russia emerged as the victor in the East, the West would be powerless to stop her recovery of eastern Poland and the Baltic states, except by military action, which would almost certainly not be an option. Therefore there was nothing to be lost by acceding to Soviet demands.[2]

At a later stage in the war. Churchill was to be much criticized for suggesting a *de facto* division of military responsibility in the Balkans between the West and Russia, which both the Americans and (probably) the Russians saw as paving the way for a post-war division into 'spheres of interest' or 'spheres of influence'. The episode is discussed at greater length in the next chapter. Here no more need be said than that such an agreement seemed to Churchill a realistic division of military responsibilities, in the light of the current military situation. As to what would happen later, the West would no doubt exert what influence it could: but the lack of Anglo-American troops in the area would in any case mean that the USSR would call the tune.[3]

There was a difference, certainly, in the way the two men approached the problem of Soviet relations. This difference had relatively little to do with Churchill's well-known opposition to Communism: Roosevelt, after all, was in no sense pro-communist, except in the eyes of those who thought anyone to the left of Ronald Reagan (or to take an example from his own times, Robert Taft) could be classified as 'pink'. It had more to do with the fact that Churchill remembered only too well the year of British isolation in 1940–41, when the USSR had behaved more like an ally of Nazi Germany than an ally of Britain. He felt no particular sense of obligation when the USSR, very much against its will, was eventually forced to fight the Germans. He expected Soviet policy towards the West to be tough, unsentimental and realistic, and though sometimes angered and disappointed by the suspicion and obduracy of Soviet reactions, he was not really surprised. His own policy towards Russia was conducted, by and large, on the same realistic principles. Nor did Churchill have the same confidence in his ability to charm and influence other men as Roosevelt had in his own persuasive abilities. Churchill did his best, during two visits to Moscow and three other meetings with Stalin, to explain and justify British policy, and to achieve some sort of relationship with the Soviet leader. But he was never very confident that he had succeeded. The Soviet mind always remained something of a mystery to him. His celebrated description of Soviet policy as 'a riddle wrapped in a mystery inside an enigma' is an adequate reflection of this general attitude of exasperated bewilderment. In October 1942 he cabled to Roosevelt apropos of Soviet attitudes, 'I am frankly perplexed'. Not for the first or last time, one might add. Towards the end of the war a particularly gross example of Soviet suspiciousness prompted him to write to Stalin that there was not much of a future to look forward to, if the world were to be divided into two hostile camps, and their relations were to be conducted on a basis of mutual bickering and suspicion. But it is doubtful if he expected this to produce much of a change in Soviet behaviour. Perhaps indeed it was written mainly for the record.[4]

Roosevelt had, with some reason, more confidence in his ability to get on with people of all kinds, and all nationalities. In peacetime, he had been a good deal more successful in this line with his fellow-countrymen than had Churchill with his. Stalin presented a new and intriguing problem, but surely not an insuperable one. He thought he could crack it. In March 1942 he cabled Churchill, 'I think I can personally handle Stalin better than either your Foreign Office or my State Department. Stalin hates the guts of all your top people. He thinks he likes me better and I hope he will continue to do so'. This touching faith remained with him almost until the end, though by 1945 even Roosevelt's unquenchable optimism was hard put to survive. Churchill often admonished him to be more robust in his attitude to the Russians, not to allow them to think that they could get away with anything and everything, above all, not to allow Stalin to sow suspicion, or drive a wedge between them; but these appeals usually fell on deaf ears. So far as Roosevelt was concerned, they came from a suspect source.

There was of course something to be said (there usually is) on the other side of the case, that is the Soviet side. Stalin had no particular reason (quite apart from the Marxist view of the capitalist world) to trust the West. Britain and France had sought to crush the Bolshevik Revolution at birth, and Churchill, as a member of the Lloyd George government, had played a leading part in this. In 1922 the French Army had aided the Poles to inflict a crushing defeat on the Red Army, and connived in the seizure by the Poles of much disputed territory. The French had then forged alliances with many of the anti-communist governments of eastern Europe. For most of the remainder of the 1920s and the 1930s the attitude of Britain and France towards Russia had been one of wary suspicion, and their policies amounted to virtual ostracism. With the rise of the threat from Nazi Germany in the 1930s

French governments, particularly of the Left, had begun to make friendly overtures to Russia, but the British government had not participated in these. The keynote of British policy (to the frequent dissatisfaction of the French) had remained one of 'appeasement' of Germany. Only at the eleventh hour, after the German seizure of Czechoslovakia in March 1939, had the British government agreed to join the French in an attempt to create an Anglo-French-Soviet bloc against Hitler – and then reluctantly and ungraciously. It is not altogether surprising that Stalin in 1939 preferred to strike a bargain with Germany, rather than embrace these apparently reluctant allies. The course of Anglo-French policy during the first two years of the war did little to alter the Soviet view. The ridiculous and ill-fated attempt to intervene in the Soviet–Finnish war of 1940 on the Finnish side, while the Anglo-French and German forces sat and faced each other idly on the Western Front, confirmed Soviet suspicions that there were powerful figures in the West who preferred fighting Russia to fighting the Germans: and Churchill was now a member of the British Government. It did not perhaps occur to Stalin that his own policies had led the Anglo-French leaders to write off the possibility of the Russians as allies – that they now regarded the Soviet Union, however mistakenly, as in effect an ally of Nazi Germany. What was apparent to Stalin was that, in the midst of a mortal struggle with Germany, the West was prepared to launch an attack on Russia. It made no sense, unless the real enemy was Russia, not Germany. The collapse of France seemed to confirm the unwillingness of the West to fight seriously against the Germans. What, in any case, could you make of a people who offered paper guarantees and assurances to Poland, Romania, Greece and Finland which they had no power to make good, and who entered a war with Germany which they were manifestly unprepared to fight? The British claimed to be continuing to fight after 1940, but seemed to be doing little about it, except launching what were, in the early stages of the war, not very effective air-raids on Germany. Then there was the Hess mission to Britain in March 1941. Clearly he was bringing peace-terms from Hitler. If there was no intention by the British of closing with the offer, why were they so secretive about the whole business? Perhaps they were keeping Hess on ice until the favourable moment came for serious negotiations – and possibly meantime encouraging Hitler to attack Russia?[5]

When Russia became an ally, therefore, there were ample grounds for suspicion on both sides, at any rate between Britain and the Soviets. The United States ought logically to have been a different case. Although the Republican administrations of the 1920s had joined in the general ostracism of the USSR, Roosevelt had inaugurated a new approach in 1933, recognizing the Soviet regime and encouraging contacts and technological exchanges with Russia. True, the United States had not taken any effective steps to resist Nazi Germany, but at least she had not connived with the Nazis. Roosevelt was entitled to feel that he ought to have built up some degree of credit, as a friend, with the Soviet leaders. He did not realize how deeply ingrained was Soviet suspicion of all capitalist states.

THE PROBLEM OF AID TO RUSSIA: THE ARCTIC CONVOYS AND THE SECOND FRONT CONTROVERSY

The point must also be made that the wartime policies and actions of the Western powers must sometimes have been as baffling to the Soviet leaders as theirs were to the West. Roosevelt, for example, had promised a 'Second Front' in Europe in 1942: and then the Western Powers had invaded North Africa! The promised Second Front had not come, in Soviet eyes till 1944. Similarly both Roosevelt and Hull had given Stalin the impression, in two conferences held in 1943, that they were not overly interested in eastern Europe. The Soviet leader probably deduced from the attitude of the two men, and particularly their manifest unwillingness to support the various British initiatives, that the USSR was being offered virtually a free hand in eastern Europe, subject to a few cosmetic gestures in the direction of self-determination. But then in October 1944, after backing on and off from the British proposal of a short-term division into 'spheres of interest', Roosevelt had chosen the beginning of a Soviet–British conference on eastern Europe to say 'there is literally no question of this kind in which the United States is not interested'. On Germany, too, as will be seen, the Americans and British first put forward harsh proposals for a post-war settlement, then backed away from them. There seemed to be no consistency about Anglo-American policy: so often, it seemed, they would say one thing, then do something else. How could you do business with such people? In the end, Stalin probably drew only two firm conclusions about his allies from all this: first, that you could never really be sure they meant what they said; second, that when they proved unwilling to do what the USSR wanted, Churchill was usually to blame.[6]

Immediately after the German attack on Russia in June 1941, Roosevelt and Churchill both indicated that they supported the USSR in its resistance, Churchill as an ally, Roosevelt as a friendly neutral, anxious to help. Stalin could have no complaints here. Hopkins was dispatched almost at once to London to concert measures with the British, and Roosevelt readily agreed to his going on to Russia. Hopkins' report stressed that, in spite of their initial defeats and loss of territory, Soviet resistance was holding and would continue to do so. The Soviets were worth assisting. At the Argentia conference in August that year, Churchill and Roosevelt agreed on the necessity of supplying Stalin with arms and other necessities, and a high-powered mission was sent to Moscow, led by Beaverbrook, a close friend of Churchill, and Harriman, a trusted associate of Roosevelt. Agreement was reached on supply matters. So far, so good. Roosevelt wholeheartedly admired the tenacity of Soviet resistance, at a time when the West was hardly engaging German troops at all. He tried hard to meet Soviet requests for supplies, both through the Persian Gulf–Middle Eastern route, and through the much more dangerous, if shorter, Arctic convoy route. The greater part of the dangers, however, even after Pearl Harbor, fell upon the British Navy and merchant service: and though Churchill was willing to do his best, he was not willing to commit suicide. In the first six months of 1942, German submarine warfare made serious inroads on allied shipping resources: the outbreak of the war with Japan in December 1941 had also created fresh demands on these resources, and added to the losses. In April, Churchill felt bound to warn Roosevelt that 'a serious situation' was developing in regard to shipping. Roosevelt, now of course a full ally, replied that it would be a grave mistake to halt Soviet supplies: it would have 'political repercussions' in Russia and have an 'unfortunate effect' on Stalin. What the President feared was that the Russian armies might collapse completely, or be so near collapse that Stalin might feel obliged to sue for peace. To prevent that, even severe losses of merchant ships and escorting warships were a justifiable price to pay. Churchill, for his part, did not see that it could help anyone to weaken the overstrained Royal Navy beyond a certain point. He did not regard the navy as expendable. 'With very great respect', he asked Roosevelt not to press him too hard on this point, in the light of the fact that his senior naval adviser regarded the shipping situation as sufficiently serious to warrant six months' suspension of the convoys. Only between a third and a quarter of the ships were getting through: that was not good enough.[7]

In the end, the result of the argument was that the convoys continued in fits and starts throughout the crucial year of 1942 – in June, then in September, then again in December. The losses were fearful. Stalin was well aware that Churchill, not Roosevelt, was responsible for the shortfall in convoys. At the Moscow meeting of the two men in August 1942, he upbraided Churchill for letting him down, prompting a vigorous defence by the latter. To Stalin's sneering suggestion that the British should try fighting the Germans and they wouldn't find it so bad, the Premier replied that the British understood the problems of naval warfare – with the clear implication that the Russians did not.[8]

During this same period, of course, the argument over the 'Second Front' was at its height, and it was also Churchill's unpalatable task during the Moscow talks to break the news to Stalin that there would be no invasion of Europe in 1942. Not surprisingly, relations between the USSR and its Western allies worsened considerably, and did not really recover until the Moscow Foreign Ministers' Conference, over a year later. Stalin correctly identified the British as being mainly responsible for the disappointment of his hopes in this area. Logically the Americans should have escaped some of his resentment. On the other hand, the British had at least made it clear, during their earlier discussions with Molotov, that they were making no promises, whereas Roosevelt had given the distinct impression, at that time, that a new European front *would* be opened in 1942. An attitude of wary suspicion seemed therefore as appropriate towards the Americans as towards the British.

THE QUEST FOR A SUMMIT MEETING: SOVIET-AMERICAN ENTENTE AT TEHERAN

Anxious, as always, lest Stalin should be provoked into signing a separate peace, Roosevelt redoubled his efforts to reassure him that the allies were making every possible effort to assist Russia. He continued to press Churchill to resume the Arctic convoys; suggested sending an Anglo-American staff mission to explain more fully to Stalin the strategic possibilities flowing from a successful North African operation; and raised the possibility of sending Western air forces to the Russian front. 'Nothing,' he cabled to Churchill in October, 'is more important than that Stalin feels we mean to support him.' Above all he sought eagerly to bring about a personal meeting with Stalin. It was not until the following year that American policy-makers committed themselves whole-heartedly to the view that US relations with the USSR were going to be more important for future world stability than relations with Britain. But already, in 1942, Roosevelt was convinced that he must do his utmost to win Stalin's confidence – and the best way to do that was to meet him personally. Immediately after Pearl Harbor he had proposed to Stalin a four-power meeting (i.e. including the Chinese) in Chungking; but Stalin was not disposed to risk annoying the Japanese by associating with Chiang Kai-shek, and in addition could fairly argue that, as commander-in-chief, he could not leave Russia at a time when his country was fighting for its life. Roosevelt was not discouraged, however, and the events of 1942 added fresh urgency to his efforts – all the more so after both Churchill and Eden had visited Moscow during the course of the year. If the British had had personal talks with Stalin, so should he: with the British present if need be, but even better perhaps without them. He could talk much more frankly with Stalin if Churchill were not around – and as he told Churchill the following year, Stalin would probably talk more frankly to him. It was not to prove an easy matter to bring such a meeting about, since there were many difficulties in the way, difficulties created partly by Stalin's role as commander-in-chief, and partly by the constitutional limitations imposed on Roosevelt as president. But Roosevelt was convinced it was necessary. Churchill, of course, regarded the possibility of a meeting between Roosevelt and Stalin *à deux* with no particular enthusiasm. By June 1943 when Roosevelt again revived the idea, he was becoming increasingly suspicious about the President's intentions. Roosevelt sought to placate him. He assured the Premier, with no particular regard for the truth, that a 'two's company' meeting was not his idea. Stalin had asked for it. Reasonably enough, Roosevelt argued that he wanted a personal opportunity to 'explore Stalin's thinking'. Eden had done so on Churchill's behalf as early as January 1942, and Churchill himself had met the Russian leader in August of that year, without Roosevelt. It was only fair, indeed essential, that the President should have the same opportunity. He and Churchill could have a personal meeting soon afterwards, perhaps in August, and than all three could meet together in the autumn. But Churchill's fears were not be reasoned away. They were based on substance – the substance being that he knew Roosevelt to be either indifferent or actively hostile to what Churchill regarded as vital imperial interests; Stalin even more so. He was afraid of what the two men would hatch up together. As it happened circumstances were on the Premier's side, and enabled him to win his point. It will be evident from what follows that Stalin was in no mood to gratify the President's wishes during most of 1943, even if the military situation on the Eastern Front had permitted his absence. He was angered by the renewed suspension of the Arctic convoys in April, 1943 – 'a catastrophic diminution', he cabled angrily to both leaders – and even more so by the Anglo-American decision, at the Washington Conference in May, not to attempt an invasion of Western Europe in 1943. The most his allies were apparently prepared to do was to invade Sicily, and perhaps Italy. The cross-Channel attack must wait till 1944. Understandably, Stalin was bitterly disappointed. 'The Soviet Union cannot align itself with decisions to which it was not a party and about which it was not consulted,' he protested. But he knew the decision was irreversible. Churchill, of course, was again to blame, and Roosevelt had weakly allowed himself to be persuaded to follow in his trail.[9]

These two causes of contention continued to rumble on throughout most of 1943, and it was not until the Moscow meeting of foreign ministers in October that for various reasons the climate improved and Stalin indicated his willingness to meet Roosevelt and Churchill. But in the meantime, a fresh cause of dissension had arisen, and once again it was with Churchill rather than Roosevelt that Stalin found himself at odds.

The problem of Poland, together with other Eastern European problems, is discussed in the next chapter. Here it is sufficient to say that what historians know as the 'Katyn incident' blew up in April 1943 and provoked Stalin into breaking off relations with the London-based Polish government-in-exile, and that Churchill from this date onwards devoted much effort towards healing the breach, while Roosevelt for the most part stood aloof. It was an early indication that Roosevelt was not prepared to risk antagonizing Stalin over Eastern European issues which did not effect vital American interests. To Churchill the Polish problem was a source of constant anxiety, not only because of British obligations to Poland, but because of what it might point to as an omen of Soviet intentions in Eastern Europe. To Roosevelt it was little more than a source of irritation as a possible impediment to good relations with Russia. It was against this unpropitious background, in which there were disagreements with Russia over crucial issues, and interchanges between Churchill and Stalin which occasionally resembled more the exchange of salvoes between enemy battleships than communications between allies, that the year 1943 must be seen, and against which one can judge how far attitudes to Russia contributed to the distinct worsening of the Roosevelt–Churchill relationships during that year.[10]

The year began propitiously enough, in February, with Churchill agreeing with Roosevelt that the USSR had 'suffered horribly' and 'must be aided'. True, in the same message Churchill reverted to Stalin's designs on Poland and the Baltic states, but events were to show that, Wilsonian principles notwithstanding, the President was now prepared to be accommodating on this issue. A month later he indicated as much to Eden, when the latter visited Washington. During these discussions the two men agreed in their hopes that the

Soviet Union would prove 'reasonable and co-operative' after the war: and the Foreign Secretary expressed the belief that Russia would not seek to 'communize Europe'. There was indeed no reason at this point, other than Marxist rhetoric, to suspect any such intention. But the talks also provided the occasion for some preliminary discussion of the future world organization, and this must have helped to reinforce Roosevelt's belief that post-war amity between the US and Russia would be of supreme importance. In line with this he gave cool approval of Churchill's attempts to heal the breach between Stalin and the London Poles, while indicating privately to the Soviet leader that he thought the Poles 'misguided' in their reaction to the Katyn affair. There were, indeed, quite enough causes of dissension with Russia as it was, with the convoys suspended in April and Stalin's angry reaction to the Washington Conference decision on the cross-Channel attack. It would be best to leave contentious territorial issues like Poland on one side for the moment, and meanwhile press the London Poles to show some sense and recognize that their future interests demanded good relations with Russia. But Roosevelt must have been struck by one observation of Churchill's during the further discussion of the future UN at the Washington Conference. The Prime Minister expressed the view that 'the prospect of having no strong country on the map between England and Russia was not attractive'. Roosevelt did not agree. During the months that followed he was to indicate on more than one occasion, amongst others to his son Elliott, his own view that a more powerful Russia would not necessarily be a bad thing, either for the United States or Europe. Nor did it matter too much if there were to be no powerful state west of her. It was a difference of view which was to lead to disagreements with Churchill over the future of both France and Germany. But at this moment, what was most apparent was that Churchill's attitude to Russia was far more wary and suspicious than his own. He would have to take care to ensure that neither Churchill's well-known dislike of Bolshevism, nor his predilection for balance of power politics should prejudice US relations with Russia.[11]

All this led to further attempts by the President to bring amount the much-desired meeting with Stalin. In June 1943 he sent the former US ambassador to Russia, Joseph E. Davies, on a mission to Stalin. Churchill suspected one important purpose of the mission was to cajole Stalin into an early meeting, perhaps 'à deux'. The President's replies to his queries tended to confirm these fears. In fact Stalin's mind was moving towards accepting such a meeting, but he replied that it would not be possible until later in the year, after the end of the summer and autumn campaigns on the Eastern Front. In the meantime, he suggested a preliminary meeting of 'responsible representatives' to prepare the ground. This was taken to mean a Foreign Ministers' conference. Churchill heaved a sigh of relief. The British would, it was clear, be present at both meetings. For his part, and unlike Roosevelt, he was not disposed to be particularly conciliatory towards Stalin. In response to the latter's protest about the Washington Conference decision on the cross-Channel attack, he had cabled robustly to Stalin that the Western Allies could best help him by winning battles, not by attempting operations which courted defeat. An even rougher exchange took place in October on the perennially thorny topic of the Arctic convoys, two of which had been cancelled. At one point Churchill refused to accept a particularly surly message from Stalin, and returned it to the Soviet ambassador. In the end he told Eden, who was about to leave for the Foreign Ministers' Conference, to handle the matter on a personal level and deal with it as he thought best; and Stalin, when it came to the point, was far more conciliatory than expected, which may provide some justification for Churchill's view that a robust approach in dealing with the Russians was best.[12]

In fact the Foreign Ministers' Conference, and the Teheran Conference which immediately followed it, were in many ways the high point of Soviet relations with the West. Certainly both the British and Americans thought so, and the unusually amicable approach adopted by both Stalin and Molotov gave Roosevelt and Hull considerable encouragement in their efforts to achieve a closer relationship. There were a number of reasons for this change in Soviet behaviour, most of which, unfortunately, had no lasting effect on inter-allied relations. One important factor was the Soviet military successes of the past year. The Red Army had inflicted two crushing defeats on the Germans at Stalingrad and Kursk, and driven the invaders back. The Soviet leaders undoubtedly came to these conferences with a greater sense of self-confidence than before, and suffering less from the strain and anxiety which had probably sharpened Soviet responses in the past. Amongst other results, the more genial and relaxed atmosphere allowed Stalin to admit what he had probably always fully realized, that Allied Mediterranean operations *had* been of service to the Soviet cause, in drawing significant forces from the Russian front, and Allied successes had helped to weaken German morale, besides knocking Italy out of the war. This was a major concession on Stalin's part. Another factor was Soviet gratification that the Western foreign ministers had agreed to meet in Moscow. For the first time a major international conference was to be held on Soviet soil, and in the Soviet capital. It marked the moment when the Soviets felt they had come in from the cold, and been recognized as allies and equals. They were all the more anxious that the two conferences should be a success, and made every effort to bring about that result. At Moscow Stalin's unexpected amiability when Eden raised the vexatious topic of the Arctic convoys, and the even more surprising readiness of the Soviet leader to consider a possible further short postponement of the Overlord operation, proposed by Churchill, were no doubt due to this. Churchill's *démarche* indeed produced a much more angry reaction from the Americans than from Stalin.[13]

Stalin's mood must have been improved by an unexpected discovery at these two conferences. Far from presenting a united front to the Soviets, the British and Americans seemed to be divided on a good many issues – on strategy, on Eastern Europe, on Germany and France, among others. The Americans made no bones about the fact that they were by no means lining up with the British, and on many issues in fact agreed more with the Soviet viewpoint. This was a very different story from what had apparently been the case in the very recent past. Stalin must have been much encouraged. This development was due partly to a positive determination by Roosevelt to court Soviet goodwill, if necessary at the expense of relations with the British, but it also reflected a positive deterioration in Anglo-American relations and in the Churchill–Roosevelt relationship. There were many reasons for this, some of which have been explored in Chapter 3. Apart from the differences over strategy – or at any rate strategic timing – there had been sharp differences of view over the French political imbroglio which had developed in North Africa. On Eastern Europe, too, especially Poland, clear differences of view were emerging, which were a source of concern, and some resentment, on both sides. For Roosevelt and Hull there was anxiety lest the British concern for the Polish cause and other East European problems should draw the United States into controversy with the USSR. On the British side there soon developed resentment, when it emerged at these conferences that they could apparently expect little support from the Americans on East European issues. However, more important than any of these factors was almost certainly a conscious reappraisal by the Americans of the respective importance of relations with the British and the Russians. An important milestone in this process had been an American military-strategic estimate of Russia's post-war position, which Hopkins had received in August. This document asserted that the Soviet post-war position would in fact be militarily 'a dominant one'. The British position would clearly be much weaker, and they would not be able to oppose Soviet wishes without US support. The conclusion drawn was much that which Roosevelt was already coming to: that during the war the Soviet military contribution would be the decisive one, therefore the Russians must be given 'every assistance': and that since after the war the Russians would be the dominant power in Europe, it was even more important 'to develop and maintain the most friendly relations with Russia'. There is no doubt that the editor of the Churchill–Roosevelt correspondence, Professor Kimball, is right in thinking that this conscious reappraisal was the most important factor in the deterioration of the relationship. That it *had* deteriorated is very evident from the tone of Roosevelt's discussions with his chiefs of staff en route to the Cairo and Teheran conferences. Roosevelt here displays an almost pathological suspicion of British motives. It is so marked as to suggest that Roosevelt was subconsciously and uneasily attempting to justify to himself the change of front which he proposed to adopt, and the lack of support which he intended to demonstrate for British policy in various areas, and which Hull had already, at Moscow, denied to British policy on Eastern Europe.[14]

Roosevelt then set out to make the situation plain to both men. He refused to meet Churchill separately to concert a common policy on strategic and other matters before their meeting with Stalin. The opportunity was allowed to pass by both before the Cairo Conference with Chiang Kai-shek – a conference at which Roosevelt spent more time with the Chinese leader than with Churchill – and again at the end of that conference. Once at Teheran, he accepted Stalin's invitation to stay at the Soviet Embassy rather than Churchill's invitation to the British Embassy; sedulously avoided any private conclaves with the British Premier; and adopted on occasion a teasing, facetious attitude towards the British leader which Churchill did not find funny, and which the Russians no doubt regarded with astonishment. It was very much a case of 'Codlin's the friend, not Short', and Churchill, not the Russians, who must have felt out in the cold. It will be clear that the foundations already existed, both on the American and the Soviet side for what may be called without too much exaggeration, a 'Soviet–American entente' which emerged at both these conferences. It applied to Grand Strategy, where the British were forced to reiterate their commitment to the May 1944 date for Overlord – and further, to swallow an operation against southern France (Anvil) for which they had no enthusiasm. British suggestions for operations in the eastern Mediterranean got nowhere, and the Italian campaign got pretty short shrift. It applied also to Eastern Europe. In this area Hull had offered little support for Eden's various initiatives at Moscow, which partly for that reason all fell by the wayside. At Teheran, Roosevelt curtailed as far as possible tripartite discussion on the Polish issue, and confined himself to expressing pious hopes that the conflict between Russia and the London Poles would be resolved. Privately at the same time he was assuring Stalin that the US would take a benevolent attitude towards Soviet territorial demands on Poland. Churchill and Eden were left, in fact, to 'carry the ball' on Poland and Eastern Europe. Not surprisingly, they did not get very far, then or later. On Germany, too, Roosevelt and Stalin seemed to be agreed on a drastic solution which would wipe Germany from the map, in contrast to Churchill's earlier hope that something substantial would be left between Russia and Western Europe: while on France Roosevelt agreed with Stalin that she deserved very little of the Allies, and would, in fact, not amount to much for at least twenty years.[15]

By comparison with the short shrift which the British had received at both conferences, Roosevelt and Hull felt after Teheran that the US shift of emphasis had already paid dividends. Thanks to Stalin's whole-hearted support, they had finally been able to outface and beat down Churchill on strategic matters, particularly Overlord in May 1944, and had put an end to the East Mediterranean nonsense. For the first time, too, Stalin had committed himself to a definite undertaking to enter the Far Eastern war when the European war had ended. Apart from some minor differences over Italy, there seemed a wide measure of agreement with the Russians on European problems. They saw eye-to-eye very largely on France and Germany, which could not be said of the US and Britain. Further east Stalin had shown himself reasonably amenable over Finland, which ought to be a good omen for Soviet policy towards the rest of Eastern Europe, and even on the difficult Polish problem, there seemed to be tripartite agreement on the aspect which Stalin was most insistent on – that is the territorial aspect. If that part of the problem was solved, it ought to be possible to patch together some sort of compromise on the governmental issue, if Churchill could get the London Poles to behave. Most important of all for the future, Stalin and Molotov had accepted Hull's Four-Power Declaration on International Security at Moscow, and at Teheran Stalin had confirmed his acceptance in principle of US proposals for a new international organization. This was the best possible omen for future Soviet–US cooperation in peace. Reviewing the overall results, Roosevelt and Hull felt well-satisfied with their reappraisal of alliance necessities.

By contrast Churchill was momentarily much depressed by what had happened. It had revealed all too clearly just how much the British weight in the alliance had declined, and to what extent his personal pull with Roosevelt and the Americans had weakened. He had been forced to swallow more than one unpalatable dose on strategy, and Roosevelt had seemed to have no conception of the possible dangers ahead which might follow from an over-mighty Russia or the implications that had for policy towards France, Germany and Eastern Europe. British wishes and ideas on all these matters had seemed to count for little compared with Soviet desires. It was a black look-out.

All of this is faithfully reflected in the Churchill–Roosevelt correspondence before and after Teheran, as well as by what happened at the two conferences – or rather three, if one includes the acrimonious US–British–Chinese conference at Cairo, which had certainly not improved Anglo-American relations. The tone was set by Roosevelt at the very outset of the Moscow conference, when he cabled to Churchill, 'our relations with Russia are of paramount importance'. In response Churchill sought to hark back to the close relationship they had enjoyed: in particular he asked that they should meet to concert policies, particularly strategic policies, before the meetings with Chiang Kai-shek and Stalin. 'The Russians ought not to be vexed if we concert operations for 1944 on fronts where no Russian troops are involved', he remarked plaintively. Roosevelt was eventually forced to say plainly that he was above all anxious to avoid giving Stalin the idea that the British and Americans were 'ganging up' on him. The President now, in fact, came up with a further idea for 'increasing Stalin's confidence in our sincerity', an idea which seemed to Churchill both wrong-headed and impracticable. He proposed that Soviet representatives should 'sit in' on meetings of the US–British Combined Chiefs of Staff. Needless to say, the idea did not appeal to Churchill, and he was able to present a very strong case against it. On 27 October he cabled in reply: (1) that the need for simultaneous translation would cause unacceptable delays in reaching decisions; (2) that, unlike the American and British Chiefs, the Russian military representatives would enjoy no real independence, but would simply reflect Stalin's wishes: they would sit and 'bay for the Second Front', as he put it. Finally, it would be a very one-sided arrangement, since the Russians were not inviting the Anglo-Americans to 'sit in' on their military discussions. In the upshot, the proposal was quietly allowed to disappear from the scene at Teheran.[16]

A further proposal from the US War Department also had an unpleasant resonance for the British, namely that there should be supreme 'overall' commander for the whole

European theatre, including, that is, both the Mediterranean and the forthcoming Overlord sphere of operations. The obvious choice for such an exalted post would be General Marshall. Such an arrangement would virtually have cut off Churchill and the British Chiefs from any influence on European operations. It would be almost impossible to overrule such a commander, especially if the post were held by the most highly respected US soldier of his generation. The idea had, of course, no chance of acceptance with Churchill and his Chiefs of Staff. But the fact that it could be made at all was a unpleasant indication of US thinking about the alliance. It was clear that now the Americans were developing their full military and industrial strength, they would expect the British to accept unequivocally the status of junior partner in the alliance, and not go on raising constant objections to US strategic proposals the way they had in the past. Lest his allies should have missed the point, Roosevelt took the opportunity at the second plenary meeting in Cairo to read out the disposition of Anglo-American land and air forces at home and overseas, reminding Churchill that, once Overlord had been launched, the US would become the major contributor – and would therefore expect predominance in every way. The 'overall commander' proposal would have had, from the US point of view, the advantage that it would ensure the priority of Overlord versus the Mediterranean, and by so doing, provide further reassurance to the Soviets.

THE US REFUSAL TO DETER STALIN: POLAND AND EASTERN EUROPE

It was, of course, a vain hope to suppose that Churchill's eloquence could be stifled by any considerations of junior or senior status. But the writing on the wall was clear. At Teheran Churchill's attempts to allay Stalin's suspicions of British motives, and resentment at the British part in the alliance – suspicions, Churchill felt, exacerbated by Roosevelt's misrepresentations – got nowhere. Stalin's suspicions were too deep-rooted, and not altogether, it must be said, unfounded. Fortunately Churchill did not realize how profound Roosevelt's suspicions of British motives had also become. If he had been able to overhear the President's conversation with his Chiefs of Staff on board the *Iowa*, or his *obiter dicta* to his son Elliott during these conferences, he would have been even more worried than he was. Even before this, Roosevelt's comments on British proposals for Eastern Europe at the time of the Moscow Conference had shown how distrustful he was of British objectives in that area. In the sixteen months that followed Teheran until Roosevelt's death, the tendencies manifested then in US policy towards its two Allies were confirmed. The principal issue between the Soviets and Britain continued to be the Polish issue, and, as will be seen, Roosevelt continued to give benevolent, but mostly distant approval to Churchill's efforts to reach agreement, while taking care not to offend Stalin; and when the US offered mediation, the offer was vitiated by an unwillingness to tackle the central issues head-on. Quite possibly Churchill would have failed anyway, but the lack of any positive US support certainly did not help matters. And although Cordell Hull says in his memoirs that the Balkans – and particularly Soviet relations with the Balkans – 'came to the forefront of our diplomacy' in early 1944, US policy in these matters was very much a matter of fits and starts, and showed little consistency except in its constant desire to avoid getting embroiled with the USSR. This was very apparent in the uncertain US attitude to Churchill's moves towards a *de facto* division of responsibility in the Balkans. Even more could this be said of Roosevelt's manifest unwillingness to bring pressure to bear on the Russians during the tragedy of the Warsaw uprising in August. In regard to Greece, too, Roosevelt's approval of the dispatch of British troops to forestall a Communist coup was perhaps dependent on Stalin's apparent prior agreement. The attitude of the State Department was certainly more lukewarm towards the British action in Greece, and soon became highly critical. The key to all this is to be found in the US judgement of the fruits of their policy towards Russia, shared by Roosevelt and Hull, and summed up by Hull as follows: 'Relations between the United States and Russia, as 1944 began, were closer than they had ever been. Through the Moscow and Teheran Conferences we had brought Russia into a program of real cooperation for the remainder of the war, and, we hoped, for the future.' Before the conferences, Hull had said to Eden,

'Let's talk Stalin out of his shell of suspicion and into practical international cooperation'. Hull and his chief believed they had made a substantial beginning on this programme at Moscow and Teheran. It was vital that the process should continue, and not be halted.[17]

One would have thought that Churchill would have fully grasped by this time how different Roosevelt's priorities and indeed whole attitude *vis-à-vis* Russia were from his own. Yet even as late as the Anglo-American conference at Quebec in September 1944, the British leader does not seem fully to have appreciated this fact, together with the extent to which his own influence had waned – this in spite of the President's very recent refusal to bring any real pressure to bear on Stalin over aid to the Warsaw Poles – and the rebuffs that his suggestions on that subject had received. Doggedly he persisted in parading his fears of the Soviet march into Eastern Europe before the unsympathetic gaze of Roosevelt and his Chiefs of Staff. Repeatedly he stressed the necessity of forestalling the Russians in certain areas of Central Europe, retaining a stake in Central and Eastern Europe and not allowing everything to pass into Soviet hands. As he put it in the first plenary session of the conference, 'I prefer to get into Vienna before the Russians do'. His strategic suggestions (e.g. an amphibious operation in the Istrian peninsula) were geared to this presumed necessity. Given Churchill's never-say-die persistence it is not perhaps surprising that he should have continued to flog a dead horse. What is more surprising is that he should have allowed wishful thinking to prevail over past experience, and apparently believed that he was getting somewhere with Roosevelt and the Americans. In this he was misled perhaps by the general atmosphere of euphoria which prevailed at that conference, by the fact that the atmosphere was so much better than it had been at Cairo and Teheran, and by US agreement to the Istrian operation, if it turned out to be practicable. As will be apparent from the previous discussion of this operation in Chapter 3, the Americans perceived that the circumstances would simply not arise which would make the operation practicable. It cost nothing to make concessions where no consequences were likely to follow. Churchill would have been wiser to have been guided by Roosevelt's off-hand and rather brutal attitude during subsequent discussions on much-needed post-war assistance to Britain. It was a measure of how far the importance of the British alliance had diminished in Roosevelt's eyes. Be that as it may, Churchill had already telegraphed enthusiastically to the War Cabinet, 'The Conference has opened in a blaze of friendship ... the idea of going to Vienna, if the war lasts long enough, is fully accepted here.[18]

Quite why Roosevelt refrained from openly contradicting Churchill's arguments, and allowed him to retain the illusion that he had made some impact on the President's thinking, is difficult to see. Roosevelt was a tired and ailing man by this time – which must also serve an excuse for some of his less defensible behaviour at this conference. Perhaps he simply could not be bothered to consume energy in refuting Churchill's *idées fixes*. Certainly Churchill's flights of oratory on the Russian menace can have had little influence on him, save to reinforce his determination not to be drawn into supporting Britain against the Soviet Union over Eastern European quarrels. Indeed, Roosevelt's to-ing and fro-ing over Churchill's pursuit of some kind of temporary *modus vivendi* with Stalin in the Balkans ought already to have warned Churchill how little inclined the former was to follow *any* British lead in this area. At one point he had felt constrained to point out to Roosevelt that neither of them had any troops in Romania (the point at issue in this case) and therefore the Russians 'would probably do as they like anyhow'. On the question of policy towards Eastern Europe therefore, he asked Roosevelt to trust him – but that was precisely the trouble: Roosevelt did not trust him, and was deeply suspicious of British motives in the Balkans; the State Department even more so. This attitude was equally evident when Churchill pursued this policy at the subsequent Churchill–Stalin meeting in October 1944. Reference has already been made, at the beginning of this chapter, to the President's telegram to the two leaders, indicating his unwillingness to go along automatically with anything they might decide. By thus throwing a spanner into the works, Roosevelt in fact not only embarrassed Churchill, which may not have worried him, but also annoyed Stalin, which was certainly not his intention. Roosevelt at this moment was in fact more concerned with the teething troubles of the new UN organization, which Hull had been labouring to set up at the Dumbarton Oaks Conference, than with the Balkans, and was, if anything, anxious not to raise contentious issues with USSR until these problems, particularly those connected with the nature and scope of the Great Powers' 'veto' were sorted out. At all events, Churchill was, as usual, prepared to fall in with the President's wishes if possible. He assured Roosevelt he would not commit him on either that issue or on 'spheres of influence': his arrangement with Stalin would remain a personal one. Roosevelt was in fact able to secure from Stalin a satisfactory compromise on the veto, and this for him was more important than the simultaneous collapse of Soviet negotiations with the London Poles, which Churchill had been diligently fostering. He had neither Churchill's commitment to the London Poles nor his belief in them.[19]

Stalin's recognition of the rival Lublin government at the beginning of 1945 was a disappointment, but Roosevelt did not necessarily see it as a major issue. His thoughts were centred at this point on the forthcoming Yalta conference – his second meeting with Stalin. Both Roosevelt and his new Secretary of State, Edward Stettinius, saw this as an opportunity to strengthen the relationship with the USSR and his personal relationship with Stalin. To build, in fact, on the foundations which he felt had been established at Teheran. To this end, he was as determined as on the previous occasion not to allow Churchill's prejudices and conflicting aims to muddy the waters. It must again be made clear to the British that whatever kind of 'special relationship' they might think they had with the United States, it did not mean that they had priority in Roosevelt's scale of values compared with the Russians. Accordingly, when Churchill yet again sought a prior meeting between the British and Americans, the President refused. He would only agree to a meeting of the two Foreign Ministers, Stettinius and Eden, at Malta. This of course could do little to satisfy Churchill. Both constitutionally and as a very new secretary of state, Stettinius could not risk even appearing to commit the President. He could only spell out certain US lines of thought. Roosevelt went to Yalta therefore, as he intended, uncommitted to Churchill on the issues which most concerned the Premier. At Yalta, Roosevelt's tactic – not a bad one in the circumstances – was on most issues to indicate sympathy with the Soviet point of view, and then, having as he hoped conciliated Stalin, to work for some sort of acceptable compromise between the Russian leader and Churchill. The gulf between the two latter was in fact wide and deep on many crucial issues. On Poland and some other East European states, on the treatment of Germany, on the future role of France, there were clear differences of view, though on the last of these issues it was not pretence for Roosevelt to imply that he fully shared Stalin's view. Indeed on Germany also, Roosevelt's views were still at least as close to Stalin's as to Churchill's, and even on Poland Roosevelt had some sympathy with Stalin's attitude to the London government. These issues are dealt with in detail in subsequent chapters. In the context of Anglo-Soviet-American relations it is only necessary to say here that Roosevelt's purpose was to prevent an open breach in the Alliance by obtaining compromises on all these issues, at any rate on paper. It could not be said that it proved easy to do so, but in the end compromises were obtained which could be incorporated in documentary form. One must add that this amounted in the most contentious cases simply to postponing final decisions.

Yalta, in fact, was an exercise in papering over the cracks. On the question of the Polish government and its future political regime, the controversies over German partition and reparations and the future of Eastern Europe, formulae were worked out, or means found towards further negotiation and possible agreement. A complete breakdown was averted and amity on the surface preserved. This satisfied Roosevelt fairly well and achieved his main object, though it was less satisfactory to Churchill. But, ailing though Roosevelt undoubtedly was, and vague though he sometimes appeared to be, it was a not unsuccessful exercise in diplomacy. He was able to extract sufficient concessions – or apparent concessions – from Stalin on all these issues to enable Churchill to go along with what had been decided. He was even able to secure Stalin's agreement to a substantial concession of his own on the vexed question of a French zone of occupation in Germany. This was something both Churchill and Eden had very much at heart. On the face of it, indeed, Churchill emerged from the conference with not too much to complain about – if Stalin meant what he said. And this, too, was what Roosevelt intended. Neither of the two main charges which were subsequently made against him – that he had allowed Stalin to gain a substantial diplomatic victory, and that he had lost his grip on the issues – can really be sustained. If what was decided was sometimes no more than to postpone a decision for further consideration and negotiation, well, that was not so bad. Roosevelt's first instinct had always been to leave decisions on the most contentious matters to what it was hoped would be a cooler and less emotional atmosphere, after the fighting had ended. So be it. Above all, he had achieved his main object – to bring the conference to an end in an atmosphere of goodwill, and so preserve the good relationship with Stalin and the Russians that he felt had been achieved at Teheran.[20]

The sequel was less satisfactory. In the two months which were all that remained of Roosevelt's life and the Roosevelt – Churchill relationship, it soon began to seem that it was the latter's doubts and fears rather than Roosevelt's optimism which had been more realistic. It seemed that the concessions which apparently had been made by Stalin at Yalta, particularly on Poland and Eastern Europe, had somehow evaporated. Stalin's attitude, too, had suddenly become altogether more surly and truculent. Churchill was not slow to bring his feelings on the matter to Roosevelt's notice. They had been sold, he said, 'a false prospectus' at Yalta. But Roosevelt remained consistent in his policy of minimizing differences with the Soviets as much as possible. In the face of Churchill's exhortations to take a strong line, he preferred to put gentle and conciliatory pressure on Stalin. 'We are not', he told Churchill on 15 March, 'confronted with a breakdown of the Yalta agreement, until we have made efforts to overcome the difficulty.' Even Roosevelt's patience, however, was tested to breaking point by a particularly insulting and suspicious message from Molotov on the subject of some feelers which had been put out by the German High Command in Italy for possible armistice negotiations – approaches which in fact came to nothing. Roosevelt's reply was unusually sharp, for once as sharp as Churchill's. Perhaps it is cynical to reflect that it is always easier to be philosophical about insults to another than insults to oneself. Be that as it may, Roosevelt's uncompromising response undoubtedly took the Soviet leader by surprise, but he gave no ground, though he did cable to Churchill that 'he had no intention of offending anyone'. Roosevelt no doubt took the same view as Churchill that in the realm of apologies, 'this is about the best we are going to get'. At all events, and again true to his consistent policy, he cabled to Stalin a more conciliatory message, urging the importance of avoiding misunderstandings. It was the incident which occurred at the beginning of April 1945, which was in Roosevelt's mind as much as the immediately pertinent Polish issue, when he said in his last message to Churchill on the subject of allied relations with Russia, 'these problems seem to arise every day, and most of them straighten out.' Before matters could develop further, the President lay dead at Warm Springs.[21]

THE SOVIET ENIGMA

It cannot be said that either Roosevelt or Churchill was very successful in plumbing the depths of Soviet policy. Neither man was particularly familiar with the Marxist analysis of society, history and international relations. According to that analysis the interests of all capitalist states must be ultimately at war with those of socialist states. Temporary bargains based on equally temporary mutual interests might be possible, but true or lasting friendship or real confidence could simply not exist. Roosevelt and Churchill were inclined to see Stalin as a traditional Russian nationalist, the latest in a line of powerful Tsars, and there often seemed good reason for this view. Stalin was certainly a 'good Russian', with most of the attitudes that implied. He disliked the Poles, hated the Germans; he distrusted the British as heartily as any of his predecessors, and was as ready as any Tsar to seize an advantage for Russian national interests in the good old fashioned way. His language, too, often suggested it. Yet all this did not mean that he did not accept in broad terms the Marxist analysis, and this was perhaps even more true of Molotov and some of the other Soviet leaders. According to this analysis, the Americans and the British, if they had known their true interests, should have been fighting on the same side as the Germans. The Marxist theory, however, covered this problem. It pointed out that fortunately the capitalist powers sometimes fell out with each other, and temporary alliances with socialist states might then develop. But it was to be expected that the capitalist states would not fall over themselves to help a socialist ally, and would have no particular objection to seeing that ally bear the brunt of the fighting, and being much weakened in the process. Always suspicious of treachery, the Soviet leaders of course found ample cause for their suspicions, as one always does. It is not a weakness peculiar to Marxists: de Gaulle, after all, suffered from the same malaise. If Roosevelt is to be accused of simplicity or naivety in his approach to the Russians, it is because he seemed largely unaware of this deep and fundamental suspicion. He was not fully conscious of the scale and difficulties of the mountain he sought to climb.

To what extent did the joint and separate inputs of Roosevelt and Churchill amount to a common policy towards Russia? Rather more than is sometimes conceded. Churchill was always anxious to keep in step with Roosevelt, and to follow his lead if he possibly could. Indeed, for a considerable period, and on most aspects of the problem, he saw eye to eye with Roosevelt. So far as the war itself was concerned, there was no question that Russia must be kept in the fight. They could not therefore afford a complete breach with their ally, no matter what. On the future possible danger from an over-mighty Russia, Churchill's prescience has sometimes been overstated. Until 1943 he seems to have had relatively few worries on this score. He thought, with some reason, that the Russians would emerge much weakened from the conflict, and would need Western goodwill and assistance. Moreover, until that stage, the Red Army had only just succeeded in holding its own with the *Wehrmacht,* which was still fighting deep inside Soviet territory. Even after Stalingrad, when his anxieties grew greater, and Soviet behaviour more provocative, he was still willing to be half-persuaded that future cooperation might be possible. He was as well aware as Roosevelt that the alternative was not an attractive one. As he wrote, quite sincerely, to Stalin at the end of the war, a future of perpetual bickering and animosity was a bleak prospect. Neither Roosevelt nor Churchill, of course, ever succeeded in persuading the other to alter their fundamental postures. Churchill, inherently prejudiced against communist Russia, and discouraged by the rough and stormy nature of the wartime relationship, could never be persuaded to adopt as frank, open and optimistic an approach as Roosevelt thought necessary. But nor, on the other hand, could Churchill persuade Roosevelt to adopt the tough line with Stalin that he himself often thought would be more beneficial. Churchill's view was that Stalin dealt in tough language, and understood it, and he may well have been right. Tact and subtlety were perhaps wasted on Stalin. As anxieties mounted towards the end of the war, Churchill believed this more vehemently than before. But Roosevelt was not persuadable on this issue. Churchill's known anti-communism, his imperialism, his staunch conservatism, his concern for purely British interests, all made him an unsafe guide in this matter in Roosevelt's eyes. Nevertheless, in practical terms the two men managed in general to keep together and in step. Churchill would go along with the President if he could: he needed the Americans. And Roosevelt, too, for all his occasionally dismissive attitude, needed the British.

But how far, if at all, did Roosevelt achieve any success in seeking the friendship of the Russians, and Stalin in particular? The question is important. Important, because some left-wing historians have considered that Roosevelt, the leader of a great capitalist state, must in the last resort eventually have been led into the same policy of hostility to Russia as his successors. If this analysis be sound, Roosevelt's success or failure with Stalin was in the long run of little importance. But other historians, also critical of postwar US foreign policy, have seen Truman as the main villain of the Cold War, and pointed to the possibility that the outcome might have been different if Roosevelt had lived. If that *was* a possibility, then any evidence that the President did indeed crack what Hull called 'the Soviet wall of suspicion', would strengthen it. For certainty on this point, historians await the opening of the Soviet wartime archives. Such fragmentary evidence as there is about Stalin's inner thoughts on the subject is not encouraging. If the former Yugoslav Communist leader, Milovan Djilas, is to be believed, Stalin not only distrusted Churchill, which is not surprising, but apparently only distinguished between Churchill and Roosevelt in regarding the latter as a criminal on a larger scale. However,

Djilas, who became deeply disillusioned with the USSR and ultimately with Communism, is not a completely impartial witness.[22]

It will already be evident from discussion of the Second Front issue in Chapter 2, that the present writer does not regard it as very profitable, or the principal business of historians, to delve into the might-have-beens of history, which can never be proved one way or the other. The most that is perhaps worth saying on this subject is that such evidence as we have is not conclusive. Whatever the Soviet leader's attitude may have been, though, it is difficult not to believe that Roosevelt, had he lived, would have made great efforts to prevent an absolute breach with the USSR. By sheer persistence, he might have succeeded in establishing some sort of *modus vivendi*, and averting the worst excesses of the Cold War, though it would have meant swallowing some unpalatable draughts. But is equally difficult to believe that the full trust and cooperation between the two states, which Roosevelt would so dearly have liked to establish, was ever on offer.[23]

5 The Unsolvable Problem: Poland and Eastern Europe

'The first of the great causes which led to the breakdown of the wartime alliance' is Churchill's description of the Polish problem in his memoirs. That Poland should have loomed larger in his (and ultimately Roosevelt's) mind than other East European countries, and that it was regarded by them as a 'test case' of Soviet intentions and Soviet goodwill, was due to various factors. Most importantly, Poland was the largest and potentially most powerful of these States, and furthermore occupied a crucial strategic position. It was possible to judge, as Churchill and Eden did, that Romania and Bulgaria were of more importance to the USSR strategically and in other ways, than to the West, and similarly Greece to the British. But Poland was a different matter. It was a corridor connecting the USSR and Central Europe, which could provide a relatively easy passage for the armed forces of an invader. It had been so used, as Stalin pointed out at Yalta, by the German invaders. But, like all corridors, it could be traversed in either direction, a fact which Churchill did not overlook.

There was a further consideration, of particular significance to Churchill and his British colleagues. Poland had been in 1939 the original *casus belli*, the immediate cause of the British declaration of war on Germany. That declaration had itself been a necessary consequence of a prior undertaking by Britain to defend Polish independence. There was a clear British commitment to Poland. Churchill was later to argue that this promise to restore an independent Polish state did not commit the British government to any particular frontiers for Poland – specifically the frontiers Poland had occupied between 1922 and 1939. These frontiers included a large area seized by the Poles from the USSR in 1922. The British Government had disapproved of this action, on the ground that the Western allies had prescribed in 1919 a frontier much further west. The 1919 frontier, indeed, actually bore the name of the then British Foreign Secretary, Lord Curzon. The British Government saw no reason to depart from the view that this frontier was ethnically just. It could be argued, therefore, that Britain had a certain commitment to the 'Curzon Line' as well as to Polish independence. Certainly Churchill felt that it was hardly possible for him to oppose a Polish–Soviet frontier along this line, when Stalin made it plain that Russia insisted on it. Churchill drew a clear distinction between the frontier question, where one could make concessions to Stalin, especially if Poland were 'compensated' by acquisitions of territory from Germany in the west; and the principle of Polish sovereignty and independence, to which Britain was clearly committed, and on which she could not easily give way. Whether that principle could be sustained, would largely depend in practice on whether the USSR was also prepared to honour it. The touchstone of Soviet intentions and good faith lay in the question of what kind of government and political regime the USSR was willing to see installed in post-war Poland. If that government were a representative, all-party government in the period immediately after liberation, and if very soon afterwards the Polish people were allowed to choose a government in genuinely free elections, then all would be well. It would be clear that the USSR accepted the principle of Polish sovereignty and independence. If, on the other hand, the Soviets insisted on installing a puppet, pro-communist government, and permitted only rigged Soviet-style elections, Polish independence would be a farce.[1]

To Roosevelt, Hull, and American leaders generally, neither the strategic argument, nor the moral commitment were as compelling as to the British. It will already be clear that Roosevelt saw no virtue in old-fashioned power politics, and such concepts as 'buffer states', 'spheres of influence' and 'balance of power'. Rather than concern oneself with strategic frontiers and defensive alliances against a possible future threat of Soviet aggression, the aim should be to gain Soviet confidence in the good will and good faith of the West, and in the effectiveness of the new international organization -- the United Nations. The Soviet leaders would then not feel the need to dominate Poland and the other East European states, or to impose puppet governments on them. Roosevelt recognized (as did Churchill) that following their long ordeal, the Russians would be preoccupied, even obsessed, with the problem of guaranteeing future Soviet security – and understandably so. The question, therefore, of the exact line of the Polish–Soviet frontier, or the precise composition of the Polish government immediately after liberation was for Roosevelt a secondary issue. Put the foundations of the new international order in place, get the Soviets committed to it and confident in its effectiveness, and all territorial and other issues would fall into place. It was logical, then, that when the Polish problem became acute in 1943, and the British pressed them for support, Roosevelt and Hull drew back. They did not wish to antagonize Stalin, at a time when they were most anxious to win his consent to the new international order. It was a question of priorities, and this was the wrong order in which to tackle these problems. At that juncture, as with other contentious problems, 'postponement' should be the order of the day on the Polish question.[2]

THE FAILURE TO ACT OVER POLAND

At the Moscow and Teheran conference in 1943, therefore, Roosevelt and Hull made it clear to the British and the Russians that they did not regard the Polish issue as one of supreme importance, and had no intention of pressing the USSR hard on the matter. On the contrary, Roosevelt went out of his way to conciliate Stalin, by telling him privately that the United States accepted the Soviet demand for the 'Curzon Line'. By contrast, in regard to the dispute over the Polish government Roosevelt confined himself, as Hull had previously done at Moscow, to a vague hope that the Russians, the British and the Poles might work out a satisfactory solution. It was made crystal clear that the Americans did not share the British view that this might be the last real opportunity to do something for Poland and other East European states, before the advancing tide of the Red Army flooded across the area.[3]

Nor, it was plain, did Roosevelt feel any particular moral commitment to the London-based Polish government: still less to the inter-war frontiers of Poland. The United States had not participated in the British guarantees to Poland, Romania and Greece in 1939, and was not therefore bound by them. The only commitment which the United States had accepted was the general commitment under the Atlantic Charter (1941) and the United Nations Declaration (1942) to restore 'the sovereign rights and self-government' of all the enslaved peoples of Europe. This guarantee applied to Poland, of course, but did not bind the United States to any particular government or frontier. Indeed, Roosevelt and Hull had no great enthusiasm for the various exiled governments assembled in London under British sponsorship, particularly those for the East European states, i.e. Poland, Czechoslovakia, Yugoslavia and Greece. In the nature of the case, they were collections of exiled politicians who had never been elected as a government, and whose representative character was at least open to argument. In American eyes they were little more than tools to serve British interests in Eastern Europe. The American view was that the best course during the liberation of an occupied country was to create under military occupation an interim government exercising very limited powers, pending the holding of free elections for a genuinely representative government. It was probably a mistake to bring in unnecessary baggage in the form of exiles, who might or might not be acceptable to the people. Whatever the general merits of the argument, it was a point of view enthusiastically supported by the Soviet leaders, in regard to the London Polish government. They had their own interim 'government' in the shape of reliable pro-communist Poles, which they were only too anxious to install; whether as a prelude to genuinely free elections, remained to be seen.[4]

To Roosevelt, then, the Polish issue was essentially a nuisance – something that might get in the way of establishing friendly relations with Russia, and thereby obstruct the building of a new world order. The London government was merely a collection of political exiles, whose representative character was dubious. Their claim to acquire larger tracts of German territory, while simultaneously retaining the territories seized from Soviet Russia in 1922, was a typical example of the kind of nationalistic greed which had done so much harm in Europe in the past. The President's view of the Poles is summed up in his weary remark at the Yalta Conference of 1945, 'Poland had been a source of trouble for 500 years'. Churchill's view of the dilemma which Poland presented to the British government is equally well summed up in his statement at Teheran. 'The British government recognized,' he said, 'how important the question of Poland was to Soviet security. They wished to see a Poland which was strong and independent, but friendly to Russia.' Molotov had used an almost identical phrase at the preceding Moscow Conference, and said that was what *Russia* wanted. The phrase conveniently assumes that these objective are reconcilable. But were they? As Roosevelt had implied, there was a long history of Polish–Russian enmity, distrust and bitter hostility. In the light of this history, was it likely that a government freely elected by the Polish people would be particularly friendly to Russia? Churchill thought and hoped that the Poles would learn a lesson from all that had happened, and try to turn over a new leaf in their relations with Russia. Stalin, as it turned out, was not prepared to take a chance. If Poland was indeed, an 'unsolvable problem', the essence of that problem, how to reconcile Soviet security with Polish independence, is encapsulated in Churchill's phrase.[5]

Not surprisingly, it proved much easier for Roosevelt and Churchill to agree with each other, and with Stalin, on a settlement of the frontier issue than on the problem of Poland's political future. The opening salvoes in this long-drawn-out battle had been fired by Stalin as early as 1942, when he stated to Eden his minimum territorial claims. These amounted to a demand that the frontiers of the USSR should be restored to what they had been in June 1941, at the time of the German attack. Thus the USSR would include the Baltic states of Lithuania, Latvia and Estonia; it would also include the strip of territory taken from Finland in 1940, and a somewhat larger area taken from Romania about the same time, and the considerable area east of the 'Curzon Line' taken by the Poles in 1922 and taken back by the USSR in 1939. The question of the Polish government no doubt seemed an academic one at that time, when the Red Army was hundreds of miles from Warsaw, and no other allied army likely to get anywhere near it. For the moment Stalin was prepared to establish amicable relations with the London government. The question could always be re-opened later.

BRITAIN'S FAILURE OVER EASTERN EUROPE

In his memorandum of February 1943, Churchill reminded
Roosevelt of the Soviet demands as a factor which had to be
taken into account, both in their immediate dealings with the
USSR and in terms of the post-war settlement. In the same
memorandum, Churchill also discussed a proposal which was
part of the general plan for Eastern Europe which Eden and
his Foreign Office advisers had been formulating for the past
year or so. This was a suggestion that the East European states
should be encouraged to enter into 'blocs' or federations with
their neighbours, which would produce larger, more powerful and more viable states. Churchill particularly mentioned
his idea for a 'Danubian Federation', consisting of south
Germany, Austria and perhaps Hungary; but he also referred
vaguely to a 'Balkan Bloc'. Roosevelt did not react immediately to this suggestion. He had other things on his mind,
and moreover he had already begun to convince himself that
any British proposal for Eastern Europe was probably
motivated by sinister British interests and imperialist designs;
also, these proposals might cause trouble with Stalin. It would
be best to react cautiously. During further talks with Eden
in March, the President showed how far he was from
sympathizing with these ideas. He suggested that, far from
uniting with other states, Yugoslavia, for example, should be
broken up: Slovenia and Croatia should be separated from
Serbia – not incidentally an unprescient remark, in the light of
later developments. The Russians for their part had initially
given Eden's suggestion their cautious approval. The Soviet
Ambassador to Britain had told Eden that the USSR was not
opposed to the idea of federations 'in principle'. But that had
been in 1942, when the Soviet Union had been hard pressed,
and anxious to conciliate the West. In 1943, after Stalingrad,
things were different. Ambassador Maisky now told Eden that
in general the USSR was 'not attracted' by the idea of
federations. Some kind of Balkan arrangement, excluding
Romania, they might look at; and if the 'Danubian Federation'
idea involved the partition of Germany, well, they might
consider it. But as to a Polish–Czech federation, on which the
Foreign Office had made most progress with the exiled
governments, that was a different matter. The Soviet attitude,

Maisky said ominously, would depend on the kind of government the Poles had at the end of the war. In short, by the middle of 1943, it was already clear that neither the Russians nor the Americans were particularly warmly disposed towards the idea of federations in Eastern Europe.[6]

The concept of creating stronger political and economic units in Eastern Europe had, in fact, quite a respectable pedigree. A number of observers, including the economist Maynard Keynes, had pointed to the fact that the break-up of the Austro-Hungarian, Russian and Ottoman Empires in 1919 had not been an unmixed blessing. It had created in Eastern Europe a patchwork of small states, many of them politically unstable, and both economically and militarily weak. It had also erected many trade barriers which had not existed before. There was something to be said for the view that these states should be encouraged to form larger, stronger units, which would be more viable, and less of a temptation to the predatory appetites of more powerful neighbours, i.e. Germany and Russia. Unfortunately the proposal ignored or brushed aside certain basic realities about Eastern Europe. In particular it failed to take into sufficient account the fact that Eastern Europe was an area of innumerable internecine feuds and hatreds (it is not too strong a word) – Poles against Czechs, Hungarians against Yugoslavs, Czechs and Romanians, Romanians against Bulgarians, Turks against Bulgarians and Greeks, Greeks against Yugoslavs, Serbs against Croats, Czechs against Slovaks – the list is interminable. Eden and his foreign office advisers considered themselves to be experts on Eastern Europe, but experts are occasionally blinded by their own self-confidence, and are sometimes too close to the problem to see clearly. The Foreign Secretary and his senior officials were wont to be somewhat patronising towards what they considered rather amateurish and 'feckless' suggestions by Roosevelt in these matters. But Roosevelt's intuitive judgments were sometimes more clear-sighted than theirs, as when he judged that both Belgium in the west and Yugoslavia in the south-east were essentially artificial states, made up of warring elements which might be better separated.[7]

The point is academic, since all these proposals, including Churchill's 'Danubian Federation', (discussed at more length in Chapter 7) were ultimately thwarted by combined Soviet and American opposition. The federation proposals were, however, part of a general package for Eastern Europe favoured by the British Foreign Office, and proposed by Eden to the Moscow Foreign Ministers' Conference in October 1943. Some of these proposals deserved a better fate than they met with at that conference. It is not necessary to devote too much space to this matter, since most of the proposals came to nothing; moreover, the package was essentially a Foreign Office affair, and not therefore central to the Roosevelt–Churchill relationship. It is only necessary to say that Eden's East European 'package' was designed to strengthen the political and economic framework of Eastern Europe, establish democracy (and safeguard it against future threats) and make it more difficult for any one powerful state to dominate the area. It would have been tactless to emphasize the last point to the Russians, but Stalin and Molotov had no difficulty in comprehending it without explanation, and reacted accordingly. Apart from the plan for federations discussed above, the package consisted of: (1) a proposal that the three states should endorse the principle of 'joint not separate responsibility for Eastern Europe' – i.e. should renounce the idea of separate 'spheres of influence'; (2) a proposal of a rather similar nature, that the three should not seek to enter into separate agreements with the East European states, which would give them a special position with any state – the so-called 'self-denying ordinance'; and (3) a proposal that the three Allies should endorse a 'Declaration on Liberated Territory' which bound them to restore self-government in all liberated areas, with a rider in favour of permitting the exiled governments to return and fulfil the role of interim governments, pending free elections. Taken together, these proposals would have gone a long way towards installing democratic institutions in Eastern as well as Western Europe, and considerably limiting anything in the nature of a 'free hand' for the Soviet Union in the former. Molotov had no difficulty in grasping this point, and made clear his opposition to the entire package at the Moscow Foreign Ministers' Conference. Much, then, depended on the American attitude. But Hull made it clear at this conference firstly that the United States did not wish at this juncture to become involved in such matters; and secondly that he regarded the US proposals for future international security as a far more important priority than the detailed problems of Eastern Europe. In his remarks to the conference Hull stressed the latter point, but the first was equally important. Roosevelt had instructed Hull before the conference that he did not wish to be embroiled in issues which might cause friction with the USSR, or led into supporting specific British interests. The President had managed to convince himself that Eden's plans 'smacked of spheres of influence', though in fact the exact opposite was the case. It is an indication of the extent to which Roosevelt and his principal advisers had allowed suspicion of British motives to dominate their thoughts, that they could believe Eden's proposals meant the opposite of what they said. Ironically, it was precisely the lack of US support for Eden's East European policy at Moscow, which led the Foreign Secretary to turn his thoughts to a possible agreement with Stalin and Molotov on 'spheres of influence' in the following year. Whether this lack of support, which was certainly crucial in ensuring the defeat of Eden's Moscow proposals, also meant that the last chance to do something positive for Eastern Europe had been forfeited will be discussed at the end of this chapter.[8]

Eden's defeat on Eastern Europe at Moscow also weakened the British hand on the specific issue of Poland, which had become much more explosive in 1943. In April the graves of 8000 murdered Polish officers had been uncovered by the German occupying forces in Katyn Forest – murdered probably by the Soviet forces before withdrawing from the area in 1941. Gleefully the Germans proposed a Red Cross commission of enquiry: and perhaps unwisely the London Polish government supported the idea. Stalin saw his chance and took it. Immediately he broke off relations with the London government. The way was now clear for the USSR to put together its own (pro-communist) 'interim government' and install it when the time came. It was, said Churchill, 'Goebbels' greatest triumph.' He set to work at once to try to persuade Stalin to restore relations with the London government, while admonishing the London Poles that they had behaved foolishly. To Roosevelt he cabled, 'we must heal the breach', emphasizing his warning to the London Poles that they *needed* friendly relations with Russia. Roosevelt, as usual, thought the most important thing was to conciliate and avoid friction with Russia; what happened to the London government was of less importance. Accordingly, his first reaction was to cable Stalin, agreeing that the London Poles had been 'misguided', but hoping that the breach would not be permanent. Later he drafted, but for some reason decided not to send, a message to Churchill giving cautious approval to the premier's efforts at conciliation, agreeing that the Allies must avoid supporting rival governments, but urging that they should not for the moment discuss the Polish Soviet frontier issue (which Churchill thought was probably the most important consideration for Stalin). They must try to persuade both parties to 'declare a truce on contentious issues' and 'subordinate factional differences to the common victory'. It was probably of little importance that the cable was not sent, since Stalin was not in a responsive mood. One may doubt, in fact, if any arguments would have persuaded him to re-open relations with the London Poles, having been given a heaven-sent opportunity to break with them. In any case circumstances combined to make the Soviet leader par-ticularly 'bearish' towards his allies (if one may be forgiven the pun) at this time. The suspension of the Arctic convoys in April, and the Washington Conference decision in May to postpone the cross-Channel attack yet again, had put him in a bad mood. He was not disposed to play the game in Poland according to Anglo-American rules.[9]

It was eventually borne in on Roosevelt that if he wished to conciliate Stalin on the Polish problem, it would be necessary to address the frontier issue. There was, in fact, no reason not to do so, apart from a general reluctance to consider territorial problems. The President had already made up his mind that the US would probably have to give way on this point, and the rest of Stalin's territorial demands. But he was not going to be drawn into Eastern European problems any further than was absolutely necessary. Accordingly, he poured cold water on Eden's East European proposals, and approved Hull's negative stance on these at the Moscow Conference. Eden's requests for American support fell on deaf ears. Nor did the Foreign Secretary get any more response from Hull on the specific issue of Poland. It was, Hull said, 'more of a British problem' than an American one. The most he was prepared to do when the subject was discussed was to express the hope that the breach would be healed. But without some positive threat or positive inducement, the USSR was unlikely to be moved by the expression of pious hopes, and Molotov's response was, in fact, brutally negative and uncompromising. Poland, he said, was primarily a Soviet concern, and the London government consisted too largely of 'unreliable' right-wing elements to be trusted. Even its more sensible and moderate members, for example Micolajczyk, were useless, since they would never prevail over the others. Eden was forced to withdraw to London to lick his wounds. He could only hope that Roosevelt would adopt a slightly more positive line when the heads of government met at Teheran the following month. Given a reasonable amount of support from the Americans, it might be possible to persuade Stalin to re-open relations with the London government, permit it to return to Poland when liberated, and promise to hold free elections thereafter. At least the London Poles had been sufficiently frightened by the tough Soviet stance at Moscow and lack of US support, to adopt a more amenable attitude. They might now be persuaded to accept the Curzon Line, in return for the generous compensation in the west which the Allies were proposing, and a settlement which would 'safeguard Poland's future'.[10]

Unfortunately these hopes proved vain. Having assured Stalin privately that the United States would accept the Curzon Line, though they could not yet say so publicly, together with the principle of compensation for Poland in the west (i.e. at the expense of Germany), Roosevelt so arranged matters that there was little time allotted to the discussion of contentious political issues, such as the Polish government. When the latter subject did come up, on the last day of the conference, Roosevelt followed Hull's example and did no more than express the hope that somehow a reconciliation would be achieved. Sensing that Roosevelt was not prepared to press him hard on the matter, and in fact was prepared to let the problem hang fire for another year, Stalin likewise emulated Molotov, and adopted a particularly harsh and uncompromising tone. The London Government was anti-Soviet and totally unreliable: their attitude and policies amounted to virtual collaboration with the Germans, and their resistance forces in Poland were working against the Red Army and against forces friendly to Russia: moreover they were totally unrepresentative of the Polish people. He did not see there was much ground for hopes of a reconciliation, nor would he accept that a just settlement of the frontier question was in any way dependent on such a reconciliation. On the Polish question, Teheran was virtually a re-run of Moscow. Churchill was forced, like Eden, to return to London without achieving any of the progress on the issue which he had hoped for. The most he could do was to put the frontiers 'package' to the London Poles, tell them forcefully that it was generous and the best they could expect, and hope they would have the sense to accept it. He might then be able to present this to the Russians as evidence that the London Poles were after all a reasonable body, and be able to persuade Stalin to restore relations. In the face of the strong Soviet prejudice and the Polish reputation for intransigence, it was a forlorn hope, but it was the best he had.

One American observer at least shared Churchill's and Eden's fears for the future of Poland and Eastern Europe. This was Averell Harriman, the US Ambassador to Russia, who had had rather more opportunity than Roosevelt to observe the Soviet system and its leaders at close quarters. The USSR, he felt, had been allowed to have all its own way on Poland and Eastern Europe. Their successful opposition to Churchill's and Eden's proposals suggested that they were aiming at 'Soviet hegemony'. The United States ought to have given more support to the British on these matters. As it was, Stalin must assume that Roosevelt was giving him *carte blanche* in Eastern Europe. In particular, Harriman doubted if Stalin was really anxious to have 'a strong, independent Poland'. Unfortunately, Harriman did not press these views on Roosevelt as strongly as he might have done. At all events, Roosevelt ignored his warnings.[11]

The course of events during the following year (1944) and particularly the direction of British policy, should be seen in the light of these events. Churchill for his part, worked hard on the London Poles and tried to keep a line of com-munication open to Stalin on this matter. On the face of it, if one could believe what Stalin said, there was still some prospect of a solution. In January 1944 the Soviet leader assured the British Ambassador that 'after the war Poland would be free and independent – as much so as Czechoslovakia – he would not try to influence either country's choice of government'. He added that the London Poles would be allowed to return to Poland and participate in the establishment of a 'broad based government'. Meanwhile Churchill was persuading Micolajczyk, the Polish Prime Minister, and other leading members of his government, to drop their demand for the 'Riga' (1922) frontier; even if like Roosevelt they could not say so publicly. This looked promising – if both sides meant what they said. Roosevelt continued to give his cautious approval to Churchill's efforts, cabling to Stalin on 21 February that he hoped the Premier's proposals for a Polish settlement 'would be given a favourable reception'. But whenever a settlement seemed near, one side or the other raised difficulties. Towards the end of March Churchill was forced to tell Stalin that negotiations appeared to have broken down. The British leader felt bound to add that he must continue to recognize the London government, and that his government 'could not accept any territorial changes imposed unilaterally by force of arms' – an unwise threat, which could carry little weight with Stalin, since the British had no means of enforcing it. The Soviet leader's reply was characteristically harsh, and much in the vein of the previous year's exchanges on the convoys and the cross-Channel attack. To Roosevelt, however, Churchill was philosophical. Though unreasonable over Poland, the Russians had been 'temperate' over Finland, and 'helpful' over Romanian and Bulgarian affairs. 'I have a feeling,' he added hopefully, 'that their bark may be worse than their bite': and later, 'after each rude message, they have done pretty well what we asked'.[12]

SPHERES OF INFLUENCE AND 'PERCENTAGES'

Churchill's rather surprising optimism was largely based on the progress Eden had made with the Russians towards some kind of *modus vivendi* in the Balkans. After Moscow and Teheran, both men had felt that a complete re-thinking of general policy towards Eastern Europe was necessary. The total defeat of all the British proposals at Moscow by the Russians, with American connivance, meant that previous plans now lay in ruins. Churchill, it is true, had not completely lost hope that a breakthrough in Italy might make it possible to bring Anglo-American military power to bear in this area. But it was at best an outside chance, and one which seemed less and less likely as 1944 moved on. If that failed, Britain might still be able to get a small force into Greece (as in fact happened), but for most of the area, there would need to be a 'worst case' strategy. They had to explore with the USSR the possibility of an arrangement based on mutual respect for each other's vital interests. The need for some short-term administrative agreement, to avoid the possibility of disputes and 'crossed wires' during the process of liberation, provided a possible stepping stone. Molotov had made it clear at Moscow that the Russians regarded Romania and Bulgaria as primarily their concern, and that they expected to make whatever armistice arrangements were necessary with these states when the time came. Why not recognize what military logic anyway dictated, and try to get Russian recognition in turn of the prior British interest in Greece and perhaps Yugoslavia? At the beginning of May, Eden began to make cautious overtures to the Russians through the Soviet Ambassador in London. After exploratory talks, he felt that a 'gentleman's agreement' had been reached. Britain was to 'take the lead in Greece'; the USSR in Romania. Owing to the hesitations and inconsistencies of the American attitude, it seemed for a time uncertain whether Stalin felt himself to be committed. But actions speak louder than words. When, in October, Stalin neither intervened nor protested over the British occupation of Greece and the subsequent suppression of a Communist coup, it was evident that the Soviet leader was acting in the spirit of the agreement. Churchill was very grateful. The way was clear for a further extension of the agreement, though it is equally clear that, to begin with, both Churchill and Eden regarded this as a short-term arrangement for administrative purposes, rather than a long-term division into 'spheres of interest'. Nonetheless, as the British historian Elizabeth Barker has written, 'the outlines of a percentage agreement could already be seen'.[13]

Churchill, of course, was well aware of the necessity of keeping in touch with Roosevelt over these matters and, if possible, obtaining his approval. Since the Americans had apparently washed their hands of Eastern Europe at Moscow and Teheran, it was logical that they should not object to the British trying to fill the gap. Churchill also relied on Roosevelt's sense of political and military realism. Roosevelt, indeed, had already expressed the view in private conversation, apropos of Stalin's territorial demands, that there was no point in the US opposing them, since Stalin had the power to take what he wanted anyway. He must see that the same logic applied to the political future of Romania and Bulgaria – perhaps Hungary and Czechoslovakia too. There followed a comedy of errors, When Churchill hinted in a message of 19 May at the proposed 'arrangement', Roosevelt did not at first react. On 31 May Churchill repeated the information. But meanwhile Cordell Hull and the State Department had received the news from the British Ambassador, and caught a blasphemous whiff of a deal on 'spheres of influence'. Immediately the State Department had set the alarm bells ringing. Roosevelt felt constrained to say that the US was 'unwilling to approve the proposed arrangement'. Churchill was more than a little annoyed. The Americans had undermined every British attempt at Moscow to limit Soviet actions in Eastern Europe, but were now apparently unwilling to accept the logic of their actions, and would not allow him to try to pick up the pieces. 'Somebody', he cabled Roosevelt, 'must have the power to plan and act'. He urged the President to trust him, and give the arrangements a three month's trial. On 12 June Roosevelt agreed (while uttering a caveat about 'spheres of influence') – but weakly or inadvertently failed to inform the State Department. Churchill was 'deeply grateful', but took the opportunity to say that 'we should not prejudge the question of spheres of influence'. This was not precisely what Roosevelt intended, and provoked the tetchy reply that he hoped matters of this importance 'can be prevented from developing in such a manner in future', prompting an equally tetchy reply from Churchill. The Russians, he pointed out, 'would do what they liked anyway', since they had the troops to do so, and the West did not. There, in the second week of June, the matter rested. The State Department thought Roosevelt had turned down the whole idea: Churchill and Eden thought he had eventually given his grudging approval. There was ample room for further misunderstanding in the months ahead.[14]

Events now moved fast in Eastern Europe. In August the Polish Home Army rose in revolt in Warsaw and was brutally wiped out by the Germans. The Red Army sat outside the gates of Warsaw and took no action. Churchill pleaded with Roosevelt to use his influence with Stalin, and to join a joint Anglo-American attempt to succour the Poles, but with little success. The same month a royal coup in Romania led to an armistice with Russia, and opened the way to Bulgaria, Yugoslavia and Hungary. Churchill and Eden were much alarmed: the need for action was now much more urgent. Either they must get troops into these areas, or they must come to some agreement with Stalin. Meeting with the Americans at Quebec in September, Churchill continually harped on the Russians' threat in the Balkans and the need to 'forestall the Russians in certain areas of Europe', without in fact making much impression on Roosevelt and the US Chiefs of Staff, though for a time he thought he had. Only a month later it was clear that the Istrian operation could not be launched before the spring of 1945 at the earliest, by which time it would be too late to checkmate the Soviets in the Balkans and South-East Europe. Only in Greece had it been possible to get a small British force on the ground. So far as the rest of South-East Europe was concerned – and probably Central–Eastern Europe also – there was nothing left but to attempt to reach some kind of agreement with Stalin. As Churchill fully realised, it was always going to be a hand played from weakness. But he felt he had to do it, notwithstanding that Roosevelt had again created uncertainty by sending messages to Churchill and Stalin, warning that the USA *was* interested in these matters, and could not be committed in its absence.[15]

Accordingly, and in the belief that in spite of his message Roosevelt would never effectively stand up to the Russians in the Balkans, Churchill proceeded to meet Stalin in Moscow, and explore with him a possible compact based on the realities of the situation. No doubt he saw Roosevelt's messages as an attempt to obstruct British initiatives, rather than as a warning to Stalin. At all events, on 9 October, Churchill suggested to the Soviet leader that their previous 'arrangement' relative to Greece and Romania should be extended to Yugoslavia, Bulgaria and Hungary. The Russians should 'take the lead' in Bulgaria, Romania and Hungary, where their armies would control the situation. Britain and the US should retain their responsibility in Greece, where there were Western troops. In Yugoslavia, where the British had many contacts with Tito – far more than the Russians – but Soviet forces were likely to enter the Eastern part of the country, the West and the Soviet Union should have equal say. Churchill chose to express these arrangements in terms of percentages, ranging from 90/10 to 50/50. Stalin agreed. Two points should be made. It was made clear that neither side was completely abdicating its responsibility in any area. There should be consultation. Secondly, Churchill in his memoirs claims that all this was relevant merely to 'immediate wartime arrangements'. Perhaps. But it is difficult to believe that a statesman of Churchill's experience did not foresee the risk that the Russians might consider it a long-term, as well as a short-term arrangement, and feel they had been given the green light to make it just that. If one is to criticize Churchill, however, it is also fair perhaps to criticize Roosevelt for not reacting strongly. In fact he soon became pretty well aware of what had gone on, but did nothing. He was very much preoccupied with the US presidential election at the time, and perhaps felt that he had already made it clear that the United States was in no way committed to this arrangement. All of these issues could be taken up in the forthcoming tripartite meeting still to be arranged, and in further discussions after the war. Perhaps, too, Roosevelt did not disagree all that much with Churchill's view that the Russians had the power in the last resort to do what they wanted. The most the US and Britain could do would be to bring every kind of pressure to bear on them to behave decently. If this view is correct – and it is difficult to controvert it – the famous 'percentages agreement' probably made little difference to future events.[16]

Whatever might be the case in the Balkans, on the Polish issue things had, from the British viewpoint, gone from bad to worse. In June the USSR had formed a group of 'friendly Poles' into a Committee of National Liberation and installed it in Soviet-occupied Poland as the recognized 'administrative body'. In August they had allowed the Polish uprising in Warsaw to be crushed by the Germans without making much effort to help them. This 'grave episode', as Churchill justly called it, considerably weakened the anti-communist and non-communist resistance movement in Poland, and correspondingly reduced the influence and prestige of the London government which controlled it. Churchill's efforts to get Roosevelt to intervene personally with Stalin, or to join him in an effective air-lift to the beleaguered Poles, were largely unavailing. The President was not prepared to risk offending Stalin. His last message to Churchill on the subject, on 5 September, had simply said 'the problem has been solved by delay ... there now appears to be nothing we can do to assist them'. It is the language of a man who felt defeated, and perhaps slightly guilty. Both sentiments would have been appropriate. Churchill and Eden nevertheless persisted in their efforts on behalf of the London Poles, but it was a heartbreaking task. Whenever it seemed there might be a breakthrough, either the London Poles backtracked on concessions they had seemed willing to make, or Stalin raised his demands. At first it seemed that the London Poles had only to accept the Curzon Line, and all would be well. They could then return to Poland with Stalin's blessing, and join the Lublin group in a broad-based interim government. As the Red Army pushed deeper into Poland, however, Stalin's tone changed. By the time of the second Moscow conference, as Churchill cabled to Roosevelt, the Soviets seemed to be insisting on a 'preponderance' of Lublin representatives in any new government; and moreover that only Poles from outside 'who were friendly to Russia' would be allowed to participate. It soon became apparent that the Soviet definition of 'friendly' was a pretty rigorous one. Nonetheless, at the Moscow conference, the London Polish Premier, Micolajczyk, who had been summoned to Moscow, seemed prepared to recommend the Curzon Line to his colleagues, while Stalin, in the words of the British historian K.G. Ross, 'implied that once the frontier was settled, there should be little difficulty over a new government'. On 22 October Churchill cabled optimistically to Roosevelt, 'I do not think the government will prove an insuperable obstacle, if all else is settled'. On the same day Roosevelt replied, 'I am delighted to learn of your success', but because of its possible effects on the Polish-American vote, asked that the territorial agreement should not be announced till after the presidential election.[17] Once again it proved a false dawn. No sooner had Micolajczyk returned to London than he was repudiated by his colleagues and replaced by a much more right-wing Premier, Arciczewski. The expected solution therefore fell to the ground. Roosevelt, in some alarm, proposed making public a letter to Micolazczyk, endorsing the proposed territorial settlement (i.e. Polish concessions to Russia, and 'compensation' for Poland at the expense of Germany). Churchill agreed. Both men were afraid Stalin would now recognize the Lublin Group as 'the provisional government of Poland'. Churchill was furious with the London Poles, and made his anger known to Roosevelt and, perhaps unwisely, to Stalin. Yet when the British Ambassador to Russia urged him to disavow the London government, and gain a free hand for future negotiations, Churchill, with the loyalty which was one of his most attractive characteristics, refused. As for Stalin, he can hardly be blamed if he concluded finally that the London Poles were impossible. On 27 December he informed Roosevelt, despite the latter's pleas, that he intended to recognize the Lublin Government.[18]

So matters stood when the three leaders met at the Yalta Conference in February 1945. At the conference Roosevelt at last, and rather late in the day, gave the Polish problem his full attention. It may be doubted if, until that moment, Stalin had really believed that Roosevelt was much concerned. Nonetheless the Soviet leader was at first obstinate and unyielding. The question was repeatedly discussed, but Stalin's only concession finally was that Molotov and the British and US ambassadors to Moscow should begin discussions with a view to reorganizing the existing (Lublin) government on a 'more representative basis'. In other words, the matter was once again postponed for further discussion. As a further sop to his allies, Stalin agreed to a 'Declaration on Liberated Europe' which bound the allies to create democratic institutions in the liberated countries of Europe, and to restore 'sovereign rights and self-government'. The Soviet interpretation of 'democracy' and 'self-government', however,

was apt to be somewhat different from its Allies' interpretation. It is only fair to add that there was no democratic
tradition to build on in Eastern Europe, save in Czechoslovakia. It was one thing to instal Western democracy, quite
another to guarantee its continuance. What is certain,
however, is that Soviet policy after the war prevented the
experiment from being even tried.

EASTERN EUROPE – AN ANGLO-AMERICAN DEBACLE

In no area of policy was the fact that Roosevelt and Churchill
were at cross-purposes more evident than in relation to
Eastern Europe, and in no area did they fail so completely to
obtain the results they both wanted. As so often, they started
from different premises. Roosevelt believed that the only way
they could preserve a modicum of independence for Eastern
Europe – given that they had no troops in the area – was to
win Stalin's confidence in the friendship of the West and the
ability of the new international organization to protect Soviet
security. Overcome Soviet fears, and they would not feel the
need to erect iron-clad barriers against future aggression, in
the shape of a belt of pro-communist states in Eastern Europe.
Churchill for his part tried to convince himself that it would
be possible to cooperate with the USSR after the war, but
never quite succeeded. At any rate, he always felt a little
reinsurance was necessary. From 1943 onwards he believed
that the best policy would be to pin Stalin down to specific
undertakings on Eastern Europe, while trying to get troops
into the area somehow. Consistently thereafter he pleaded
with Roosevelt who had much more leverage with the
Russians, to use it in the cause of Eastern Europe. When
Churchill's strategic plans were finally defeated in 1943–4, he
redoubled the pressure on Roosevelt, but to no avail. The
'percentages agreement' was a desperate effort, as he saw it, to
extract what he could from the wreckage.
     There is a tragic note about the Roosevelt–Churchill
correspondence on Poland and Eastern Europe during the
last two months of Roosevelt's life, as things began to go very
badly in that quarter. Despairingly Churchill pleaded with the
Presid⸱ ⸱t to bring all his personal weight to bear on Stalin

over the matter. But, consistent with his whole line of policy, Roosevelt preferred to let his ambassador use gentle persuasion, rather than exert massive pressure himself. The important priority for him was still the need not to forfeit the good relations which he believed he had built up with Stalin. Believing, as he did, that this was what mattered, he could really do no other.[19]

Two questions have been much discussed by historians. Firstly, was there any moment during the war when Soviet domination of Eastern Europe could have been prevented? Secondly, if there was such a moment, was either of these two men mainly to blame that it was not taken advantage of? The one point depends on the other. If there was no such moment, clearly no one can have been to blame. Any answer to the first question, however, can only be based on speculation – on a consideration of the 'might-have-beens' of history – and it will be evident from these pages that the present writer does not consider that such speculation is the central purpose of the historian. Nor, indeed, is the distribution of praise and blame. His main task is to try to understand what happened. The reader must draw his own conclusions. The point is perhaps worth making, that in all these questions, so much depends on the particular point in time one chooses to focus on – how far, in other words, one goes back. In relation to Eastern Europe, a number of historians have highlighted the 'percentages agreement', accusing Churchill, in the words of one American historian, of 'muddying the waters'. This, it is argued, made it more difficult for Roosevelt to act effectively on behalf of Eastern Europe at Yalta. If one goes back to 1943, however, there is at least a case for the view that Roosevelt's veto of the Churchill-Eden proposals at Moscow and Teheran may well have been the decisive moment for Eastern Europe. If Roosevelt and Hull had fired a warning shot or two across Stalin's bows at this point, it could have done no harm, and might conceivably have done some good. Others, however, have put a powerful case for the view that the decision to pursue a Mediterranean strategy in 1942 and 1943, and the consequent failure to launch the decisive strike from the West until 1944 was the real cause of the failure. If so, Churchill and Roosevelt, who jointly took the decision, were jointly to blame. Others again believe that if the Mediterranean strategy had been persevered with, it would still have been possible to put enough Anglo-American troops into South-Eastern Europe to make a difference. Perhaps in the end the only safe verdict on all these conflicting theories is 'not proven'. The question after all still remains, 'whatever the military outcome, could the West have denied a predominant position in Eastern Europe to the Soviet Union by any means short of force?' And would American or even British public opinion have supported such a use of Western troops during the critical period 1944–6? These are questions to which one would hesitate to give a definite answer, or at least an affirmative one.[20]

6 The Heavy Cross of Lorraine: de Gaulle and the Future of France

'The heaviest cross I have to bear', remarked Churchill on one occasion, more in anger than in sorrow, 'is the Cross of Lorraine'. That cross symbolized the cause of those Frenchmen – the 'Free French' – who had continued to fight the Axis after the fall of France. It was also intimately bound up with the person of a brave, arrogant, obstinate and touchy Frenchman – Charles de Gaulle – who regarded himself personally as a symbol of unconquerable France.

Churchill's cross was largely of his own making. In June 1940 de Gaulle was unknown outside a small circle of French generals and politicians. A junior brigadier-general, he had recently been pulled out of a battlefield command by the French Premier, Reynaud, to become under-secretary for national defence. In June 1940 Reynaud had chosen de Gaulle as his emissary to London with a last plea to the British to commit their remaining fighter squadrons to the battle of France – a risk which the British government, judging that battle already lost, could not take. Churchill had been impressed by de Gaulle on that occasion, as well as at a previous meeting in France on 13 June. When it became apparent that France was on the point of collapse, he had encouraged de Gaulle to come to London, putting his own plane at the General's disposal. De Gaulle was accompanied by General Sir Edward Spears, a member of parliament, and an old friend of Churchill's, whom Churchill had used on various missions to France. It was Spears who persuaded Churchill to give de Gaulle some kind of status, and to permit him to broadcast on 17 June, calling on all Frenchmen who wished to continue resistance to join him. With de Gaulle's words over the radio, 'the flame of French resistance must not and will not be extinguished', the Free French movement was born.

It was not Churchill's intention at the time to commit himself unreservedly to de Gaulle and his 'Free French

111

Committee' as the sole, long-term embodiment of continued French resistance. One of the arguments which Spears had used was that de Gaulle's group might serve as simply the forerunner of a larger, more impressive and more representative body, under the aegis of a better-known and more impressive figure. But all the various hopes – that the French government might go to North Africa and carry on resistance, or some of its members might do so, supported by the French North African military leaders, or that leading political or military figures might come to London – all proved vain. Those leaders to whom Churchill looked in expectation – Reynaud, Mandel, Weygand, Noguès and others – were either prevented from coming, or chose to throw in their lot with the new Vichy French government under Marshall Pétain, which had signed an armistice with Germany. One well-known and senior military leader who did come was General Georges Catroux, former Governor of French Indo-China. Catroux was more of a name, and also easier to work with. In many ways he would have suited the British government better. But Catroux pre-empted any such thoughts by placing himself under de Gaulle's command. Churchill was therefore stuck with de Gaulle. He must often have regretted his choice in the years to come. Yet his judgement of men, often unreliable, was in this case not at fault. De Gaulle possessed the necessary courage and determination, the necessary abilities, the untarnished reputation, and the personality. Above all he had supreme confidence in himself and the future of France, two things which he regarded as interdependent. Churchill was looking for someone who would restore French pride, as a necessary prelude to restoring French power and prestige, so that France would be a worthwhile contributor to the war effort, and subsequently a convincing element in the post-war European balance. De Gaulle was the man for this purpose. That he was also rude, ungrateful, arrogant and suspicious was unfortunate.[1]

VICHY AND FREE FRANCE

The task facing de Gaulle was a daunting one. It was not simply a matter of gradually collecting together more and more French volunteers, seizing the odd bit of French colonial territory, and attracting, one by one, more Frenchmen of ability to his banner – though all of this was involved. But his ambitions went far beyond this humdrum process. To restore the greatness of France – that was his mission. In immediate practical terms this resolved itself into the aim of achieving for Free France the status of a major ally in the wartime coalition, not to be ranked with the Dutch, Belgian, Polish and other governments-in-exile, but more approximating to the status of Britain itself; and, as the alliance expanded, of the Soviet Union, the US and China. With this status would go, in the natural course of things, an accepted place in political discussions within the alliance, and in the planning of military operations. Ultimately this would necessarily involve recognition of his organization by the Allies as the provisional government of France, and the withdrawal of such recognition from the palsied group of defeatists at Vichy. De Gaulle was too much of a realist not to know that the achievement of such status depended on his building, with the utmost speed, a powerful territorial and military base. As much as possible of the French empire must be rallied to his cause, and as quickly as possible; and as various colonies rallied, the colonial troops which came with them must be brought under his control. Side by side with the building-up of Free French troops in the UK this would enable Free French divisions, corps, and at last perhaps armies to be formed. They must be kept firmly under French command, and not sent here and there as Allied military needs dictated, but used in ways for which the Free French, or rather de Gaulle himself, had given prior approval. Similarly every additional colony or territory which rallied to the allied cause must come, clearly and unequivocally, under the political authority of his organization. So long as de Gaulle had only the British to deal with, it was not too difficult to achieve these aims. As it happened, British relations with the French Vichy government were severed very soon after the Fall of France, when the British fleet attacked and put out of action a powerful French naval force at Oran, at the same time neutralizing other French warships at Alexandria. This action was seen by the British government as a painful necessity. The risk that these important naval forces might be handed over to the Germans had to be avoided. De Gaulle himself reluctantly accepted this view. But the effect was, of course, to horrify and antagonize many Frenchmen, and especially the French naval and military establishment. It also made normal relations with the Vichy government impossible. Churchill, therefore, had nowhere else to turn in regard to a political authority for French territories. French Equatorial Africa in any case rallied to de Gaulle of its own accord; and later, when British forces took over Syria and Madagascar, they in their turn were committed to Free French authority. It was otherwise, however, when the United States entered the war and the operation in French North Africa loomed up. President Roosevelt and his secretary of state, Cordell Hull, had other ideas on French policy.[2]

At the outset, the Americans had little contact with the Free French. They had little reason for any such contact. In 1940 the United States was still neutral. Accepting, as did the British government, that the Pétain government had come to power by constitutional means, Roosevelt and Hull felt bound to recognize it as the legal, as well as the actual government of Unoccupied France and of those colonies which had not rallied to de Gaulle. These latter to begin with included Syria and the Lebanon, Madagascar, Indo-China, and most important of all North-West Africa. As described in an earlier chapter, the danger of German naval and submarine bases at Dakar and Casablanca was a matter of keen interest to the United States. It was also important that the powerful French naval force at Toulon should not be handed over to the Germans. Roosevelt had committed himself to the view that Britain's survival and ultimate victory over Nazi Germany was in the vital interests of the US. The French navy and the French empire were important elements in the balance between Britain and Germany. It seemed therefore not only right but expedient to Roosevelt to maintain normal relations with the Vichy government, and necessarily – since de Gaulle had been declared a traitor and an outlaw by Vichy – to keep the latter at arm's length. By so doing he had a means whereby the powerful threats which the Germans could employ against Vichy could be balanced against carefully calculated inducements held out by the US. The essential point was to cajole, bully and persuade Vichy France not to collaborate with Germany one iota beyond the strict letter of the armistice terms. Among the inducements were economic concessions of various kinds, and as it happened, the most obvious and suitable recipient for such concessions was French North Africa. Unoccupied France itself could not very easily be the recipient, since US goods sent there might find their way to the Germans. But under strict US supervision and control, something might be done for French North Africa, which was suffering severely from the British blockade. If such concessions served a useful allied purpose, the British would not object. Under this pretext, a team of US officials was established in French North Africa. To act as his personal representative, and to mastermind any useful contacts that might be established with the French colonial and military authorities, Roosevelt dispatched a career State Department officer, Robert Murphy. If one accepts the general case for preserving an American channel of communication with Vichy, then the breach of British relations with that government made the maintenance of the US link even more necessary. Towards the end of 1940, the appointment as Vichy Delegate General in North Africa of General Maxime Weygand, who was known to be anti-German and favourably disposed to the US, seemed to offer new opportunities of weaning French North Africa from its neutrality. This development strengthened the case for keeping a link. All this, then, was the *raison d' être* for the much criticized US 'Vichy Gamble'. Too much criticized in fact. It may not have achieved a great deal in its effects on the central policy of the Pétain government – the Germans after all were on the spot, and could wield the big stick. But it certainly had some effect, and it provided a useful source of information. So far as French North Africa was concerned, it did rather more. It enabled the US to prepare the ground for the later Anglo-American occupation, by establishing a network of useful contacts, particularly with the military. Naturally enough, de Gaulle, who despised and detested 'the men of Vichy' was angered by the fact that the US government cold-shouldered him. Characteristically, he took little pains to understand the reasons for the policy: and in so far as he did understand them, denied their validity. But de Gaulle was not exactly an impartial witness. The Vichy policy served its purpose. The mistake, in fact, was not in the original policy, but in clinging to it, and the concepts associated with it, after it had outlived its usefulness. For this, however, de Gaulle himself was partially to blame, since he went out of his way to antagonize both Roosevelt and Hull during this period.[3]

From June 1940, therefore, for over two years, British and US policy towards France moved on two separate though parallel tracks, which rarely intersected. Churchill and Eden conducted relations with the Free French, Roosevelt and Hull, through Ambassador William Leahy, kept an eye on the Vichy government, and sought to restrain it from overt or close collaboration with the Germans. A policy of collaboration was certainly desired by some of the most influential figures in the Vichy regime, notably Pierre Laval and, at the beginning, Admiral François Darlan, but not by Weygand, while the aged, feeble Pétain vacillated according to circumstances. To bolster up the anti-German elements was the object of US policy, and one to which the US Secretary of State, Cordell Hull, devoted special attention. On this issue, unlike many others, Roosevelt was disposed to accept Hull's advice, particularly when reinforced by Leahy, an old friend of the President's. Churchill in no way dissented from this arrangement. His view is adequately summarized in a message to Roosevelt in May 1941, when he wrote, 'with regard to Vichy, we are more than willing that you should take the lead and work out how to get the best from them by threats or favours'. Roosevelt's own view of the purposes and appropriate techniques for this policy is well illustrated by his message to Churchill of October 1940, when the possibility that the French naval force at Toulon might be handed over to Germany seemed a real one. In this message Roosevelt summarized a stern warning he had given to the Pétain government: 'that the French government is under duress ... in no sense justifies providing assistance to Germany ... that a government is prisoner of another power does not justify serving it conqueror ... such action would constitute a flagrant breach of faith with the U.S. Government'. Similar action followed at regular intervals for the next two years, often, as in the above case, in response to Churchill's direct appeals. In May 1941 Darlan, who had succeeded Laval as deputy premier, negotiated the so-called 'Paris Protocols', foreshadowing the grant to Germany of the use of air bases in Syria and naval facilities in Bizerta and

Dakar. At a later stage, in April 1942, Laval again joined the Vichy government. On each occasion US pressure was applied, warning of the possibility of a total breach with America. Within the Vichy government, the delicate balance between pro-Axis and anti-Axis factions was probably influenced by these warnings. At all events Churchill did not criticize America's Vichy policy, and so long as British and US policy proceeded along these separate tracks, there was little, if any, Anglo-American friction on the issue, until de Gaulle himself at the beginning of 1942 precipitated a collision. Prior to that date Roosevelt and Churchill had seen eye to eye. Roosevelt's attitude to de Gaulle, and that of the State Department, was to begin with one of indifference. The man had emerged apparently from nowhere, and seemingly without much support, either from leading Frenchmen or from French public opinion. If Churchill chose to make use of him, well and good. But it seemed inconceivable that this obscure general should ever become a serious candidate for the leadership of a legitimate French government. There is little reference in the Roosevelt–Churchill correspondence to de Gaulle in 1940 and 1941. Their interchanges on French matters were concerned largely with Vichy. In fact the US ignored de Gaulle. If there was friction between de Gaulle and Churchill in these years – and there often was – it was not due to Roosevelt.[4]

Friction there was in plenty, and almost from the beginning. The personalities of Churchill and de Gaulle certainly played a part in this, though they were not the sole cause. A relationship in which one side is so much weaker than the other, and almost totally dependent, is bound to lead to an element of patronage in one partner, and to induce resentment in the other. If the two sides had been represented by someone less forceful and emotional than Churchill, or less suspicious and obdurate than de Gaulle, some of the asperities might have been modified, but the fundamental facts would not have changed. To begin with, however, this did not show itself too much. In 1940 the situation was too desperate. Free France needed Britain, and Britain, though less crucially, needed Free France, as a symbol of continuing French resistance, and the foundation on which, it was hoped, a much more formidable contribution to the allied cause could be built. This hope, indeed, was ultimately to prove fully justified. The legal situation between the two was that the British government recognized Free France as representing Frenchmen and French territories who wished to continue to fight. There was no question of recognizing the Free French Committee as in any sense a government in exile, or a 'provisional government'. As for de Gaulle himself, at this early stage he might have been willing to serve under a better known French figure, if any had come forward. When later on de Gaulle's demands became greater and more clamant, the Americans especially chose to regard this as a sign of his growing ambitions, forgetting that all other leading Frenchmen had withdrawn from the fray. If the voice of France was to be heard at all in the councils of the Alliance, then, as de Gaulle saw it, it could only be his voice: there was no one else. In 1940, however, all this was in the future. The relationship with Churchill and the British government rubbed along tolerably well, and survived such difficult episodes as the tragedy of Oran and the fiasco of the unsuccessful Anglo-Gaullist attempt to seize Dakar in French West Africa. On the latter occasion, in October 1940, Churchill publicly reiterated his confidence in de Gaulle. Nonetheless, some damage was done by the Dakar episode. Churchill was inevitably impressed by the fierceness of the Vichy resistance, and by the indications that this might even be greater when Gaullist forces were involved. Moreover there were security leaks, which the British chose, rightly or wrongly, to attribute to the Free French. Doubts about Gaullist reliability at the highest level spread to lower levels of the British government, and of the British military authorities. Inevitably some of these reservations trickled through to the Americans, and reinforced American doubts about de Gaulle – doubts which were continually fed by Ambassador Leahy and Robert Murphy, who furthermore assured Roosevelt and Hull that there was far more support in Unoccupied France and North Africa for Vichy than for Free France. In June 1941 an operation to rally Syria and the Lebanon – under British command, but including Free French troops – further exacerbated British relations with de Gaulle. The campaign itself was short and completely successful, but Vichy troops again fought fiercely against their fellow-countrymen, and the

British commander, General Wilson, judged it expedient to exclude Gaullist representatives from signing the armistice. De Gaulle was understandably affronted. Indeed, Oliver Lyttleton, the British minister in the Middle East, who had the unenviable task of soothing de Gaulle's ruffled feelings, subsequently described him as 'white with rage'. This episode left deeper scars than anything that had gone before. All de Gaulle's latent suspicions about British policy in the Middle East, based on a hundred years of imperialist rivalry between the two states, were aroused. The British were clearly aiming to supplant France in Syria and the Lebanon. As a first step, they were already seeking to win over Arab opinion. Why else, when Free France had already guaranteed post-war independence for these territories, had the British insisted on adding their own guarantee? Characteristically, de Gaulle chose to indulge his own suspicions, rather than accept the explanation that in the interests of the war effort it was desirable for both governments to conciliate Arab nationalism. Nor had de Gaulle seen any necessity to pander to Vichy susceptibilities in order to bring the campaign to an end as quickly as possible, at a time when the British Middle East Command was very hard pressed.[5]

ST PIERRE AND NORTH AFRICA: THE ANGLO-AMERICAN DISPUTE OVER FRANCE

Gradually there was being established in British minds – including Churchill's – an image of a difficult, truculent leader, leading an organization whose security was unreliable, and whose support in any attempt to win over further French territories was not worth the additional rancour it would cause between Frenchmen. Inevitably this view was passed on in part to Washington, where it fell on receptive ears. Roosevelt and Hull, as the latter notes in his memoirs, had already decided that they would not encourage any pretensions de Gaulle might have to the status of a provisional French government. Nonetheless, Churchill was still prepared to give de Gaulle his general support. En route to Washington, immediately after Pearl Harbor he drafted a memorandum for Roosevelt in which he urged, inter alia, that the two governments should act jointly to bring the Gaullists and the Vichy adherents closer together, especially in North Africa. To help win over de Gaulle, he recommended that the US government should establish closer links with the Free French than had been thought necessary or desirable in the days of US neutrality. Whether this would have borne fruit or not in view of American attitudes is impossible to say, since de Gaulle chose this moment for an act of supreme irresponsibility. The cause could hardly have been more trivial – the occupation by Free French forces of the tiny Vichy-held islands of St Pierre and Miquelon off the Canadian coast, at a time when the US and Canadian governments were negotiating with the appropriate Vichy representatives for a satisfactory solution of their status. Churchill had approved the Free French operation in principle, but had thought it right to consult the US government. Roosevelt had then personally expressed his opposition to the project, and Churchill had consequently passed this on to the Free French, and had received assurances that the operation would not be carried out. The whole affair was, or ought to have been, a storm in a teacup, but in fact it had profound consequences for future US relations with de Gaulle as well as creating difficulties in Anglo-American relations, and Churchill's personal relations with Roosevelt. And this in turn had further consequences for Franco-American and Franco-British relations, extending far into the post-war period. Roosevelt was irritated by this intrusion of minor French concerns into his conference with Churchill at a critical moment in the war; Churchill was embarrassed; and Hull was irreparably offended by what he regarded as an unforgivable breach of faith. Furthermore, he was suspicious of the role the British had played in the affair. Seldom has so much damage been done for so minuscule a reason. It was de Gaulle at his worst – obstinate, unpredictable, arrogant and even perhaps slightly malicious. It was almost as though he enjoyed making mischief between Churchill and Roosevelt, as though he wanted to force Churchill to choose between himself and the President – or as he would have said, between the US and France. Whenever he raised the question in this form, he was to get a dusty answer.[6]

Yet to begin with both Roosevelt and Churchill, unlike Hull, reacted quite well. In his talks with Churchill, Roosevelt appeared to treat the matter 'with a shrug of his shoulders' as a minor irritation. No doubt Churchill felt encouraged by this to pursue what was still his natural inclination to support Free France. He therefore took the opportunity in a speech to the Canadian parliament to reassert his view and to attack Vichy. This was a tactical mistake on Churchill's part. He had misunderstood Roosevelt's underlying feeling of resentment against de Gaulle, and had further infuriated Hull. The latter's view was simple, and at first sight not unreasonable. If, as Churchill claimed, de Gaulle had double-crossed him, why continue to support such an unreliable and vexatious ally? Why not break with him altogether, and transfer support to some more amenable figure? They had Catroux, and Admiral Muselier, the Free French naval commander, who was known to have opposed the St Pierre operation. Later on Churchill was to produce General Georges, and the Americans General Giraud, both senior military men, and relatively uncompromised by Vichy. On more than one occasion in the future the Americans were to urge the British to ditch de Gaulle, and on occasion Churchill seriously considered doing so. But in the end, usually under pressure from Eden, he always came back to the General, risking the friction with Roosevelt and the Americans that this was bound to cause. The fact was that by 1942 the British government had invested too much political capital in de Gaulle for him to be lightly cast aside. The effect of such a breach on the nascent French resistance movement alone might have been disastrous. As a consequence, the 'two-track' Anglo-American policy towards France came under increasing strain: a strain which increased when the occupation of French North Africa in November 1942 let to a final breach between the United States and the Vichy government. For it then became urgently necessary that Britain and the United States should construct an agreed policy towards France, and all the disparate elements that claimed to speak for France, and this was to prove no easy matter.[7]

In all this, it has to be remembered that the difficulties which arose were not due simply to the divergent paths which British and US policy had taken; nor were they solely due to the attitudes and prickly temperament of de Gaulle, though these factors undoubtedly added to the difficulties. A major cause lay in a fundamental difference between the American and British appraisal of France, and between Roosevelt's and Churchill's attitude towards her, which sprang directly from the fall of France. It was not the British government alone for whom the collapse of French resistance in 1940 had come as an appalling shock and an almost unbearable catastrophe. Roosevelt (and for that matter Stalin, too) had counted on the French army. Its humiliating defeat and the abject surrender of Pétain and Weygand, was taken to be a symptom of a fundamental rottenness in French society, and a reflection of a deep malaise in French character. It seemed to Roosevelt that not just a particular group of French leaders, but the French people as a whole, had to be largely written off: not merely as a significant factor in the allied war effort, but for the indefinite future. Roosevelt judged that it would be twenty years at least before France recovered and could again play a significant role in European or world affairs. Marshal Pétain and his associates were taken to be the genuine representatives not just of a French people stunned by catastrophe, but of a long-term mood and character. Part of Roosevelt's and Hull's irritation with de Gaulle, then, was due to a common human reaction when one stubs one's toe on an inconvenient fact. Here was a Frenchman who proclaimed that the real France was neither defeated nor defeatist, and who did so, moreover, in a particularly truculent fashion. He did not fit in with the Americans' preconceived ideas. Churchill, on the other hand, was a genuine lover of France. He appreciated only too well that in 1940 only a narrow strip of water had prevented the same catastrophe falling on Britain as on France. He welcomed any evidence that France would rise again. Infuriating, too, though de Gaulle was, he recognized in the General a kindred spirit – combative, awkward, individualistic, conforming to no recognizable class or national stereotype. De Gaulle was not typical of the French officer class, or of Frenchmen in general. He was not typical of anything. He was *sui generis*. Though there must have been many occasions when Churchill reflected that this was just as well, he could see de Gaulle's value in the situation in which France found herself. Neither of them were men who would accept defeat, even when it was staring them in the face. Certainly Churchill believed passionately in the Anglo-American Alliance, as a vital necessity for Britain and Europe after as well as during the war. But he was also a British statesman, accustomed to thinking in terms of a European balance of power. The American alliance did not rule out the necessity of such a balance. Indeed, unless Europe was to be permanently under American hegemony, that balance had to be restored after the war, and a restored France (and in some form a restored Germany) must play its part in this. As the war progressed, his growing fears about Russia strengthened this conviction. His views are exemplified by a cabinet paper he prepared on 13 July 1943: 'I have repeatedly stated that it is in the major interests of Britain to have a strong France after the war'. Again, on 6 February 1945, he notes in his memoirs, apropos of the need for France to share in the occupation of Germany, 'Germany would surely rise again, and while the Americans could always go home, the French had to live next door to her. A strong France was vital not only to Europe but to Great Britain'. There is no reason to doubt that this was his consistent view, or that he recognized that de Gaulle was the best hope of achieving his ends. In spite of frequent waverings, usually as a result of US pressure, or some particularly provocative act by de Gaulle, he tended to come back to this. As we have seen, at the height of the St Pierre affair, he had chosen to speak out publicly in favour of Free France. There is a clear line of policy from this incident to the Yalta Conference, when Hopkins noted that 'Winston and Anthony fought like tigers for France'. Eden, indeed, with whom Churchill's relations were very much closer than Roosevelt's with Hull, was if anything more convinced than Churchill of the need to rebuild France. To quote his own cabinet paper of the same period (July 1943), is perhaps sufficient: 'Our treaty with the Soviet Union ... needs to be balanced by an understanding with a powerful France in the west ... These arrangements will be indispensable whether or not the United States collaborates ... Our whole policy towards France should be governed by this consideration ... we are likely to have to work more closely with France even than with the United States ... [Our] policy must aim at the restoration of the greatness of France.' There is equal consistency here. It is sad that de Gaulle never quite believed it. Nor of course did many Frenchmen, then and later.[8]

If Churchill was always, in the end, a reluctant ally, Roosevelt, after St Pierre, was always an enemy. He was deeply affronted by de Gaulle's behaviour, on this and on other occasions, and his bias was consistently fed by Hull, by Leahy, and by Robert Murphy. He judged de Gaulle, not entirely unfairly, to have authoritarian tendencies and, as he put it in one message to Churchill, 'a Messiah complex'. The General accepted support from both extreme right-wing groups and from the Communists. This might be dangerous: they might end up using him, rather than he them. Yet at the same time Roosevelt was reluctant to accept the growing evidence, throughout 1941, 1942 and 1943, that de Gaulle's support in France was increasing, and his control over the French Resistance becoming stronger. All of this resulted in a preference for dealing with any other group or individual who raised his head – Weygand, Darlan, Giraud. Roosevelt and Hull rationalized this preference for dealing with France as a collection of fragmented groups as a principle – the principle that the French people must be free to choose their own government. Therefore the invasion of North Africa, and later of France, must be a 'military occupation'. De Gaulle must not be allowed to ride on American coat-tails into France and seize control, before the French people had had a chance to express their views. But this was unrealistic. The US military authorities in both North Africa and France would have to deal with some group of Frenchmen or the other, and it was impossible to endorse any group without to some degree pre-empting or at least influencing the issue. However that may be, this American attitude was to prove a considerable obstruction to de Gaulle in his attempts to rebuild a united France, and a constant source of vexation. Whatever other reasons there were for this American prejudice, the St Pierre incident had certainly much increased it. It was a considerable price to pay for one act of self-assertion. The consequences also were felt by Churchill in his personal relations with Roosevelt. It would have been difficult in any case to convince the President of the possibility of restoring French power and prestige, nor did he share Churchill's and Eden's views on the necessity of a 'European balance'. Roosevelt had little sympathy with what he regarded as old-fashioned balance-of-power politics. He pinned his hopes for post-war peace and security to a continuation of the quadripartite alliance of Russia, the US, Britain and China, working through a new international organization. To construct a common Anglo-American policy towards France in these circumstances was not easy. When one of the instruments offered Roosevelt was this obnoxious general, the task became that much more difficult.

From this point of view, it was unfortunate that the first major Anglo-American operation – that in North Africa – should have been intimately tied up with the French, and French politics. The consequences of the St Pierre affair now became all too clear. Roosevelt insisted that de Gaulle and his movement should not only have no military role in Torch but should be rigorously excluded from the planning of the operation, and not informed in any way about its details. The coldness of the exchanges on this subject between Roosevelt and Churchill in the midst of friendly discussions of the military aspects of Torch is notable. Roosevelt had proposed to send a friendly and conciliatory note to Pétain just before the operation, hoping that Pétain would instruct the French service chiefs not to offer much resistance. Churchill commented that the message was 'too kind' to Pétain, who had done the allied cause much harm, and the President thereupon toned it down – but was clearly offended. When Churchill reported a few days later that he proposed to tell de Gaulle on D-1, and let de Gaulle announce the appointment of a Free French governor of Madagascar that day, as a 'sweetener', Roosevelt not only refused permission, but added, gratuitously, that the announcement of the Madagascar appointment 'will not be of any assistance to Torch'. As Hull remarks, putting the blame naturally on Churchill, 'British support for de Gaulle was causing Anglo-American friction'. Or, looking at it from the other point of view, US support for Vichy. Although the State Department had reluctantly agreed to the establishment of more formal relations with the Free French Committee in July 1942, in September they were again urging the British government to break with de Gaulle. Churchill would not do this; but though constantly reminding Roosevelt that he had obligations to de Gaulle, he nonetheless went along with the exclusion of the Free French from Torch. By this time his own personal dislike of de Gaulle disposed

him to this course, as well as his conviction that the Free
French would muddy up the works, but he knew de Gaulle
would be mortally offended.[9]

In all this, one has to try to distinguish what was rational in
US policy from what was due to mere prejudice. Roosevelt had
been constantly advised by Murphy and Leahy that the
inclusion of the Free French in the military operation (and
even that of the British in the early stages) would result in
fiercer resistance from the Vichy troops, and on this point
Murphy was almost certainly right. Indeed, he might have
gone further and advised his Chief that no outside figure,
such as General Giraud, would cut much ice in North Africa –
that to begin with, the Allies would have to rely on one of the
senior Vichy men, such as generals Noguès or Juin – or Darlan
himself, who was fortuitously visiting Algiers at this time.
Certainly, as events turned out, French army resistance was
sporadic and ineffective, though the French navy, with its
memories of Oran, put up more opposition. Moreover,
Darlan, having thrown in his lot with the Allies, was able to
bring over the whole of North and West Africa to the allied
cause. In military terms, the 'Vichy Gamble' came off.
Politically, however, it caused a good deal of trouble. De
Gaulle was outraged, and the policy, especially the 'Darlan
Expedient,' ran into heavy press criticism in both the US and
Britain. When Darlan was assassinated, on Christmas Day
1942, and replaced by Giraud, the criticism was a little
modified, but did not cease. In all this, however, Churchill and
Roosevelt managed to maintain good relations, the President
masking his irritation under references to the 'three prima
donnas' and their 'catfights'.[10]

DE GAULLE WINS THE NORTH AFRICAN CONTEST

So far as de Gaulle was concerned, the damage might have
been somewhat lessened if the Allies had not tried to keep
him totally in the dark. The accusation that Free French
security was unreliable was little more than a pretext. The
Americans themselves were in constant contact with the
higher levels of command, and with political circles in
Algiers, which in their turn were in contact with elements in

the Vichy government. If it was not quite equivalent to a direct line to Berlin, it was not far from it. If the Allies had chosen to explain beforehand their reasons for not including Free French troops, citing the experience of Dakar and Syria, de Gaulle would not necessarily have accepted it but would have had less cause for complaint. Roosevelt, however, made no effort to conciliate de Gaulle either before, or in the aftermath of Torch. On the contrary, he insisted to Churchill in January that Allied rule in North Africa was a 'military occupation'. Far from recognizing any group as a 'representative French Government', Eisenhower, the Allied commander, should therefore deal with the French 'on a local basis'. Roosevelt cautiously agreed with Churchill that they must try to reduce inter-French rivalries – which meant bringing de Gaulle and Giraud together. But it has to be said that the first attempt to do so, at the Casablanca Conference of January 1943, was not conspicuously successful. Roosevelt meanwhile continued to resist – what no one was as yet proposing – that any group should be recognized as a 'provisional government': and to assert that 'only the French people themselves, after they shall have regained their liberty, can determine the Government they desire'. This kind of statement, made publicly, only served to further infuriate de Gaulle, who pointed out, not unreasonably, that having taken up arms against German and Italian dictatorships, and broken with the authoritarian regime of Vichy, he should not be suspected of wishing to impose a new dictatorship on France. In any case, it was for Frenchmen to decide the political future of France, not the Anglo-Americans. This attitude was neither completely fair, nor completely rational. It overlooked the fact that it was the Allies who would have the task of liberating France. They could neither be expected to be indifferent to the political consequences of their action, nor was it possible for them to avoid influencing those consequences. So far as de Gaulle was concerned, however, the problem immediately ahead of him was to assert Free French political authority in North Africa. The first stage of this process was to reach some sort of agreement with the French regime there. Now that Giraud had succeeded Darlan, that was at least possible – i.e. not politically objectionable.

However, de Gaulle had no intention of making things easy for Giraud and the Anglo-Americans, or agreeing to anything which in his eyes limited French sovereignty. If Roosevelt was angered by the delay, that was of no importance. Roosevelt and Churchill agreed in theory that this union was desirable, but they expected – particularly Roosevelt – that de Gaulle would be properly grateful, and accept whatever was proposed. When the General proved every bit as difficult and pernickety as usual – and he had the highest possible standards in this regard – Roosevelt was infuriated, Churchill hardly less so. When it further became apparent after four months' negotiations that de Gaulle would insist on the removal of the most prominent Vichy collaborators, and perhaps on their being brought to trial, both men lost their patience. In May 1943 Churchill was at Washington, in conference with Roosevelt. From there he wired to Eden that 'there was a very stern mood developing in Washington' and he feared 'estrangement from the U.S. government'. Roosevelt, he reported, mentioned the subject 'every day'. The time had come when they should consider a rupture with de Gaulle. Eden replied firmly on behalf of the War Cabinet that agreement between de Gaulle and Giraud was now very close, and it would be wrong to upset the applecart at this point. He reminded Churchill (who was well aware of the fact) that de Gaulle's support had grown considerably in both North Africa and France, and that most of the Free French Committee would support no one else. The problem was, he suggested, that Murphy, Leahy (and by inference Roosevelt himself) were unwilling to admit they had been wrong in assessing the degree of Gaullist support. Having relieved his feelings, Churchill withdrew his proposition, and risked Roosevelt's displeasure. Perhaps, indeed, he expected the War Cabinet's reaction, and, as on other occasions, found it a useful alibi. At all events he offered Roosevelt a soothing syrup of excuses, arguing that in the newly-formed 'Committee of National Liberation' de Gaulle would be outvoted by five to two (a totally false assumption), and therefore his influence would be 'merged in the Committee.[11]

Certainly the President's ruffled feelings need soothing, as de Gaulle continued to assert himself, especially in relation to control of the French Army. This was a subject on which the

Americans were particularly sensitive, since they were largely arming and supplying the French armed services, and looked to them for a useful contribution to the Allied military effort. In May Roosevelt had described de Gaulle's 'whole course and attitude' as 'intolerable'. In June he was cabling Churchill 'I am fed up with de Gaulle ... there is no possibility of our working with him ... the time has come when we must break with him'. Similar expressions of presidential wrath were poured out to General Eisenhower in Algiers. Eisenhower, more cool and clear-headed than Roosevelt on such matters, was bold enough to ask Marshall to restrain the President from forcing a crisis, thus reinforcing the British view. Roosevelt's principal grievance was that de Gaulle was a 'disloyal ally', and in this he was right. De Gaulle was loyal to no one and no cause except that of France.[12]

RECOGNITION AND LIBERATION: DE GAULLE TRIUMPHANT

Churchill was placed in a difficult position in his attempts to keep the peace between two hostile powers. His greatest fear, he told the War Cabinet, was that 'the anti-Gaullism of the US Government might harden into a definite feeling against France'. But he was equally concerned that differences over de Gaulle might harm his precious relationship with the President. Nor was this fear entirely misplaced. Amongst the various causes of the deterioration of that relationship during the summer and autumn of 1943, the irritation which Roosevelt felt with de Gaulle, and, by transference, with Churchill the 'creator' of de Gaulle, was a significant if minor factor. This irritation was in no way assuaged by the fact that from the time the new Committee was formed, it became increasingly obvious that the Americans had backed the wrong horse. Giraud's influence within the Committee continuously waned, while de Gaulle's became stronger. Meanwhile, the Committee's control and influence generally was growing. The now powerful French Resistance for the most part acknowledged its authority; a substantial French force was fighting with the Allies in Italy; Corsica had been won over. All this made it seem the more appropriate to Eden and

Macmillan, and increasingly to Eisenhower, that some more generous form of recognition should be extended to the Committee. If that was taken to mean in effect recognition as a 'provisional government', did it matter? Roosevelt's prejudices, however, ensured that concessions on this matter had to be extracted from him as with a corkscrew, and Churchill's desire not to offend the President any further kept British policy in line. As he wrote to Roosevelt in July, 'my chief desire is to keep in step with you'. Later the same month, however, he wrote that he was 'under increasing pressure from the Foreign Office' to offer a measure of recognition. Roosevelt's reply, concocted after much consultation with Hopkins, Leahy and the State Department, was again grudging. 'Acceptance' of the Committee as the principal French authority, rather than 'recognition', with its unfortunate 'governmental' connotations, would be the appropriate term. Moreover, the President wished to include specific conditions that the ultimate choice of government must be left to the French people, and that the Committee must not function 'for the promotion of factional movements [i.e. Gaullism]'. De Gaulle would certainly have found this insulting, and those conditions may indeed have been designed to make him reject the formula. Under pressure from Eden and the Cabinet, Churchill submitted his own more generous formula, but Roosevelt stuck to his insistence on limited 'acceptance' only. Roosevelt, of course, like the rest of us, wanted to have his cake and eat it. He wished to see de Gaulle's authority over those territories and forces which had previously rallied to him limited by a Committee which would include the 'Giraudists'; while at the same time continuing to deal exclusively with Giraud as French C.-in-C., in relation to French forces in Italy and North Africa. This was an impossible demand. In the end, after further argument at the first Quebec Conference in August 1943, each government went ahead separately with its own formula; but further damage had been done to Anglo-French and Franco-American relations in the process. De Gaulle might console himself with the thought that events were moving steadily his way, but he resented American attitudes bitterly. Nor did he feel particularly grateful to Churchill and Eden for their efforts on his behalf. They might have done more. One day he would show the British that France was not to be trifled with. When that happened, it was ironical that de Gaulle's malice should have been visited on Macmillan, who had been his friend and advocate when de Gaulle needed friends.[13]

As it was, further events occurred to keep de Gaulle's relations with both Roosevelt and Churchill at a less than cordial level. Giraud was pushed out of the French Committee, Roosevelt, Churchill and Stalin met at Teheran – without France – and troubles blew up in Syria, where the British Government's heavy-handed intervention reawakened all de Gaulle's suspicions of 1941. In December 1943 Boisson, Peyrouton and Flandin, all former protégés of the Americans and former Vichy supporters, were placed under house arrest, to await trial in a liberated France. It is not surprising, though regrettable, that in April, with the invasion of Europe pending, Roosevelt gave Eisenhower categoric instructions that he should personally choose which French authority to work with, nor that the President should insist that de Gaulle be kept in the dark about the planning, exactly as had been the case with North Africa. Eisenhower, for his part, thought it only common sense to recognize the status of de Gaulle and his Committee, and to make rational arrangements with the Committee and with General Koenig, de Gaulle's 'Chief of Resistance'. Eisenhower also ensured that Leclerc's French Armoured Division should be on hand to take part in the liberation of Paris. Churchill, following Roosevelt's lead, dutifully told the House of Commons on 24 May 1944 that 'he was not convinced that the Committee represents the whole body of the French people' – and was contradicted the next day by Eden, who informed the House that the Allies would deal with the Committee 'as the French authority which will exercise leadership in France as liberation progresses'. Immediately Roosevelt cabled to Churchill that 'Allied military power should not be used to impose a particular group as a government'. With Roosevelt, Churchill, Eden and Eisenhower all pulling different ways, Allied policy towards France was in fact a shambles. De Gaulle took advantage of the confusion to proclaim that the Committee was now the 'Provisional Government' of France. How much Churchill's attitude was dictated by his own dislike of de Gaulle, and how much by his desire to conciliate Roosevelt is not certain. It has to be borne in mind that Britain was now definitely the weaker and the junior partner in the alliance, and, as Churchill was to say in a different context, 'we had much to ask of the Americans'. Certainly Churchill's celebrated meeting with de Gaulle on the eve of D-Day was as acrimonious as Roosevelt could have wished, with displays of affronted grandeur on one side and furious rage on the other. Yet five days later, the Prime Minister let slip in his correspondence with Roosevelt, apropos of a currency question, the phrase: 'shall we get de Gaulle to take responsibility for these notes as President of the Provisional Government of France?' Roosevelt's reply, as might be expected, was uncompromising, but the slip is revealing.[14]

The inexorable pressure of events was in fact making inevitable the recognition of the committee as a 'Provisional Government', as Churchill must have foreseen. As France was liberated, de Gaulle's officials took control, with Eisenhower's approval, and by the end of August the General was establishing his government in liberated Paris. Belatedly, the necessary allied agreements for civil administration had been signed with the Committee. By the time the Allies again assembled in conference at Quebec in September, Churchill was prepared to press the case strongly. By now even Hull had been converted, but Roosevelt still held out, in the face of pressures from the British and from Eisenhower. Perhaps the firm handling of the more radical elements in the Resistance by Eisenhower and de Gaulle finally tipped the scale. Eventually, on 23 October, Roosevelt capitulated, and the French Committee was recognized as the 'Provisional Government of France'. It had taken fifteen months of bitter argument to bring it about, and had done untold damage to Franco-American and Franco-British relations.[15]

All in all, Anglo-American policy towards France was a muddle, and a muddle which, largely because of de Gaulle's return to power in 1958, had long-term consequences for Anglo-French and Franco-American relations. The causes of the muddle have been sufficiently set out above, and some part of the responsibility must rest on both Roosevelt and Churchill, as well as de Gaulle. For a considerable part of the wartime period Roosevelt and de Gaulle operated on the highest plane of unreason in their dealings with each other.

De Gaulle was unnecessarily sensitive and touchy, always on the look-out for slights, and sometimes finding them where none were intended; sometimes, too, mistaking petulance for firmness. More often than not he was right in his essential position. The more reason for being gracious, when graciousness cost nothing. Roosevelt for his part, egged on by Leahy and Hull, let his judgement be too much influenced by his anger over the trivial St Pierre incident, and allowed himself to be trapped into an obstinate insistence on propositions which became increasingly unrealistic as events moved on. Churchill, it could be argued, might have tried to restrain and influence the President to wiser courses more than he did. Certainly Eden and other members of the War Cabinet thought so. His own annoyance with, and dislike of de Gaulle was partly responsible for his failure to do so. But fundamentally, it was his constant need not to try Roosevelt's patience too hard over French problems, when even more important matters had to be decided, which held him back. He was conscious, more than any other member of the British Cabinet, of Britain's waning power, and of his own waning influence with the President. As Napoleon remarked, 'God is on the side of the big battalions'; and Roosevelt, not de Gaulle, had the battalions.[16]

7 The Problem of Germany: Destruction or Reconstruction ?

All men are to some extent captive to past impressions, and particularly in their images of other nations and the problems associated with them. Most powerful are the impressions formed in youth and early manhood. Roosevelt and Churchill were no exceptions to this rule. Faced with the central problem of how to deal after the war with their main enemy, Germany, both men were powerfully influenced by their early impressions of and prejudices against the German nation, and also by what they conceived to be the lessons to be drawn from the failure of the earlier peace settlement of 1919 and the mistakes of the inter-war years.

Roosevelt seems to have had an anti-German prejudice from his early days, derived partly from his parents, and partly from his own experience of Germans, when visiting Germany as a child and a young man. An impression was fixed in his mind of a people who were militaristic, arrogant and yet unduly susceptible to regimentation and obedience to authority. As with many Americans (and British), his prejudices were powerfully reinforced by the First World War. He accepted the dogma that Germany was mainly responsible for the war, without recognizing that this was a gross oversimplification of a highly complex issue. Furthermore, the Germans had introduced new elements of barbarity into that conflict – submarine warfare against neutral civilians as well as belligerents; bombing of civilians from the air; poison gas. They had shown no respect either for international law or human decency. Not surprisingly Roosevelt, then Assistant Secretary for the Navy in Wilson's administration, was a partisan of US entry into the war, and not sorry when eventually Wilson capitulated to events. Afterwards, however, the United States – along with the other Allies – had made the mistake, as he saw it, of not taking sufficiently strong measures to ensure that Germany could not again become a threat to

European and world peace: and the US had compounded this
mistake by withdrawing from the League of Nations and
failing to take its proper share of the burden of maintaining
world peace and security. Both of these mistakes must be put
right this time.

Churchill was equally in some ways the prisoner of the past
in his attitude to Germany, but in his case, it was the image of
Imperial Germany that he saw, and above all the Prussian
military caste, which had been the social and political basis of
support for the Hohenzollerns. Contrasted with 'the
Prussians', who were the root of German evil, Churchill had a
vision of peaceful South German peasants, pipe-smoking,
music-loving and beer-drinking who, left to themselves,
without the malign influence of Prussian militarism, would do
no harm to anyone. This rather romantic vision of Churchill's
was, of course, old-fashioned, rose-coloured and, to put it
bluntly, plain wrong. As Eden more than once pointed out to
him, whatever might have been the origins of Imperial
Germany's militarism, the roots of the support for Nazism
were to be found in south Germany and rural Germany
generally, more than in Berlin and Prussia or the industrial
heartland of the Ruhr. Stalin was to make a similar point to
Churchill when they met: he could detect no difference in the
nationalistic fervour or military spirit of Germans whether
from the south, north, east or west. They were all much of a
muchness. Therefore, Roosevelt's view, that support for the
Nazi regime was equally widespread in all parts of Germany
and all Germans were equally to blame for the war, was in fact
nearer to the truth than Churchill's. But though derived from
a mistaken premiss, Churchill's image of the Germans did
enable him to take a slightly more discriminating view of the
German problem. Because he distinguished between different
kinds of German, it was easier for him also to distinguish
between different levels of guilt – the more heinous guilt of
the active, evil minority at the top, and the lesser guilt of the
inert mass of the German people, who acquiesced and obeyed
orders. At the Teheran Conference, indeed, he suggested to
Stalin, during one discussion, that one could (and perhaps
should) distinguish between the Nazi regime and the ordinary
German working people; but Stalin, the proletarian, would
have none of it. The Germans were all the same – dangerous,

because they would always obey orders – and willing to fight like devils. It was not at all surprising that it was Stalin's view of the German problem which Roosevelt found initially much closer to his own than Churchill's.[1]

There was, of course, another reason why Churchill's view of Germany was bound to differ from the simplistic approaches of Roosevelt and Stalin, namely the 'European View'. Churchill was after all a European, and Britain, with all due allowance for its insularity and the psychological importance of the Channel, was still a part of Europe. Europe was a family of nation-states, and Germany, however aberrant and misguided, was a part of that family, just as France, however weak and temporarily diminished, was a part of it. Churchill was influenced by this traditional view of Germany, and Eden even more so. In a paper for the War Cabinet in March 1943, the Foreign Secretary had specifically said, 'when regenerated, Germany should eventually find a place again in the family of nations'. Churchill did not always go along with Eden, but was inclined to regard his judgement in foreign affairs as pretty sound. By contrast, Roosevelt often paid little attention to the opinions of his Secretary of State, Cordell Hull, whose views on a German settlement were as it happened more moderate than his Chief's – though for different reasons than Eden's. In addition to this difference between the British and American approach to the German problem, and all other European problems, there was a further reason for the divergence between British and US attitudes – the traditional British concern with the maintenance of an equilibrium or balance or power in Europe. Germany was a part of that balance, as was France. To eliminate Germany completely, either politically or economically, or both, would be to take an important weight from the balance and alter its entire nature. Churchill saw at a very early stage that if Germany in the form it had worn since 1870 were removed, something would have to be put in its place. As the threat of Soviet military and political dominance began to loom larger in his mind towards the end of the war – as it became apparent indeed that it would extend to much of Eastern Europe – this consideration assumed greater importance. The US treasury secretary, Henry Morgenthau, whose 1944 Plan did, in effect, seek to eliminate Germany from the map, both politically and economically, attributed right-wing American opposition to his plan to hatred and fear of Russian 'Bolshevism'. The right saw that a weak Germany would mean a stronger Russia. Churchill certainly was also motivated by fear of Russia, thought it was fear of the power and might of the Soviet State, more than his well-known ideological opposition to Communism, that weighed with him, and inevitably affected his attitude to the future of Germany.

Here was a fundamental difference. The point has been made that Roosevelt, like other liberal Democrats, had no sympathy with balance-of-power politics, which in his view were not merely a mistaken, but a positively harmful approach to the problem of security. The Americans, who had been drawn into two European wars against their will, could indeed hardly be blamed for thinking that the balance of power had not worked particularly well. Nor was Roosevelt worried by the thought that Germany, France and, for that matter, Britain would emerge from the war much weaker than before, and therefore European influence as a whole would be much less than it had been for several centuries. The European 'Great Powers' had not made a particularly good job of running affairs, either at home, or abroad, where their colonial empires, in Roosevelt's view, had done little for the welfare of their native subjects. As for Europe itself, two appalling internecine conflicts in less than half a century were certainly no advertisement for European political sagacity. The thought, therefore, that wiping Germany off the map would create a power vacuum in the heart of Europe, which Russian influence might fill, was not as alarming to him as it was to Churchill. If genuine Soviet–American cooperation post-war could become a reality – which Roosevelt believed possible, and on which he had set his heart – then they might together do a much better job of running European and World affairs than the old Great Powers of Europe.[2]

A HARSH OR A MODERATE PEACE? PARTITION, REPARATIONS AND THE MORGENTHAU PLAN

The problem of Germany can be easily stated. How could the victorious allies ensure that Germany, populous, disciplined, rich in industrial resources and know-how, and centrally placed, would not rise again after defeat? How could they guarantee that it would not again become a threat to peace, unless they destroyed it utterly? To break up Germany into a number of smaller states might seem to be the answer, but how ensure that they would not some day reunite? To guard completely against the dangers of a unified Germany, only the permanent destruction of German war-making capacity, i.e. the total obliteration of Germany heavy industry, especially the Ruhr, would suffice. Stalin and the Russian leaders could see no objection to that programme. Within both American and British governing circles, however, but more acutely in the US there arose, as the end of the war approached, two schools of thought on the problem. There were those who accepted the severe logic of the argument stated above, and favoured the most rigorous and punitive post-war measures against Germany – the so-called 'Carthaginian Peace'. Even if this meant the growth of Soviet power and influence, and a general reduction in European living standards, these consequences must be accepted. Opposed to them was the other school, who thought the German people could be purified of the Nazi infection; the German State reformed on democratic and decentralized quasi-federal lines; and total disarmament imposed, supplemented perhaps by some form of international control of the Ruhr. Given the shock of total defeat, unconditional surrender and the occupation of their country, the German people, rid of the Nazi corruption, might respond to these reforms. Eventually, after a period of probation, Germany might again take its place as an acceptable, even useful member of the European 'family of nations'. In the United States Henry Morgenthau and a group of his advisers emerged as the principal champions of a 'Carthaginian Peace', on the other side, Cordell Hull, with his State Department advisers, put forward in general a more moderate line, supported as a rule by Henry Stimson and the War Department. Roosevelt, with his simplistic approach to the German problem, was instinctively drawn to the Morgenthau school. His natural tendency, indeed preference, for seeking advice on foreign affairs from sources other than the State Department, gave Morgenthau on occasion the opportunity to exercise considerable influence on the

President's thinking. Within British governing circles the 'Carthaginian' school of thought was represented by Lindeman, Churchill's trusted scientific adviser and associate of many years, who was fanatical in his dislike of Germany. On the other side, looking to a future European balance, in which Germany might be a necessary element, were Eden and the serried ranks of the Foreign Office 'mandarins'. In the British case, however, the influence on Churchill of Lindeman, and those who thought like him was on most occasions more than counterbalanced by other powerful forces. Firstly by Churchill's natural sympathy for the balance of power argument; secondly by his trust in Eden's judgement; and thirdly by the traditional weight and influence of the Foreign Office within the British political system. In the final stages of the argument, these powerful forces were reinforced by the British Treasury and its much respected chief, Sir John Anderson. Unlike Morgenthau and Lindeman, Anderson was not prepared to take a complacent view of the consequences for European prosperity of the total destruction of German industry; nor did he think this likely to benefit British economic interests.[3]

It was only, therefore, when Morgenthau and Lindeman were both present, at the Quebec Conference of September 1944 – while not only Hull, but momentarily Eden as well, were absent – that Churchill temporarily wavered in the direction of a 'Carthaginian' approach to Germany. But on that occasion there were probably, as will appear, other reasons for this aberration. In general Churchill remained faithful to the traditional, and therefore more moderate view of Germany's future place in the scheme of things. But Churchill would not have been Churchill, if he had not had his own idiosyncratic contribution to the debate, particularly on the central question of whether or not Germany should be partitioned.

During the critical early years of the war, neither Churchill nor Eden was disposed to give too much attention to the future treatment of Germany. Their minds were concentrated on the immediate problems of the war. When the US became involved, Roosevelt was similarly disinclined to commit himself to precise plans for Germany, and very anxious, as was Hull, that Britain should not do so either. All territorial and frontier questions were best left to peace treaty discussions after the end of hostilities, when these issues could be considered coolly, and when the US could exercise its full weight. Therefore, when Stalin raised the issue of the East European territorial settlement, with implications for Germany, during Eden's visit to Moscow in January 1942, the US reaction was to urge that no commitments be made. Nor was Churchill disposed to give his mind to these detailed problems at this stage. Eden was therefore obliged to tell Stalin that neither Britain nor the US was prepared to commit itself at that time. It became apparent during the talks, however, that Stalin would demand the return to the USSR of the territories taken from her by Poland after the First World War, and that Poland should be 'compensated' by acquisitions of German territory to the west. Stalin further suggested that Hitler's acquisitions of territory in the thirties and forties should be disgorged, i.e. Alsace-Lorraine, the Czech Sudetenland, and Austria. What remained of Germany might be divided into at least three independent states. Thus the issue of German partition or 'dismemberment' was for the first time formally raised between the Allies. It also marked, for Eden, the beginning of a long period of tacking backwards and forwards on the issue of German partition, which left both Allies and colleagues in doubt as to his real views, and does not add to his reputation as Foreign Minister. Indeed during a period of a few months in 1943, he appears to have simultaneously given Roosevelt (who had come to favour partition) and Hull (who was dubious about the idea) the impression that he agreed with each of them. At this early meeting with Stalin, Eden went perhaps further than it was wise to do in saying that 'he had no objection in principle' to the idea of partitioning Germany. It was a weakness of Eden's that he was sometimes inclined to tell people what they wanted to hear, rather than what he really thought. It is a temptation to which statesmen should not succumb, though it is only fair to say that Churchill himself gave in to it on one or two occasions, as did Roosevelt.[4]

Another thorny question was raised by Stalin for the first time at these meetings, namely how far the Germans could be made to compensate the Allies for the loss, damage and suffering they had inflicted? This issue – the issue of reparations – was to become inextricably bound up with the question of partition, and how far this might impede the ability of the Germans to pay up. On this issue, both the British and Americans had uncomfortable memories of the long-drawn-out attempt to extract reparations from Germany after the First World War. To Stalin Eden expressed his doubts about large-scale financial payments across the exchanges, as compared with possible transfers of manufactured goods, or perhaps machinery. There the matter rested for the moment.[5]

The question of partition having been raised, however, led Churchill naturally to turn his fertile mind to this problem. Possibly Stalin's desire to split up Germany could be made to serve the purpose of separating the rest of Germany from the bad influence of Prussia. But something would have to be put in place of the old German state, not only to maintain the balance of power, but also to give the 'good' Germans some worthwhile object to attach themselves to. Otherwise they would soon begin to hanker after reunion with their German kinsfolk in the East. Why not a fusion of the 'peace-loving' south Germans and Austrians, or better still, because larger and more weighty, bring the Hungarians also into a new state, which would be something like the old Austro-Hungarian Empire – but without the Slavs? The important overriding consideration in all this was the need, as Churchill and Eden saw it, to reverse the disastrous fragmentation of central and eastern Europe after the First World War. Eden had ideas of creating more powerful states in Eastern Europe through the federation of the smaller states. To these 'castles in the air' Churchill added the notion of a 'Danubian Federation', on the lines indicated above.

The fate of Eden's plans for Eastern Europe has been discussed earlier. Churchill's 'Danubian Federation', like them, was to founder on the rock of the combined opposition of Roosevelt and Stalin. At this early stage, however, Churchill did not impart his ideas to Roosevelt. The President had made it clear that he did not wish to embark on any discussion of future territorial changes in Europe. In 1942 Roosevelt's thoughts were concentrated on the need to aid Russia and keep her in the fight: the best way to do that was to send the Russians as much material aid as possible, and to bring

Anglo-American military power to bear as soon as might be, in a way which would take some of the weight of the hard-pressed Red Army. As will be apparent from the discussion of the 'Second Front' controversy in Chapter 2, however, Churchill was determined not to be pushed into any disastrous military adventure in Europe. He would rather have given the Soviet Union encouragement by some indication that Britain and the United States were not completely opposed to its territorial demands. For the moment, however, Churchill (and Eden) had to keep their thoughts on the future of Germany and Eastern Europe to themselves. But it was already evident that, when the British and Americans did begin to discuss these matters seriously, Churchill's views on Germany – and Eden's also – would differ from Roosevelt's. Fortunately for his peace of mind, Churchill did not, at this moment, appreciate just how much.

Roosevelt was not unmindful, of course, of the need to reassure and hearten the Russians in their hour of need, and even more so after the decision had been made not to attempt the invasion of Europe in 1942. At the back of his mind, and of many American minds throughout 1942 and 1943, there was always the possibility that the Russians might surrender, or prefer a peace even on disadvantageous terms to further hardship and sacrifice. Even after the stunning Soviet victory at Stalingrad in February 1943, reports were still reaching Washington that Stalin would be satisfied when the Red Army drove the invaders off Soviet soil, and would then negotiate a peace on much the same lines as the 1939 Molotov – Ribbentrop agreement – i.e. including a division of Eastern Europe into German and Soviet 'spheres of influence'. By that stage of the war, the Germans might well be glad to sign such a peace. British opinion on this subject had veered sharply, from the earlier view of the British military that Russia would be knocked out in six weeks, to the more relaxed view, after Stalingrad, that the worst was over, and that the Russians, having gone through so much, would probably not settle for anything less than total victory. In Washington, however, the attitude was not quite so relaxed even after Stalingrad, and certainly not before. It was partly, Roosevelt thought, a question of persuading Stalin that he could trust his allies. He himself was not as yet willing to discuss the future of Germany.

Even less was he prepared to match a possible German offer of 'spheres of influence' in Eastern Europe. His solution to the problem of reassuring the Russians was to make it clear to them that the United States and Britain, for their part, would fight to the bitter end and until total victory, would never negotiate with the Nazi regime, and would, in fact, accept nothing less than 'unconditional surrender' from the German armies. There were to be no bargains with the Germans. They would have to accept what terms the Allies chose to impose on them. Stalin need have no fears that the West would sign a separate peace with Germany.[6]

THE PROS AND CONS OF UNCONDITIONAL SURRENDER: CONFLICTING SCHEMES FOR PARTITION

There was a further reason why, in Roosevelt's (and Churchill's) opinion the doctrine of 'unconditional surrender' should be proclaimed. After the First World War, German historians had maintained that the German army had never been defeated. Germany's leaders had surrendered and laid down their arms voluntarily, in the belief that the peace settlement would be based on President Wilson's celebrated 'Fourteen Points', or more accurately, 'Twenty-three Points'. These had included, *inter alia*, a promise that the settlement would not be based on 'private understandings' (i.e. secret agreements) between the Allies; that peoples and provinces should not be 'bartered about like chattels'; that the independent state of Poland would be restored, but would include only 'territories inhabited by indisputably Polish populations'; and in general that 'every territorial settlement must be in the interests of the populations concerned'. There was no specific promise that every part of the territorial settlement would be based strictly on the principle of 'national self-determination', but the principle was implicit in much that was said, both about the general settlement and specific parts of it, such as Poland, Italy, and the treatment of the old Austro-Hungarian and Ottoman empires. It was not too difficult for German propagandists to argue subsequently that the principle had been breached in various ways in the eventual peace treaties, and thereby to create a sense of grievance in the mind of the German people, of which the Nazis took full advantage.[7]

Therefore, along with the desire to reassure Stalin that the Western Allies would in no circumstances sign a separate peace with Germany, Roosevelt had the additional motive of excluding any such evasions by the Germans in future. Their armies must suffer total defeat, beyond any possibility of misrepresentation, and there would be no promises, commitments or conditions this time. The Germans must surrender 'unconditionally', that is, in the full knowledge that they were signifying their willingness to accept whatever terms the Allies chose to mete out to them. Churchill, for his part, could see the force of these arguments. When the two men met at the Casablanca Conference of January 1943, the British leader certainly agreed to the general 'unconditional surrender' proposition, though he was, he says, slightly taken by surprise by Roosevelt's actual timing of the announcement, which came towards the end of the conference. It is not worth devoting much attention to the question whether this proclamation stiffened the German will to resist, a question much discussed by historians. All that need be said here is that the Nazi propaganda machine would have distorted and put to effective use whatever was said on the subject. The alternative of 'spelling out' possible conditions of peace, given the frame of mind of both Roosevelt and Stalin then and later, would certainly have alarmed the Germans and stiffened their resistance even more, as was apparent when details of the 'Morgenthau Plan' later became widely known. As late as April 1944, soon after Roosevelt and Stalin at the Teheran Conference had spelt out their wishes to inflict a harsh peace on Germany, Churchill fobbed off the suggestion that some indication should be given to the Germans of the kind of treatment they might expect. Roosevelt and Stalin, he pointed out – and indeed popular opinion, so far as it could be ascertained – were evidently set on 'a peace of retribution'. It would not be possible to say anything about Allied intentions to the Germans, with any honesty, that they would be likely to find reassuring. Privately, as opposed to what might be said publicly, Churchill was clear that the Germans must not be treated too harshly. Indeed his first contribution to the debate after Casablanca was the suggestion to Roosevelt in February

1943 that the German people (and those of the other Axis partners) should not suffer ' total destruction', but should be able to look forward to the possibility of 'a decent life'. He also urged that the Allies should accept the impossibility of making the Germans and their allies pay for the war through reparations: on the contrary, the Allies themselves would have to shoulder the burden of rebuilding Europe and aiding the Soviet people, who had suffered most of all. In forecasting that 'severe exertions' would be necessary on the part of the victors, Churchill was in fact anticipating both the long period of sacrifice and austerity, which were the principal fruits of victory for the British people, and the massive flow of US dollars for European recovery which was to be asked of the Americans. Roosevelt's and Churchill's views on the treatment of Germany were in fact already beginning to diverge, though this was not fully evident as yet to either man. That Roosevelt's views did not accord fully with the above is demonstrated by various 'straws in the wind' during 1943 and eventually – and conclusively – at the Teheran Conference in November. The President had not, in fact, replied specifically to Churchill's note of February 1943 – which may have meant no more than that there were other issues (such as the behaviour of generals de Gaulle and Giraud) that he regarded as more worthwhile subjects for his correspondence with Churchill. More probably he had not yet made up his mind on the issues raised by Churchill's memorandum.[8]

During 1943, in fact, Roosevelt was in the process of working out his views on the question of German partition in his usual way – that is by throwing out ideas, and using both Americans and allied visitors as a 'sounding-board'. One such occasion was the Eden visit to Washington of March 1943. That this was not a more successful exercise was Eden's fault. He had expressed considerable doubts about the practicability of German dismemberment in a paper for the War Cabinet a week or so earlier. Yet, when Roosevelt made it clear that his mind was moving in favour of dismemberment, Eden now said that he personally favoured it! Putting together Churchill's known desire to separate Prussia from Germany with Eden's apparent willingness to back the general principle of partition, and Stalin's expressed approval of it, it must have seemed to Roosevelt that there was the basis for a tripartite allied agreement on these lines. At the very least they could all agree on detaching Prussia from the rest of Germany, while in what was left they should certainly encourage all 'separatist tendencies' which might exist – as such tendencies certainly did in the Rhineland for example. Morgenthau was already at his ear, suggesting that Germany should be thoroughly dismembered, as well as weakened in other ways. On the other side of the fence, Cordell Hull had set up a State Department Committee the previous year to consider the issue of German partition, but it had not yet reported. When it did report, in July, the committee spent a good deal of time summing up the opposing points of view, while being cautiously in favour of maintaining a unified state. But it is significant that the party in favour of partition in this committee was led by Sumner Welles, widely regarded as 'Roosevelt's man' in the State Department, and one who might be presumed to know the trend of presidential thinking. Certainly the State Department's views seem to have made little impression on Roosevelt, since in September he sent to Hull, with obvious approval, a letter from the *New York Times* recommending a very drastic partition of Germany, as well as measures for the control of the Ruhr industries – in short a 'Morgenthau programme'. Hull's sharp rejoinder that such a settlement would be 'a disaster both for Germany and for us' made no lasting impression, though Hull thought it had.[9]

However that may be, neither Roosevelt nor Hull were attracted by Churchill's idea of a 'Danubian Federation' which had been mentioned in the Prime Minister's February note, and explained by Eden in more detail. By the time of the Quebec Conference in August 1943 Roosevelt was already saying definitely that Germany should not be reconstituted in any form, but divided into three or four states. On the reparations question, too, Roosevelt favoured a fairly brutal line, and did not flinch from imposing on the Germans after victory the kind of forced labour they had imposed on the subject-peoples of occupied Europe. Partly this was because another 'folk memory' by which Roosevelt was influenced was the (incorrect) belief that the United States had largely financed the payment of reparations by Germany to Britain and France in the 1920s. He was determined this should not happen 'again'. If possible, they should avoid monetary payments. Instead, Germany's industrial plant should be dismantled and sent to Russia and other countries by way of compensation, and German prisoners-of-war should also labour to help restore the damage they had done. Here again, his views were very close to Morgenthau's, and may well have been influenced by them.

The whole question came to a head in November, on the last day of the Teheran Conference between Roosevelt, Churchill and Stalin, as a by-product of Stalin's demand that Poland should be compensated with German territory in the west, for the lands which would be transferred to the Soviet Union in the east. Roosevelt and Churchill both signified that they were prepared to agree to this. Roosevelt then went on to propose a fivefold division of Germany into smaller states, obviously assuming, as was not unreasonable, that the general principle of partition was already agreed between the three of them. Churchill, however, was taken aback by a proposal far more sweeping and wide-ranging than anything he had envisaged. It ran directly counter to his own belief that the Germans should have a state substantial enough to claim their allegiance. It would have been tactless to mention Churchill's other reason for wishing this, namely as a bulwark against an over-powerful Russia, but Stalin was quite shrewd enough to work that one out for himself. Partly, perhaps, to head off Roosevelt's proposal, Churchill brought up his project of a 'Danubian Federation'. Roosevelt immediately showed how little he cared for the idea that the Germans should be left with anything substantial; they had been far less dangerous, he remarked, before 1870, when they had been split up into a large number of small states. Stalin must have been somewhat relieved by the President's *démarche*, since he had derived the impression from Eden and Hull during their visit to Moscow a little earlier, that neither the US nor Britain much favoured dismemberment. Now Roosevelt was proposing something more drastic than Stalin's own proposals of two years earlier. The Soviet leader hastened to say that he much preferred Roosevelt's proposals to Churchill's. It was already pretty evident that Churchill's 'Danubian Federation' was a non-starter. It served its purpose, however, by preventing Roosevelt's drastic scheme (which in fact was an improvisation, and had not been really thought out) from becoming agreed Allied policy. Eventually Churchill was able to secure the agreement of the other two to the proposition that this discussion constituted only a 'preliminary survey' of the problem of Germany. The whole question of German partition was referred to the London-based European Advisory Commission (EAC), which Eden had persuaded the Americans and Russians to set up during the Moscow talks referred to above.[10]

It was this discussion at Teheran which led Churchill to feel that for the present it would be advisable not to make any statement to the enemy on the probable conditions of peace, and to warn members of his government off any such course. To give the Germans any inkling of the kind of terms that looked like being inflicted on them would only stiffen their resistance. Much better tell them nothing at all for the present. Ironically, Stalin had expressed some doubts about the 'unconditional surrender' formula and wondered if it was advisable to leave the Germans completely in the dark about their fate: Eden, too, thought the point might be worth considering. This led, in January 1944, to some discussion in the correspondence between Churchill and Roosevelt, in which the latter summed up his view that they should stick to the simple 'unconditional' formula. He pointed out that he had already stated publicly that the Allies had no intention of 'enslaving' the German people. That should be sufficient reassurance for them. As Churchill also felt that this was not the best time to say anything on the matter, the subject was allowed to drop.[11]

It will be noticed that at this juncture, only eighteen months before the end of the war, it was not only the case that Churchill and Roosevelt were thinking along different lines on the subject of Germany. Their foreign ministers also were pursuing their own separate lines of thought, though both Hull and Eden were gradually coming to have more and more doubts about the wisdom of trying to enforce partition on Germany. However, all this led to a certain confusion about Western intentions which must have puzzled Stalin. The latter, although generally in favour of treating the Germans as harshly as possible, was not unwilling to adapt his ideas as far as might be necessary to achieve an agreed policy with his allies. Indeed he saw the necessity of doing so. But what exactly *was* the policy to which he would have to adapt? At this stage it was not at all clear. Meanwhile Roosevelt continued to shy away from announcing any detailed surrender terms for Germany, or even agreeing on detailed conditions with his allies. At the end of February 1944, the European Advisory Commission, impelled by the desire of the British Foreign Office to introduce some sort of order into the confusion, came up with fairly detailed provisions for an eventual armistice with the Germans. This led to further discussion between the two leaders. Roosevelt was not minded to let any subordinate body, particularly one based in London, decide such important issues, nor was he yet ready to do so himself. He reiterated to Churchill the argument that it was better for the Allies not to commit themselves to any rigid set of terms or conditions – the Germans would only argue subsequently that the Allies had not stuck to the terms they had promised. Perhaps Roosevelt also felt that even terms confidentially agreed between the Allies would 'leak out' and be distorted by German propagandists. By all means tell the Germans again that the Allies were not barbarians – they would not seek to destroy the German people. Eisenhower, who would shortly have the task of overcoming German resistance in Europe, had been pressing for some such statement, to offset the possible damage done by the 'unconditional surrender' announcement. For the rest, all that the Allies need agree among themselves was what they were going to do immediately after victory – i.e. the necessary arrangements for the occupation and total disarmament of Germany, the liberation of Allied prisoners-of-war, the surrender of war criminals and so forth. Churchill, slightly annoyed no doubt by the sweeping aside of the EAC replied rather petulantly that if they kept on assuring the Germans that they had nothing to fear, it would look as though they, the Allies, were suing for peace.[12]

This desultory discussion of the subject had gone on virtually from the time of the Teheran Conference at the end of the previous year, until the eve of the invasion of Europe (June 1944), without achieving any positive result. Various factors, however, now stimulated Roosevelt into a more urgent consideration of the matter. In July Hull submitted a memorandum expressing considerable doubts about the partition of Germany, which in Roosevelt's mind was still in some form agreed Allied policy. Although Hull's memo did not suggest anything more drastic than simply a further postponement of any decision, it was clear that the State Department's views on this and other aspects of the German problem were widely different from Roosevelt's, and the President was aware too that Stimson and the War Department, who would have to grapple with the immediate task of administering a US zone of occupation, also favoured moderate treatment of Germany. In August the crushing Allied victory in Normandy and subsequent break-out provided a further stimulus. The Red Army was advancing in Eastern Europe, and in Italy the Allied armies had taken Rome and advanced to the Pisa–Rimini line. It looked as though the war might even be over by Christmas. Meanwhile Morgenthau, aware that the State and War Departments were not on his wavelength, was pressing Roosevelt to come down on the side of a severe settlement. In September the three departments formally submitted their views to the President. The Treasury memorandum included the recommendation for a threefold division of Germany and the dismantling and removal of virtually all German industrial equipment. In complete opposition to these proposals, the State Department recommended a loose federation within a unified state, while the War Department was unalterably opposed to the complete wrecking of the German economy. There was obviously no room for compromise between these extremes. Roosevelt felt that he had to make a decision. It was necessary to resolve the dispute, not only so that practical plans for the German occupation could be worked out, but also because they really could not postpone any longer the process of getting agreement with the British and the Russians.[13]

In fact, Roosevelt had already made up his mind. In mid-August, he had written to Morgenthau, 'we've got to get tough with Germany'. This naturally encouraged the latter to stick to his guns during the interdepartmental discussions the following month, the more so when Roosevelt then intimated to Morgenthau that he agreed with the Treasury memo-randum. As a final demonstration of his opinion, Roosevelt invited Morgenthau to come to the Quebec Conference with Churchill in September, while accepting Hull's decision to stay in Washington. In his memoirs, Hull says that he had imagined the conference would be mainly concerned with military matters. Even so it might seem strange by British standards that Hull did not insist on attending, or threaten resignation, when he learnt that Morgenthau was to be there. The British system operates on the basis of a powerful Foreign Office, working within a framework of 'collective responsibility', and it is as well for Britons to remind themselves that the American political system has quite different parameters. It will be evident that Roosevelt was following his natural instincts in turning to Morgenthau; he had all along believed that Germany should be dealt with drastically. But he must also have thought that inter-allied agreement would be possible along these lines. From what he knew of Stalin's mind, there would be little Soviet resistance to a harsh settlement. Churchill might be more difficult. But the British Premier apparently favoured some form of partition, and on the reparations issue too, Churchill seemed to agree that any long-drawn-out attempt to extract large sums of money or quantities of manufactured goods from Germany was not desirable. Yet he also thought that the USSR should receive some practical compensation for the appalling losses and damage she had suffered. An immediate transfer of German industrial equipment to the Soviet Union would partly meet the case, and could be supplemented by German forced labour. Just how far the dismantling of German industry should go, was something they could work out together. Roosevelt, moreover, knew that he had a powerful lever where Churchill was concerned. Britain would be exhausted financially and its industry sorely dilapidated when the war ended. She would need the continuation of Lend-Lease, or some other form of US assistance, while the problems of reconstruction were tackled. Churchill was only too well aware of this.[14]

At Quebec, when it came to the point, discussion focused on the linked issue of German war-making capacity and the possible dismantling of German industry, rather than on the question of partition, though the latter was part of the overall plan. Roosevelt, with Morgenthau's assistance, put the proposals – the so-called 'Morgenthau Plan' – in its extreme form. Whatever happened to other German industrial areas, the Ruhr at least should be wiped out completely. All its industrial equipment should be dismantled and removed for reparations; anything which was left should be wrecked; the mines should be flooded. The wretched inhabitants would have to convert themselves – at very short notice – into farmers and agriculturists. Churchill's first reaction, prompted one would like to think equally by humanity and common sense, was one of horror, particularly in view of the fact that the British were likely to be administering the Ruhr. 'We should be chained to a corpse', he exclaimed. Further discussions, however, persuaded him not to oppose the proposals. On the one hand Morgenthau had outlined to him a scheme for a $3 billion loan to the UK on generous terms, after Churchill had admitted frankly that 'Britain was broke'. Roosevelt, however, seemed teasingly unwilling to commit himself on this proposal, and Churchill knew exactly what lay behind the President's slightly malicious playfulness. Secondly, Lindeman set himself to convince Churchill that the destruction of the Ruhr could be to Britain's advantage. The British would need to rebuild their export trade after the war; the Morgenthau Plan would remove a powerful competitor; that could not be bad. Maybe these arguments convinced Churchill, who was no student of economics. Maybe not. At all events he agreed that the Ruhr should be – to use his own word – 'pastoralized'.[15]

At this juncture Eden arrived, and in contrast to Hull's passivity, immediately launched a powerful counter-offensive. The plan could not possibly work to Britain's advantage, he argued. Churchill was furious with this display of independence before the President. All the more so because, characteristically, he had not been able to resist the temptation to improve on Morgenthau's drafting. The document which he and Roosevelt had initialled was therefore partly his own, and he had assumed proprietary rights towards it. He refused to change his mind, and significantly told Eden that they had to choose between 'our own people' (i.e. the possible US loan) and the Germans (i.e. resisting the Morgenthau Plan). There could be no clearer indication that, rightly or wrongly, Churchill felt US economic pressure had been applied to make him agree. But Churchill knew very well that Eden would return to the charge when they got back to London.

A good deal of discussion by historians has centred around the question, 'why did Churchill agree?' A good question. Anyone who reads the reports of the Quebec Conference, however, will not have much difficulty in deciding that Churchill himself felt that there was an element of *force majeur* in the Quebec decision-making. As he puts it, in his memoirs: 'we had much to ask from Roosevelt and Morgenthau'. Perhaps it was as simple as that. Perhaps he half convinced himself that Lindeman was right. Perhaps too, as on one or two previous occasions, Churchill was half expecting that subsequent consideration, and the pressure which would come from Hull and Stimson, would cause the President to have second thoughts. He knew about the differences of view within the US administration. As it turned out, the second thoughts were not long in coming. Some historians think it an indication of Roosevelt's failing powers – he had only six months or so to live – that a few months later he seemed to have half forgotten what he had signed, claiming to Stimson that he was 'staggered' by the terms of the memorandum. Since Churchill for his part asserts in his memoirs that he 'had not had time to study the terms of the memorandum in detail', it would seem that the two leaders initialled a document which neither of them had properly considered – notwithstanding that one of them had helped to draft it. This seems difficult to swallow. A classic case, one might think, of the difficulty all politicians feel in the simple admission that they might just have made a mistake. It was in keeping with this disclaiming of responsibility that Roosevelt described the whole affair as 'Henry Morgenthau's boner' – not 'Winston's and my boner'![16]

At all events, the pressure from Hull and Stimson soon did its work with Roosevelt. Amongst other considerations, he realized that the Morgenthau Plan might lengthen the war – and be used against him in the forthcoming presidential election. He reverted to what historians have called 'the policy of postponement' declaring airily to his associates, 'I dislike making plans for a country we do not yet occupy'. Unfortunately, but inevitably, the details of Morgenthau's scheme had leaked out, and were made good use of by

German propagandists: but the plan itself, in the sweeping form that Roosevelt and Morgenthau had envisaged, was dead. It was some little while before Churchill became fully aware of this. In October he journeyed to meet Stalin in Moscow, to whom he certainly gave the impression that the Morgenthau principles were still the basis of the Western approach to Germany – and that he, Churchill, favoured them. He also derived from these talks, surprisingly, the impression that Stalin might, after all, be prepared to consider his 'Danubian Federation' scheme. By this time the Soviet leader must have been thoroughly confused by the various indications he had been given of his allies' thinking about the German problem, and perhaps had received some information that Roosevelt had changed his mind about the Morgenthau Plan. Certainly Churchill soon became aware of this, and advised the War Cabinet accordingly. He also advised Roosevelt that he still favoured the 'Danubian' idea. Roosevelt for his part, in a complete *volte-face*, now told Stettinius, who succeeded Hull as Secretary of State in January, that the Germans should be 'allowed to recover', at the same time advising caution on the reparations issue, at least so far as monetary payments were concerned. Roosevelt, in fact, now reverted to his previous notion, that the German people should receive some reassurance, and suggested this to Churchill, but unsuccessfully. Both the two Western leaders, having taken up this 'hot potato' at Quebec – and burnt their fingers – now seemed inclined to postpone all decisions on Germany at least until the forthcoming Yalta meeting with Stalin, if not to an eventual peace conference. Churchill emphasized this to Eden, who was pressing for some decisions, and making it abundantly clear that he regarded the Morgenthau approach as both disastrous and impracticable. The British Premier came back to a point he had stressed in the past – if they tried to make a final settlement now, public opinion would insist that it should be a harsh and vengeful one. Better allow time for the dust to settle and emotions to cool.[17]

In the run-up to the Yalta Conference – a conference much written about, and whose importance has been overstressed – the only thing that was clear about Anglo-American policy on Germany was that it was not clear. Yet this was not altogether surprising. Roosevelt and Churchill had started from totally opposite premises, and, at the end of the day still hankered after their original ideas on Germany, even if Roosevelt had backed away from the logical outcome of his. It is not surprising either, that historians have found it difficult to agree on what was actually decided on this matter at Yalta. It had become clear at least that there were two separate problems: namely, what to do with Germany immediately, and what to decide on the final German peace settlement – the short-term and long-term aspects of the problem. It was not too difficult, in fact, for the three allies to agree on the short-term decisions. After unconditional surrender, there should be a total occupation of Germany by Allied forces; the German armed forces should be disarmed and disbanded; all military, naval and air installations not required by the Allies for occupation purposes, should be destroyed – Germany, in other words should be totally demilitarized; the Nazi regime at the centre should be liquidated, while at lower levels of government Nazi party members should be removed, in a process of 'denazification'; the Nazi leaders should be severely dealt with, and lesser war criminals punished. There had been some differences of view between Roosevelt and Churchill on the question of their respective occupation zones, as well as on the thorny question of a possible French zone. Roosevelt's prejudices were still well to the fore on the latter topic, and his written interchanges with Churchill on the subject were curt and irritable. On the question of occupation zones, the main difference between Roosevelt and Churchill was on the point whether US or UK forces should occupy north Germany. In the end, the point was settled in Churchill's favour, but in the process of argument over US and UK zones, the boundaries of the Soviet Zone were agreed almost without discussion, and it was these boundaries, reinforced by the military dispositions at the end of the war, which mainly determined the post-war shape of Germany. At Quebec, however, the question of the British and American zones had been settled, and at Yalta Roosevelt and Stalin reluctantly gave way to strong pressure from Churchill and Eden, and agreed to a French Zone. It had long been agreed that the Soviet zone should extend well west of Berlin – to the Elbe. In view of their enormous sacrifices, the Russians would not have agreed to less. It was assumed that there would be no problem about arranging communications between the Western zones and their occupation sectors in Berlin, which was also to be divided – an assumption which did not seem as unreasonable then as it did later.[18]

So far, so good. There remained the question of a long-term settlement for Germany, particularly the three key questions: (1) Should what was left of Germany, after its ill-gotten gains had been lopped off, be divided or left as one state? (2) should any serious attempt to be made to extract reparations from Germany? (3) should an attempt be made to control German industry in the long term, perhaps by a scheme for international control of the Ruhr? or should the Allies rely on a modified programme of dismantling industry for reparations purposes, thus temporarily reducing Germany's war-making capacity? Obviously any solution of one of these three problems had repercussions for the others. In fact no decision – not even provisionally – was made at Yalta on any of these issues. The reason is not far to seek. The crucial fact was that the war in Europe had not yet been won – and the Germans appeared to have plenty of fight left in them. It was better to postpone such decisions, if that was the only way of maintaining a facade of allied unity. The verdict of an American historian thirty-five years ago is apposite enough: 'they could not agree, and they could not afford to disagree'. Moreover, anything which they *did* agree was certain to be so harsh as to stiffen German resistance. On the question of partition, Stalin continued to press in favour of it; Roosevelt, now much more willing to pay heed to the State Department than before, wanted to postpone a decision, but at the same time avoid offending Stalin; Churchill recognized that his pet project of a Danubian Federation stood no chance of realization, and was under considerable pressure from Eden to opt for a decentralized, federal Germany: he too favoured postponment. The most the Big Three could agree was that 'dismemberment' should be included in the German armistice terms *as a course that the victors might follow, if they thought it necessary.*[19]

The story on the reparations question was very similar. Stalin again pressed hard with unusual but understandable emotion, for a substantial sum to be fixed then and there, no matter how the Allies eventually decided to exact it. Twenty

billion dollars was the figure named, of which half was to go to
the USSR. Not an unreasonable figure, in relation to Soviet
losses. But the State Department had warned against naming
large sums in monetary terms, and raised the spectre of the
US financing reparations payments, which aroused an old fear
of Roosevelt's. Churchill was equally dubious about massive
reparations payments, and consistently with this view
maintained his opposition: he would not countenance even
the acceptance of the $20 billion figure 'as a basis for
discussion'. In the end the most that could be agreed was that
the whole question should be referred to a tripartite
Reparations Commission, to meet in Moscow, on which the
Soviet and US representatives would take the Soviet figure as
an agreed starting point. Nor was there any concession to the
Soviet demand that up to 80 per cent of German heavy
industry should be dismantled for reparations purposes, and
that there should be a three-power board to supervise and
control this process.[20]

In short the picture of Yalta as a 'sell-out' to the Soviet
Union, once fashionable and useful for Republican Party
propaganda, is very far from the truth. Stalin indeed regarded
Yalta as a defeat. He had not got what he wanted, so far as
Germany was concerned, nor any firm assurance that he was
likely to get it in future. It probably required only a brief
experience of the arguments in the newly appointed
Reparations Commission to convince him that there was little
chance of getting what he wanted through inter-allied
agreement, and that he had better look to other means.

THE LONG-TERM CONSEQUENCES

It might seem that the story of Roosevelt and Churchill's
impact on the German problem can be reduced to two simple
propositions. Firstly, after the two years' discussion the two
men were both uncertain what to do, and could think of no
better course than to postpone a decision on the fundamental
issues. In the face of War Cabinet doubts about these matters
and his own growing concern about Soviet power, virtually the
last word from Churchill on the subject of partition before
Roosevelt's death was, 'I am reluctant to consider the

dismemberment of Germany, while Russian intentions are uncertain'. Roosevelt's very last word on the reparations problem was to instruct the US representative 'to put off any final decisions for the moment'. Secondly, since neither Roosevelt's original sweeping plan for the dismemberment and economic weakening of Germany nor Churchill's Danubian project was realised, it might seem that neither man very much influenced the future of Germany. If that were all, an unjustified amount of space has been devoted to the topic. One can, however, go a little further than this. In the end, for reasons that are largely not germane to the Roosevelt – Churchill partnership, considerable elements of the Morgenthau Plan found their way into Allied policy towards Germany between 1945 and 1946. In particular, a substantial programme of dismantling of German industry for reparations took place, and for ten years the German people and many German prisoners of war suffered a good deal, as Roosevelt thought they deserved to, before a change of heart brought Marshall Aid to their rescue. In the last few months of his life, Roosevelt did not try to prevent the infiltration of Morgenthau's ideas into Allied policy: in fact he aided it in certain ways. Churchill, for his part, started with two simple assumptions, firstly that Prussia should be separated from the rest of Germany, and secondly that something substantial should be left in Central Europe to play its part in the balance of power. To this end, so far as the latter purpose was concerned, he fought a long delaying action against the extreme courses on which Roosevelt and Stalin seemed to be agreed: until, in fact, the march of events and pressures within his own administration led Roosevelt to conclude that it would be best not to impose any drastic solution without careful and prolonged consideration. The one real exception to this generalization occurred when Churchill initialled the Morgenthau Plan in September 1944. His reasons have been discussed earlier. It is quite possible that Churchill foresaw that the intense opposition to the plan which would emerge in Washington and London would lead Roosevelt to change his mind. It would not have been the first time he had pursued such tactics when faced with an unacceptable US proposal. What emerged finally, though in ways that Churchill had not fully foreseen, was a powerful West German state, allied to the

West, from which Prussia had been detached, thus satisfying, it could be said, Churchill's two main criteria. One can claim at least for Churchill that his long delaying action on Germany made this possible. In the broad sense, the post-war future of Germany, was determined by the limits of Soviet and Western military power. Within this overriding factor, however, for the next fifty years the fate of Germany was shaped by two things. Firstly by the destruction of much of German industry at the end of the war and immediately after it, which paved the way for its massive reconstruction and modernisation, and so, ironically, for the future prosperity of Germany. The second major factor was the acceptance by the West of the *de facto* partition of Germany into two states. Roosevelt and Churchill contributed to both these results. In the long run, of course, the partition of Germany proved no more durable than most things in international affairs. But fifty years is a pretty long run.[21]

8 The Generalissimo: Chiang Kai-shek, China and the Far East

It is perhaps inevitable that the historian should focus mainly on those aspects of international relations which are particularly stormy, contentious and controversial. To the journalist bad news is news: good news by and large is not. One would not apply the same simple statement to the historian. But it remains the case that the more peaceful and productive aspects of any historical relationship provide less material for exposition, discussion and argument than its contentious and less successful aspects. So it is with the Churchill–Roosevelt relationship, with the consequence that this survey of various areas of that relationship may seem cumulatively to present a picture of two partners quite unsuited to working together, temperamentally incompatible, pursuing different ends, and not unnaturally often producing unsatisfactory results. This is not, of course, the whole story. The partnership did, to point the obvious, make a major contribution to winning the war. But it was not, obviously, always the harmonious and easy-going relationship that Allied propaganda presented to the world.

This was true of the Far East, as elsewhere. Far Eastern strategy and diplomacy involved four main areas. These were (1) Allied strategy against Japan in the Pacific (2) Allied strategy in South-East Asia (3) relations with the Chiang Kai-shek regime in China and coordination of that strategy with the Chinese, and (4) the future peace settlement in the Far East and South-East Asia. In the long run Allied strategy in the two main areas had to be coordinated. But for a considerable part of the war, the Americans in the Pacific were effectively cut off from direct contact with their allies in China, India and Burma by Japanese control of South-East Asia and the western Pacific. Thus the two had to be run as separate theatres of war, which ultimately would link up. Similarly, the problem of coordinating strategy with the Chinese became inextricably

connected with Roosevelt's vision of a future Chinese role in
world affairs, and also with Churchill's objective of restoring
the British Empire in South-East Asia, and Britain's role as a
world power in the East. It was not possible to separate strategy
and politics, since whatever strategy was pursued in South-East
Asia would affect the future status of China on the one hand,
and the British Empire on the other. It so happened that, of
the two main strategies which could be followed, one would
serve US objectives *vis-à-vis* China, but not necessarily British
long-term aims; while the other would help to achieve British
purposes, but would not serve US aims in China – or so the
Americans thought. The issue was further complicated by the
fact that Roosevelt and most of his military and political
advisers were opposed to British imperial objectives, or at best
had little sympathy with them. This attitude of mind was
matched by a similar British lukewarmness and scepticism
towards US aims in China. The result was the situation fully
described, in brutal and uncompromising detail by
Christopher Thorne, and by other historians of the Far
Eastern War, namely that in the Far East Britain and the
United States, to a much greater extent than in Europe, were
only 'Allies of a kind'. The two Allies were, in fact, fighting
different wars, for different purposes, and in widely separated
theatres.[1]

All of this affected operations in the Pacific far less
than it impinged on strategy in South East Asia. There was
very little conflict between strategy and politics in the Pacific,
or between US and British political aims. In general the policy
of amphibious 'island-hopping' operations across the Pacific,
from US bases in the east and from Australasia in the south-
west, was accepted as the most effective strategy against Japan.
It also served the US long-term political-military aim of
regaining American bases and restoring the US strategic
position, and facilitated the further strengthening of the
American position in the western Pacific through the
acquisition of bases from the Japanese. None of this conflicted
with British political aims, provided always that the defeat
of Japan resulted in the recovery of British possessions in the
Far East. There were, of course, political as well as military
problems in this area. One of these was the rivalry between
the US Navy and the US Army, personified in Admiral Nimitz,

Supreme Commander Pacific, and General MacArthur, whose South-West Pacific Command competed with the Pacific Command for resources of all kinds. Another was the need to cater for Australian and New Zealand susceptibilities, and the ties between them and the UK. But none of these problems impinged very much on the Roosevelt–Churchill relationship, or Anglo-American relations generally, once Churchill had accepted the absolute primacy of the US in the Pacific area. And this he was obliged to do by the total collapse of British naval and military power in South-East Asia in 1941–2, and with it a large part of the British Empire in that region.

THE CHINESE PROBLEM

It was quite otherwise with what was originally referred to as the 'China-Burma-India Theatre', which later became the China Command under Chiang Kai-shek and the British South-East Asia Command under Mountbatten, with its supply base in British India. Here strategic problems, relations with China, and Anglo-American relations were inextricably combined. Roosevelt, deeply concerned both for China and for the US forces there, and Churchill, equally concerned for the British Empire and British forces in India, Burma and Ceylon, were inevitably drawn into the melée. It could not be otherwise. The personality, status and future of Chiang Kai-shek, the leader of the Chinese Nationalist Government, was a key factor. The Nationalist regime was effectively a one-party state, and Chiang a dictator, but a dictator in a far weaker position than Hitler or Stalin. By the spring of 1942 the Japanese controlled the whole of Manchuria and North China, a large part of the Yangtze Valley in Central China, and the whole of the China coast, including the great Yangtze port and commercial centre of Shanghai, and Canton and Hong Kong in the south. The Chinese Communists, opposed to the Nationalists, but operating independently against the Japanese, controlled important areas of north-west and western China. Soviet power and influence had encroached on Mongolia, and the vast province of Sinkiang in the west. Chiang had been driven back into the far south-west of the country, its most backward and feudal area. He was dependent

on the support of semi-independent warlords and cor-
rupt financial cliques. His armies, nominally very large,
were demoralized, ill-equipped, ill-trained and often unpaid.
Not surprisingly, after ten years of unequal combat against
the Japanese, and continuous defeat, the Nationalist military
effort against the Japanese had slackened. Indeed Roosevelt
was to complain, two years after Pearl Harbor, that Chiang
appeared to be doing very little fighting against the Japanese:
he seemed as concerned, or more concerned, with staving off
his rivals, the Chinese Communists. What fighting was being
done was mainly by the large US air forces, at first volunteer,
later official, under General Chennault, and about thirty
American-trained divisions, the only ground forces really
capable of carrying on offensive operations against the
Japanese.

Quite possibly no leader, however capable, could have
coped successfully with so desperate a situation. Certainly,
however, the personality of Chiang – usually referred to as the
'Generalissimo' in recognition of his status as Commander-in-
Chief of the China Theatre – was not helpful. He was vain,
obstinate and narrow, conservative in outlook, deeply opposed
to both Communism and European imperialism, and
therefore equally suspicious of the USSR and Britain. He was,
however, inclined to trust Roosevelt and the Americans. He
does not appear to have had any outstanding military or
administrative skills, though politically he could be quite wily.
Isolated and hard-pressed as he was, he could hardly be
expected to look at things from any point of view but a narrow
regional one, and showed few signs of the ability to take a
global view of strategic problems. His demands on the
Americans for help of all kinds – economic and military –
were inordinate and equally heedless of the needs of other
theatres. Roosevelt, for his part, was aware of Chiang's defects;
aware too, as the war progressed, how the Chinese military
effort was steadily declining and Chiang's political support
steadily ebbing away. The main facts were reported to him by
his military representatives in China, Stilwell and later
Wedemeyer, and various diplomatic representatives – Gauss,
Hurley, and others. Yet Roosevelt felt bound to continue
supporting Chiang and the Nationalists *faute de mieux*. There
was no other Nationalist leader in sight, and virtually no

contact with the Communists in their remote fastnesses, even if it had been thought desirable to support them. He was committed to Chiang, as Churchill was committed to de Gaulle, and however much both men may have sometimes regretted it, the longer the commitment continued, the more difficult it was to end it. Marshall, too, retained to the end a belief that some positive military use could be made of the Nationalist forces, given enough American training, equipment and leadership; though in his case it was probably as much loyalty to his subordinate, Stilwell, as regard for Chiang that motivated him.[2]

If there was a considerable difference between British and American aims in the China-India-Burma theatre, there was an equally marked difference between the respective attitudes of Roosevelt and Churchill towards the role of China in the war, and the future Chinese role in world affairs. It would be said that both men were right about China in one sense, and wrong in another. In the long perspective of history, Roosevelt was surely right in judging that a nation which included so large a proportion of the world's population, and which was rich in resources – and therefore potentially powerful both economically and militarily – should not be ignored. The President summed up the point succinctly when he said 'I would rather have millions of Chinese on our side than against us'. Enlarging on this point to Eden in 1943, he also pointed out that a powerful China would be a useful counterpoise to the USSR in the Far East. Both remarks strike one as being very prescient, though the latter one shows that Roosevelt was no more capable of absolute and invariable consistency than are most human beings. Although Roosevelt was apt to disregard the 'balance of power' argument when used by the British in relation to Europe, he was not unaware of its application to the harsh realities of world politics, and quite capable of using it as an argument when it suited him. Nor does the remark show the absolute confidence in Soviet good intentions which he normally evinced. Churchill, on the other hand, never seemed able to escape from the 'pigtail' image of the Chinese, or from the attitudes formed by generations of British freebooting in China. He could not make the imaginative effort necessary to see beyond contemporary Chinese weakness, confusion and corruption to its potential in the future.

In regard to the contemporary scene, however, Churchill was the more clearsighted. He thought, rightly, that many Americans, including Roosevelt, over-estimated the military role that China could play in the winning of the war, and the political role it could fill in the immediate post-war international order; and he considered Chiang's reputation over-inflated, and American regard for him excessive. Churchill, of course was prejudiced. He knew that Chiang was an enemy of British imperial interests, and suspected him of having his own imperialist ambitions in Thailand and Indo-China, as well as casting covetous eyes on Hong Kong. If Churchill resented American advice on British policy in India, he resented even more occasional attempts by Chiang to influence that policy through Roosevelt. He thought it impertinent that a semi-autocratic ruler should read him lectures on regard for democracy and national rights in India, and that someone who was unable to control the situation in his own country should tell the British how to run their affairs. Nor did he particularly want to see a powerful and united China in the future, which might, under a compliant and pro-American Chiang, serve US interests in the Far East, but would be no friend to the British Empire. Ironically, it was a point of view probably shared to some extent by Stalin. It was not a Soviet interest, either, to help create a strong and united China, and Soviet policy was certainly not directed to that end. Prejudiced or not, however, Churchill was basically right in assessing Chinese military capacity during the war, and its political capacity in the immediate future. To his British colleagues he made no secret of his views on China. 'It is an affectation', he minuted to Eden in October 1942, 'to suppose China could be a Great Power'. In any future international body, China would simply be a 'faggot vote' for the United States. To Roosevelt, however, and to Americans generally, Churchill was more muted in expressing his views, in contrast to his frank and vehement expressions of opinion in other areas.[3]

There was good reason for this. The Americans had considerable leverage with Chiang through the vast amounts of supplies they were sending him, most of it flown in US aircraft over the Himalayas, from Ledo in north-east India to Kunming in south-west China. They had military advisers in

China and a substantial air force. Moreover Chiang appeared to trust the United States, as he definitely did not trust Britain. In every way Roosevelt was in a more favourable position to deal with China, and obviously was going to shape Allied policy there. Churchill fully realised this. The maintenance of the Anglo-American alliance was cardinal to him, and he was often reminded by Eden that it was expedient, in the interests of that alliance, to be tender towards US prejudices about China, and not to rile the President by arguing with him about the perhaps excessive regard he seemed to have for Chiang. Churchill on the whole accepted this with good grace. What mattered was winning the war in Europe first of all. Until that was achieved, the Far Eastern War, and even more the relatively unimportant Chinese contribution, should be regarded as secondary issues. At the very outset of the war against Japan, in February 1942, Churchill was saying to Roosevelt 'Chiang Kai-shek is primarily your concern', in much the same language as he applied to US conduct of relations with Vichy France. The Americans should liaise with Chiang and coordinate Chinese military efforts with the West. He asked only that Roosevelt should keep him informed about all of this. The position, then, was the same in regard to China as it was in relation to the Pacific theatre. The Americans would make the decisions, but would keep the British informed. It was only when Roosevelt's or his advisers' views on the Chinese role in the war, or the future peace, impinged on the British-Indian campaign in South-East Asia, or directly on British interests, that it might be necessary to argue with them. Not infrequently during the war this did happen, and controversy arose. Roosevelt and Marshall both had strong views on the political and military aspects of the matter, and were not disposed to emulate the British attitude to the Pacific, namely that SEAC was their allies' proper sphere, and not theirs. They felt, with some justice that the US stake in China and the fact that the US was supplying a considerable part of the sinews of war in South-East Asia gave them some *locus standi* in the area. Although there were very few US ground troops in the theatre, there was a large Air-Transport Command, manned by US pilots: and in addition, Roosevelt and Marshall felt they had a certain responsibility for the Chinese troops which operated in Burma under the American

General Stilwell. The point was fully ventilated when the Ceylon-based South-East Asia Command (SEAC) was set up in 1943 under Mountbatten – and on this point Roosevelt and Marshall got their way. Churchill's first proposal had been that Mountbatten's ultimate responsibility to the 'higher command' should follow 'the MacArthur model'. MacArthur as Supreme Commander, South-West Pacific, reported to the US Joint Chiefs, *not* to the Combined Chiefs, on which the British as well as the Americans were represented. Mountbatten, it was implied, would similarly be responsible to the British Chiefs of Staff, not to the Combined Chiefs. Roosevelt replied firmly 'I could agree only to this command relationship following the Eisenhower pattern'. In the Mediterranean, and later in north-west Europe, Eisenhower as Supreme Commander was ultimately responsible to the Combined Chiefs. Churchill resisted, but eventually gave way. General Brooke, the CIGS, reluctantly agreed, accepting the advice of his friend Dill from Washington, that it was better that the Americans should be involved, since their support and aid was necessary for any successful operations in South-East Asia.[4]

SEAC AND THE BURMA CAMPAIGN

Dill, as so often, was right, and acting in the best interests of the Alliance. However, much argument had already taken place about Burmese and South-East Asian operations, and more was to follow. Both the British and the Americans were well aware of the political ends they had in view, but both also had sound military arguments to advance. In political terms, Roosevelt wished to bolster up Chiang's prestige and strengthen the Nationalist regime generally, so that China could become one of the 'Big Four' in the post-war international order. He also wished to sustain the Chinese military effort. The Chinese, after all, were keeping large numbers of Japanese troops employed. The usefulness of that to the Allied war effort could not be questioned. Besides, Roosevelt wished to see some return on the large quantities of military supplies sent to China, so much of which seemed to be swallowed up in the morass of Chinese corruption and inefficiency. In all this he was supported by Marshall, who was influenced by Stilwell's view, that Chinese troops could be a useful military force with proper training, leadership and equipment. Much the best way of achieving all these objectives would be a campaign in Upper Burma which, if successful in reconquering that region, would permit the so-called 'Burma Road' from Burma to southern China, to be reopened. Such a campaign would make full use of the resources of British India, and provide an opportunity for Chiang to participate with formations from China. Once land communications had been reopened, it would be possible to step up supplies to the Chinese Nationalists, and thus pave the way for more vigorous and large-scale operations against the Japanese in the China theatre. It had the additional advantage from Roosevelt's point of view that no American resources would be diverted to the dubious purpose of operations for the recovery of British imperial possessions in the South-East Asia. Churchill, by contrast, as we have seen, had no great sympathy with Roosevelt's political aims in China, was doubtful about Chinese military capabilities, questioned the strategic arguments, and disliked the whole idea of a campaign in Upper Burma. 'To fight the Japanese in the Burmese jungle', he complained, 'would be like going into the water to fight the shark'. The elements themselves would fight for the Japanese. British-Indian troops were largely untrained in jungle warfare; disease, especially malaria would be rampant; and during the monsoon season – or so it was thought – large-scale military operations would be almost impossible. Moreover, Allied superiority in tanks, airpower and artillery could not be brought effectively to bear, nor could use be made of Allied naval and amphibious resources. Churchill and his military advisers Brooke (and from mid-1943 Mountbatten) would have preferred to make use of the growing naval and amphibious power of the Allies in the Indian Ocean, to launch a series of amphibious operations on the Burmese, Malayan and north-west Indonesian coast, in conjunction with a land offensive southwards from India along the Burma coast. Such operations would be aimed at capturing the main Japanese coastal bases and supply ports in South-East Asia, especially Rangoon and Singapore, thus cutting off supplies to Japanese armies to the north; these large Japanese armies could then be left to 'wither on the vine'. This would be far better than fighting a costly and gruelling campaign in the swamps and jungles of Upper Burma, a campaign which in any case might be rendered unnecessary by the success of the increasingly powerful American thrust across the western and south-western Pacific. If, eventually, the Russians joined the fray, and attacked the Japanese in Manchuria, there was even less necessity for a campaign in Burma. From the autumn of 1943 onwards, the West had a promise to this effect from Stalin. As for the Chinese, they could be kept going, as a military distraction, by the maintenance of air-supply over 'the Hump'. It was foolish to expect more of them. By the time substantial Chinese forces had been trained and brought up to scratch, the war, it was hoped, would have been won by other means. Taken together, all of this constituted a formidable case, both on practical military and broad strategic grounds. Yet in the end Roosevelt's political ends were to prevail over purely military and strategic consideration, and Churchill himself was, in effect, to 'sell the pass' so far as the Burma campaign was concerned.[5]

It is not necessary to describe in detail the course of the strategic argument. In the critical period from Pearl Harbor to mid-1942 the Japanese had crippled US naval power in the Pacific, destroyed British and Dutch naval power, and conquered the Philippines, Malaya, the Dutch East Indies and Burma. In the latter half of 1942, the Japanese advance was halted and the line of Allied resistance painfully stabilized in the Pacific, Australasia, in the Indian Ocean and on the frontiers of India. The question of an Allied counter-offensive in Burma immediately came up. As early as January 1943, just before the Anglo-American conference at Casablanca, Roosevelt was cabling to Churchill, 'offensive action by the Chinese and the timeliness of the thrust into Burma *this spring* are all important ... I would like to give the Generalissimo the necessary assurances to prevent the Chinese attack [into north-east Burma] from stalling' (emphasis added). At the subsequent conference Churchill felt constrained to yield to strong pressure from Roosevelt and Marshall, and commit Britain to a campaign for the reconquest of Burma, though he was able to persuade the Americans that it could not begin till the end of the year. Churchill's views at this time are adequately reflected in his remarks at a meeting of British South East Asia Commanders in April 1943. 'Burma,' he said, 'appears a disadvantageous area to fight the Japanese'. British superiority in weaponry could not be effective in jungle warfare... 'we should concentrate on the support of China by air...' and try to find the most favourable area of attack 'by-passing Burma and making the fullest use of seapower'. After further discussion and argument, the whole issue came to a head at the two Cairo conferences of November–December 1943. Roosevelt had invited Chiang Kai-shek to the first of these conferences because he wished to get to know the Chinese leader, and have a full discussion of Far-Eastern strategy with him, at which the British would be present. This also served the purpose of minimizing the amount of time that could be spent discussing and rehashing the Overlord–Mediterranean argument, which the Americans did not want reopened. Once closeted with the Generalissimo, however, Roosevelt was exposed to the full force of Chiang's (and Madame Chiang's) complaints, fears, blandishments, and what General Brooke called 'impossible demands'. Roosevelt, in fact, did not need to be told how dire the Chinese situation was, and how poor their morale. He had gained a pretty fair impression from the reports of Stilwell and others. He decided that Chiang's prestige and Chinese morale must be bolstered up, both by the promise of large political gains and by military assurances. Politically they should be assured of recognition of their status as one of the 'Big Four', both in the war and in the post-war international organization. Furthermore, he told Chiang, China should regain all her lost territories, including Formosa, which had been Japanese since 1895. Perhaps, too, China would share 'trusteeships' for Korea and Indo-China. On the military side, Chiang had been demanding that there should not only be a powerful land campaign in Burma, but that it should be supported by an amphibious operation against the Andaman Islands (Operation Buccaneer) which would pave the way for a sea-borne attack on Rangoon. This, too, Roosevelt was prepared to promise. There was only one snag. Buccaneer would have to be carried out by British forces under Mountbatten. Mountbatten was more than willing. This was the kind of operation he understood and believed in. Unfortunately, Roosevelt had not secured Churchill's prior agreement. The latter in fact was not willing to agree. Amphibious operations meant landing-craft, always in short supply, and Churchill wanted all the landing-craft which Admiral King had not got his hands on for Pacific operations, to be used for Europe – for Overlord, and Mediterranean operations against Italy and the Greek Islands. When the Americans added an additional European operation – a landing in the south of France (Anvil), this merely reinforced Churchill's objections to Buccaneer. Moreover, Roosevelt was behaving as though he were commander-in-chief of British as well as US forces, and Churchill could not allow that. Eventually, Roosevelt had to give way. In addition to all the other arguments, Churchill had been able to make use of Stalin's promise, reiterated at Teheran, to enter the Far Eastern war once the defeat of Germany had been accomplished. In view of this undertaking, he told Roosevelt, 'operations in South-East Asia have lost a good deal of their value'. But Churchill for his part felt that, having thwarted the President over Buccaneer, he must put the full weight of his authority behind the land campaign in Burma.[6]

The ironical and paradoxical result of the Roosevelt–Churchill argument over South-East Asian operations was, therefore, that the British were finally committed to an arduous land campaign which neither Churchill nor Brooke had really wished to fight, and which they regarded as wrong in principle and practice. It ended in the British, Indian and Chinese forces fighting the largest single land campaign against the Japanese in World War II. On the other hand, they rejected an amphibious operation which was in line with Churchill's broad strategic thinking, and favoured by his area commander. It is reasonable to ask the question whether Churchill's obsession with Mediterranean operations did not lead him astray here. Would it not have been better to have given up on his cherished plan for an attack on Rhodes, and accepted Buccaneer? Roosevelt had sternly refused to take landing-craft from the Pacific for unspecified Mediterranean operations, but later had shown more flexibility when it was a question of landing-craft for Anvil, an operation in which he and the US Chiefs believed. Would he not have done the same for Buccaneer, which they also wanted? Given the necessary resources, and their successful employment against the Andamans, would it not then have been possible for Churchill to argue that those same resources should be used, not only against Rangoon, but in further operations on the Malayan coast? In that case, the land campaign in Burma became less important. It is an interesting speculation, but can be no more than that.

On Roosevelt's generous political promises to Chiang, Churchill had relatively little to say, in accordance with his acceptance of the principle that China was largely Roosevelt's affair. This did not mean he had altered his opinion of Chiang and the Chinese Nationalists. During the Quebec Conference in August–September 1943 he had proposed to speak publicly of the efforts of the three Allies, leaving China out, as his principal foreign affairs adviser put it, 'in the most pointed and wounding way'. He had to be restrained. It was pointed out to him that Roosevelt had stressed during their meetings that he wanted the proposed Declaration on International Security to be a four-power document, thus emphasizing his desire that China should be recognized as one of the 'Big Four' both now and in the post-war world. A little later, at a time when Churchill was feeling particularly disgruntled by the relative failure of Allied operations in the Mediterranean, and by Roosevelt's insistence on inviting Chiang to Cairo, a revealing interchange took place. Churchill had quoted the Bible, apropos of the forthcoming meeting with Stalin at Teheran, referring to 'three tabernacles in the desert'. In his reply Roosevelt said that at some stage there would have to be a fourth 'tabernacle' for the Chinese leader, whom he jokingly described as 'your old friend Chiang'. Roosevelt was teasing Churchill, knowing pretty well just how much and how little friendly the latter's feelings were. Churchill replied that he had an option on 'Tutankhamen's tomb' for Chiang. Not entirely a joke one feels.[7]

However, paying attention to Eden's advice as he usually did, Churchill went along with Roosevelt's policy. At the Moscow Foreign Ministers' Conference, Eden was allowed to support Hull on Chinese signature of the International Security Declaration; and at the subsequent Cairo Conference, Churchill endured the presence of the Chinese with reasonable patience. Indeed he formed quite a favourable impression of Chiang. He was not present at the private meeting when Roosevelt promised Chiang the return of all lost Chinese territories, and also appears to have at least hinted that China must make some concessions to the Soviet desire for the use of Chinese warm-water ports, and some measure of 'influence' in Manchuria. But though not present, Churchill subsequently accepted the inclusion of the territorial promises in the official communiqué of the conference (the 'Cairo Declaration'). On the subject of concessions to Russia he went further. He was clearly as determined as Roosevelt that Chiang should make a contribution to good relations with Russia, in return for largesse promised to him. At Teheran the subject of Soviet access to Chinese warm-water ports came up. According to the US record, indeed, it was Churchill who brought it up. Whether it was Churchill or Stalin who did so, the Premier undoubtedly expressed sympathy with the Russian need for access to ports in the Far East which were ice-free all the year round – which could only be Chinese ports. Roosevelt mentioned his idea that the Soviets might have the use of Dairen (Talien) for commercial purposes and Port Arthur as a naval base, possibilities which almost certainly he had already discussed with Chiang. He thought the Chinese could be 'persuaded' to agree to this. In return Stalin indicated, as Roosevelt had hoped, that he might look sympathetically on the proposition that the Chinese should regain all their lost territories.[8]

It is clear, therefore, that Churchill, though not a prime mover in the affair, was quite prepared to go along with Roosevelt's proposition that Chiang should concede important privileges in north-east China and Manchuria in return for the recovery of Chinese territory. The Premier's reservations about the proposed Far Eastern settlement were focused on quite a different point. From the British point of view, there had been a glaring omission and discrepancy in the first draft of the Cairo Declaration which they had been asked to approve. By contrast with the lavish promises on the restoration of Chinese territory, there had been no mention of the recovery of British, French and Dutch territories. Churchill, Eden and their advisers had to fight hard for a

concession on this point, in the face of Roosevelt's obvious
objection to any such general promise, particularly where the
French were concerned. In the end the most the British could
obtain was the statement that the Japanese should be forced to
disgorge *all* their conquered territories – but with no
reference to what should then happen to those in South-East
Asia.

Two points are worth stressing and re-emphasizing in
relation to these discussions. Old myths die hard, and the
myth of Yalta as the crucial conference where all important
decisions were taken, and particularly where Nationalist China
was sold down the river to the Russians, has continued to
persist, in the popular mind, if not in the minds of scholars. It
is worth saying again, therefore, that the outlines of a tripartite
– or possibly quadripartite – agreement on the Far East
emerged at Cairo and Teheran, and to a large extent was only
ratified at Yalta. It is an equally important element in any
account of the Roosevelt–Churchill partnership to recognize
that, if Roosevelt made the running, Churchill adhered to his
principle of accepting the US lead in this area, and was a
consenting party. He must share the responsibility with
Roosevelt.[9]

The remainder of the Far Eastern story can be briefly
summarized. Militarily there was no going back from the
decisions reached at Cairo. Churchill continued throughout
1944 to argue against concentrating everything on Burma,
and in favour of amphibious operations in the Bay of Bengal
and further south, as and when resources allowed. In March
he was writing to Roosevelt that amphibious operations across
the Bay of Bengal should play the highest part' in the next
eighteen months; and in August that he 'would deprecate the
policy of allowing the whole British-Indian effort to be bogged
down in North Burma'. 'The Fourteenth (British) Army', he
complained in August, 'is fighting in the worst possible
conditions, in order to guard the US airline over the
Himalayas into their overrated China' – but this remark was
made in his private correspondence, not to Roosevelt! At the
Quebec Conference in September, however, he did say to
Roosevelt directly, 'it is most undesirable that fighting in the
jungles of Burma should go on indefinitely'. But these
lamentations were fruitless, so far as the main objective was

concerned. By his persistence, Churchill was able eventually to get authorization for Mountbatten to carry out a sea-borne attack on Rangoon and subsequent operations against the Malayan coast, but these operations could now be only a *coda* to the campaign in Burma, not a substitute for it. The Burma campaign had acquired an unstoppable momentum, and Churchill himself had brought this about. By a tragic irony, thousands of British, Indian and Chinese troops were to struggle and die in the Burmese jungles in a campaign which may well have been superfluous to Allied requirements.[10]

Politically, Roosevelt had done all that he could to bolster Chiang's image and the prestige of Nationalist China. He had ensured that the Generalissimo would emerge as the man who had regained China's lost territory and secured recognition of her position as an equal in status of the 'Big Three'. It was now up to Chiang to settle China's internal problems. Churchill meanwhile remained sceptical. In July he relieved his feelings to Hopkins, though fully aware that the remark would be passed on to Roosevelt. It was very difficult, he complained, 'to get concerted action between the three Great Powers', adding dismissively, 'or four, if you still include China'. This was unwise. Roosevelt was already becoming paranoiacally suspicious of British intentions and British policy everywhere. Six months earlier he had told the US Chiefs of Staff that the British would try to. 'undercut' US policy in occupied Germany – though he never explained what he meant by this. He was aware that Churchill did not share his regard for Chiang, and, instead of treating the remark as an expression of frustration, which it was, he began to think the British were actively opposing his China policy. Just before the Yalta Conference, in January 1945, he was telling his new secretary of state, Stettinius, that the British did not want a strong China, and were 'undermining U.S. policy in China'. The truth was that Churchill and British had very little power to undermine Roosevelt's China policy. Chiang Kai-shek, the Chinese Communists and the Japanese were doing a very good job in this respect on their own, without British interference. Churchill, in fact, was not the only one who had doubts about US policy in China. There were critics nearer home, as Roosevelt knew full well. As early as June 1944, the Vice-President, Henry Wallace, had returned from a visit to

China, and reported gloomily that Chiang was losing the three-cornered struggle in China. 'China', he concluded, 'is not a Great Power, but a fragmented, chaotic mess!' Morgenthau, too, complained that the President was 'badly misinformed' on China. This was an unjust reflection on US diplomatic and military representatives in the area. Roosevelt *was* informed, but chose to minimize the significance of the unfavourable reports on Chiang. The truth was, he felt he had no option but to continue with a policy which was already crumbling into ruins. US policy in China, like the Burma campaign, had acquired a momentum of its own, and the ailing President, with so many other problems on his mind, had neither the time nor the energy to stand back and reassess his China policy. Yet he knew something had to be done, and that the division and rivalry between the Nationalists and Communists was a major source of Chiang's weakness. At Cairo he had already brought pressure to bear on Chiang to heal the breach and bring the Communists into a coalition government. In July 1944 he sent Patrick Hurley to China to see if he could assist in bringing an end to the civil war, but to no avail. This attempt to reconcile the irreconcilable – the first of many by the Roosevelt and Truman administrations – was doomed to failure. Stimson commented that there was no (Nationalist) 'drive' against the Japanese. Chiang was not carrying out the democratic reforms and reform of land tenure in China which might have won him greater popularity, and stolen the Communists' thunder. Yet nor was he seeking a settlement with his rivals, which was the alternative to winning the propaganda as well as the military battle.[11]

Churchill, meanwhile, wisely did not seek to interfere or influence affairs. He remarks in his memoirs that he had never shared the excessive American estimates of Chiang's or Chinese power, but, as before, he was willing to follow the president's lead, and give Chiang the benefit of the doubt. When they again met with Stalin at Yalta, in February 1945, he let slip the revealing phrase at the first plenary meeting 'world peace depends on the friendship and collaboration of the Three Great Powers'. But it was only a slip. Subsequently Churchill agreed that the final ultimatum to Japan should be a four-power ultimatum, and that China should join with the three in sponsoring the forthcoming San Francisco

Conference on future international organization. The question of the territorial concessions to Russia at China's expense, agreed at Yalta, has already been touched on. They amounted to little more than a ratification of the provisional agreement reached at Teheran, with some modifications to soothe Chinese susceptibilities. Russia was to lease Port Arthur as a base. Dairen was to become a 'free port', i.e. not charging customs duty on Soviet commerce. Russia was to have a predominant influence in Manchuria, and joint control of the vital railway communications to these ports. Eden said to Churchill that these arrangements should not have been made without prior agreement by the Chinese, but Churchill, probably wisely, refused to protest. He knew it would only anger the President and Stalin to no purpose. 'China', he told Eden, 'is a United States concern'. At least, Eden urged, they should not themselves sign what he felt was a discreditable document. But Churchill felt that Britain's status, as one of the Big Three, required that he did. At the end, therefore, as at the beginning, Churchill accepted and associated himself with Roosevelt's China policy, no matter how much he may have privately felt it to be mistaken.[12]

'THE BEST-LAID SCHEMES O' MICE AN' MEN GANG AFT AGLEY'

The ultimate outcome in the Far East may be regarded as an eloquent comment on the vanity of human wishes, for neither Roosevelt nor Churchill ultimately achieved what they regarded as their long-term aims. Roosevelt hoped to see a Far Eastern settlement emerge in which a strong and united China would take its place as an equal partner in a Soviet-American-Chinese hegemony over the region. On the other hand, he was opposed to the restoration of British power and influence, and that of other European colonial powers. He thought this influence should disappear: if not immediately, then certainly over a relatively short period of time. In fact, China at the end of the war was still hopelessly divided and in any case, even when its internal divisions were healed, would take a generation to recover from fifteen years of civil war and war against Japan. At the end, Roosevelt admitted that it would take a long period of reform, reconstruction and education for China to match up to his wishes. China, he conceded, was incapable of acting as one of the 'Four Policemen' in South-East Asia and the Far East. This accounts for some inconsistencies in Roosevelt's actions at the end of the war. Although he jibbed at allowing Mountbatten full authority to restore the French colonial regime in Indo-China, he ordered US air forces to assist those French troops who had taken up arms against the Japanese; and allowed Mountbatten to carry out amphibious operations in Burma, and finally Malaya, which for the moment restored British authority in full. It might seem, therefore, that Churchill achieved his objective of restoring the British Empire and British power in South-East Asia. But it did not take long for it to become apparent that this was a false dawn. The rise of Asian nationalism, stimulated by the Japanese, the decline of European prestige as a result of their catastrophic defeats, and the economic weakness of the European colonial powers combined to create a momentum for independence which could not long be resisted. In that sense, Roosevelt's policies for South-East Asia ultimately prevailed over Churchill's. The moral justice as well as the historical inevitability of this process is not likely to be questioned nowadays. Whether this large-scale reshaping of the political scene in South-East Asia and the Far East was in the interests of the United States, at any rate in the short term, is another matter. It certainly was to produce a number of problems for subsequent US administrations, and there would be times when the United States sought to call on British power in the Far East – only to find that it was no longer there.[13]

9 'By Their Fruits Ye Shall Know Them': The Roosevelt–Churchill Partnership Assessed

Any judgement of the Roosevelt–Churchill partnership must be based on the actual results of that partnership for both their countries, and for the future course of events after the Second World War. An attempt has been made in the preceding chapters to assess the results of their joint efforts in relation to some of the most important wartime problems. On the basis of these results, what conclusions can be reached? Obviously the first consideration must be the effect their joint deliberations had on the strategy of the Alliance. Gallons of ink have been split on various theories relating to alternative decisions and alternative strategies to those which in fact prevailed. Plausible arguments have been put forward for the view that some of these might have ended the war sooner. The present writer has already indicated that he does not wish to add very much here to his previous conclusions on this general point, mainly for the reason that, fascinating as it is to speculate, no definitive conclusion can ever be reached in the world of 'might-have-beens'. This certainly does not mean that all the books written on the subject have been valueless. They have forced historians to examine even more closely the actual results of the decisions which were made, the reasons which lay behind them, and the real possibility of alternative decisions. On the second and third of these points – the consequences and rationale of the strategy adopted – I have suggested that in reaching the most crucial early decision for Torch, Churchill did not so much influence Roosevelt by persuasion as block the main alternative, thus enabling Roosevelt to take, in appearance by *force majeur,* a decision which perhaps he was inclined to take anyway. I have also suggested that quite possibly, a decision to launch *no* major Anglo-American operation in 1942, but instead to concentrate

179

all efforts on building up a powerful force in Britain for a major invasion of Europe in 1943 (Round-Up) might have been the best and quickest war-winning strategy. Roosevelt, however, held that because of the need to reassure the Soviets, it was politically impossible for the West not to act in 1942 *somewhere*; Churchill believed that Sledgehammer would probably be disastrous, and that it was necessary to invade North Africa in 1942, to 'clear the Mediterranean' and facilitate success in the Middle East. Therefore the decision was taken which set Allied strategy on a Mediterranean course for the next eighteen months. It was a decision for which Roosevelt and Churchill were jointly responsible. Their responsibility is all the more personal and unequivocal, since 'Torch' was an operation which Roosevelt's principal military adviser, Marshall, strongly condemned, and even Churchill's principal adviser, Brooke, had had at times considerable doubts about the feasibility of the operation. It is of course perfectly possible that the Sledgehammer–Round-Up scenario might have produced better results, just as there might have been advantages in forging ahead with a Mediterranean strategy in 1944 and postponing Overlord till later. But neither of these contentions can ever definitely be proved – or disproved. [1]

It is one thing, however, to consider whether the strategy actually followed was that most likely to win the war as quickly as possible. It is another question whether it was in the best interests of the parties concerned, particularly the weaker partner in the alliance. Here the question of Churchill's personal responsibility must be more closely examined. The decision to invade North Africa, and so inaugurate an extended period of Mediterranean operations, became inevitable because Roosevelt was determined to put US troops into action in 1942, and Churchill vetoed Sledgehammer, thus leaving only North Africa as a possibility. But it would of course have been possible for Churchill *not* to have taken this line: to have accepted the Sledgehammer–Round-Up plan for 1942–3, instead of North Africa. His insistence on North Africa led to certain consequences. One of these was that General Marshall ceased to fight hard for absolute priority for European over Pacific operations. The principle of 'Europe First' to which Churchill attached such importance, was effectively abandoned. Secondly, Marshall was very unwilling to put more than the bare minimum of US ground troops into operations which he regarded as secondary: and the abandonment of 'Europe First' would have made it difficult for him to do so, even if he had wished it. The paradoxical result, therefore, of Churchill's 'victory' in the strategic argument was that Britain, the weaker partner in the alliance, actually had more ground troops fighting in Europe in 1943, the fourth year of the war, than the United States, and it was not until August 1944 that this situation was reversed, and the US really brought its massive weight to bear *on the ground* in Europe. The strain on British manpower need not be emphasized, and it led to difficult problems for Britain during the last year of the war. It is not necessary to have absolute certainty about the results of the alternative Sledgehammer–Round-Up strategy – which in the nature of the case cannot be obtained – to hazard the opinion that the latter strategy might have imposed much less strain on British manpower and other resources, since the more probable result of that strategy would have been that US manpower would have been fully committed in Europe from mid-1943 onwards. [2]

It is also possible – a possibility discussed in Chapter 8 – that Churchill's preoccupation with Mediterranean operations may have worked to Britain's disadvantage in the Far East also. Whether this was so turns around the question whether the campaign in Burma was essential to Allied strategy or not. As events turned out, the nuclear weapon brought the Far East War to an end, and would have done so had the Burma campaign never been fought. But even without the nuclear weapon, there is a persuasive case for the view that better results could have been obtained by a programme of amphibious operations, starting with Buccaneer and proceeding from there. Such a programme could well have followed if Churchill had not vetoed Buccaneer for fear of jeopardizing the projected attack on Rhodes and other Mediterranean operations. As it was, Britain was saddled with the Burma campaign – and a further heavy strain on British manpower and resources. These possibilities must form a part of any judgement of the British–American arguments about strategy, and Churchill's part in them.

However, whatever qualifications are made, and whatever speculations are indulged in, Roosevelt and Churchill did succeed in agreeing on a common strategy, and that strategy was ultimately successful. The Roosevelt–Churchill partnership was rather less effective in forging common political policies and making them work. The two men had different ends in view, and approached almost every problem in a different way. It might be said that Churchill hoped to restore the old world, while Roosevelt aimed to build a new one. Roosevelt's object was to create a new and more secure international order, and his chosen instrument was the United Nations Organization.

It was a Wilsonian concept, a new League of Nations, but one that sought to learn the lessons of the League's failure and repair its deficiencies. The League had failed, it was thought, firstly because it lacked the support of all the Great Powers. Neither the United States, nor Russia, nor to begin with Germany, were members. It was for this reason that Roosevelt and Hull worked so hard to secure Congressional and public support for the UNO and worked equally hard and patiently to secure Soviet approval and membership. Secondly, the failure of the League was attributed to its lack of adequate powers, and its inability to move quickly to settle disputes. The UN (to give it .its present title) was by contrast to be in permanent session, and to have the authority to mediate and arbitrate in any dispute. If mediation failed, it would also have the authority to impose economic sanctions, or in the last resort to use military force. There would not be the requirement of unanimity among the member-states of the Council before action, a requirement which had crippled the League. A two-thirds majority of the Council would suffice, provided the decision had the support of the five permanent members (France being added to the 'Big Four'). Moreover, even the 'Big Five', it was intended, should not be able to prevent *discussion* of an issue, so that the voice of the UN would always be heard on a dangerous dispute. All this, it was hoped, would make the new body an effective instrument for the peaceful settlement of disputes and the actual enforcement, if necessary, of peace and security. Roosevelt's hope was that the various sources of international friction could be contained within this framework. Potential troublemakers, particularly Germany and Japan, should be so weakened and confined in the post-war settlement as to destroy their capacity to make mischief for a very long time. Another potent source of future trouble, as Roosevelt saw it, as well as an affront to human dignity, was the European colonial system. By the end of the war he had accepted that it would not be possible to prevent the colonial powers from resuming control of their possessions for the time being. But he hoped to contain, reform and make the system acceptable, by bringing it within the scope and under the authority of the UN in a 'trusteeship' system. All the colonies should ultimately come within this system, the colonial powers accepting that they were 'trustees' for their territories, and responsible to the UN for their welfare and progress. It would be an inherent part of the function of a trustee power that it would prepare its territories for eventual self-government, and facilitate their progress to this goal. [3]

Churchill, by contrast, essentially hoped to restore the *status quo*, in Europe as elsewhere, based as before on the traditional 'Great Powers of Europe'. France and ultimately a reformed Germany, in some form, should take their places in this system, alongside Britain and the Soviet Union, forming an effective 'balance of power'. But there would be one new and all-important element which would keep the balance stable. The Anglo-American Alliance, which had proved such an effective war-winning instrument, must be kept in being to provide the ultimate guarantee for world peace. It was this to which Churchill pinned his hopes. Without it, no international organization would have a chance of working. They must all hope that the UN would prove effective, that the USSR would be cooperative in maintaining the peace, that Germany and Japan would have learnt their lesson, that other potential troublemakers would profit by this experience, or be overawed by the authority of a powerful world body. But the Anglo-American Alliance must be there to provide some final insurance against the worst.

It hardly needs to be said that Churchill's plan for Africa, Asia and the Middle East also amounted, in effect, to a restoration of the pre-war *status quo*. In other words the maintenance and where necessary restoration of the British Empire and the other European colonial systems. In Churchill's eyes they might have their defects, but they were still the best guarantee of order and stability over wide areas of the globe. Self-government might be an aim in the far distant future, perhaps. But progress towards it should take place in a manner and at a speed appropriate to the condition of each territory, and should remain at the absolute discretion of the administering power.

In summing up, it only remains to say that both men failed to achieve their main long-term objectives, Roosevelt being more fortunate than Churchill in not living to see the failure of his hopes. The UN did not become in the post-war world, and has not yet become, the force for peace and security that Roosevelt hoped, and relations between Russia and the West declined with catastrophic speed to the bleak depths of the Cold War – two developments which were, of course, closely related. China, far from becoming an effective part of a constructive system for world peace, relapsed into civil war, and then emerged in a form which made Western hopes totally unrealistic. But Churchill's dream of a restored and revitalized imperial system has also faded into oblivion. The course of history had turned permanently against the European colonial empires. So far as the individual states of Western Europe were concerned, and in particular Germany and France, Roosevelt and Churchill never successfully aligned their policies, even to the extent that was achieved in policies towards Russia and China. The result was a muddle, but the outcome of that muddle was perhaps more favourable to Churchill's hopes than Roosevelt's. Germany ultimately re-emerged as a powerful force in European affairs, first and for a long period in the shape of West Germany, later as the united Germany of the past. France, too, regained something of her old status in Europe, not always to Britain's advantage. The balance of power *vis-à-vis* Russia was restored, and the United States threw its decisive weight into the system. Only in Eastern Europe, for fifty years, were Churchill's hopes completely falsified. One cannot say, therefore, that Roosevelt and Churchill were really successful, either individually or as a partnership, in creating the world they wished for. But it is probable that, even if they had seen eye to eye and worked more effectively to produce common policies, they would still have failed in large measure to overcome the tides of history and the forces which worked against them.

Appendix A
List of Persons and Code-
Names Mentioned in the Text

(Wartime Posts, Ranks and Titles)

Acheson, Dean	US public servant and Democratic politician.
Alexander, Field Marshal Sir Harold	British soldier. Allied Ground Forces C-in-C, Tunisia and Italy. Later Supreme Commander, Mediterranean.
Anderson, Sir John	British public servant, Chancellor of the Exchequer (Treasury), 1943–5.
Anderson, General Sir Kenneth	British C-in-C, First Army, Tunisia.
Anvil	Allied landing in southern France (later Dragoon), 1944.
Arciszewski, Tomasz	London Polish Government Premier, 1944–5.
Arnold, General Henry	C-in-C, US Army Air Force, Member, US Joint Chiefs of Staff.
Attlee, Clement	British Labour leader, Deputy Prime Minister, (Postwar Premier)
Avalanche	Allied landing at Salerno, Italy, 1943.
Beaverbrook, Lord	British newspaper proprietor and politician. Minister of Supply, etc.
Bevan, Aneurin	British Labour politician. (Post-war minister).
Bevin, Ernest	British trade union leader. Minister of Labour. (Post-war Foreign Secretary).
Birkenhead, Lord	British Conservative politician and minister during the 1920s.
Blum, Léon	French Socialist leader. Prime Minister pre-war and post-war. Imprisoned by the Germans.
Bohlen, Charles	US public servant and Soviet expert, State Department.
Boisson, General Pierre	Vichy Governor, French North-West Africa. Ousted by de Gaulle.

Bolero	Movement of supplies from US to UK.
Bracken, Brendan	British Conservative politician. Minister of Information.
Bradley, General Omar	C-in-C, US First Army, and later C-in-C, US 12th Army Group, NW Europe
Brooke, Field-Marshal Sir Alan	Chief of Imperial General Staff (British Army Chief of Staff), 1942–46. Chairman, British Chiefs of Staff.
Buccaneer	Proposed Allied landing on Andaman Islands, Indian Ocean, 1944.
Cato, Marcus Porcius	Politician in Ancient Rome, at time of Punic wars.
Catroux, General Georges	Free French (Gaullist) soldier and politician. Member FNCL.
Chamberlain, Neville	British Conservative leader. Prime Minister, 1937–40.
Chennault, General Clare	C-in-C US Air Forces, China.
Chiang Kai-shek, General	Chinese Head of State and C-in-C.
Churchill, Lord Randolph	British nineteenth-century Conservative politician.
Clark, General Mark	C-in-C, US Fifth Army, and later 15th Allied Army Group (Italy).
Clausewitz, Karl von	German nineteenth-century writer and soldier.
Clemenceau, Georges	French Prime Minister, 1916–19.
Cunningham, Admiral Sir Andrew	British C-in-C Mediterranean, later Allied C-in-C, and First Sea Lord.
Curzon, Lord	British Conservative politician. Foreign Secretary, 1919–23.
Darlan, Admiral François	Vichy C-in-C, Armed Forces and deputy to Marshal Pétain.
Davies, Joseph E.	US public servant. Pre-war US Ambassador to USSR.
De Gaulle, Charles	Free French leader. Prime Minister, 1944–6.
De la Chapelle, F. Bonnier	Resistance leader, Algiers.
Dill, Field Marshal Sir John	British CIGS 1940–41. British Military representative, Washington, 1941–4.
Djilas, Milovan	Yugoslav Communist politician and writer. (Post-war dissident).

Eden, Anthony	British Conservative politician. Foreign Secretary. (Post-war Premier).
Eisenhower, General Dwight	Allied C-in-C, North Africa and Italy, 1942–4. Supreme Commander, NW Europe, 1944–5.
Flandin, Pierre-Etienne	French right-wing politician and pre-war Premier.
Gauss, Clarence	US Ambassador to China.
Georges, General Alphonse	French soldier and politician. Member, FNCL.
Giraud, General Henri	French soldier and politician. Joint President FNCL 1943–4.
Goebbels, Joseph	Nazi propaganda minister.
Goering, Marshal Hermann	Nazi leader and airman. Hitler's designated successor.
Gymnast	Proposed Allied landing in French North Africa (later Torch), 1942
Harriman, Averell	US Democratic politician. Presidential Envoy to Churchill, 1940–3. Ambassador to Russia, 1943–6.
Hiss, Alger	US State Department official. Imprisoned for perjury, post-war.
Hitler, Adolf	Nazi German Head of State and C-in-C.
Hopkins, Harry	US Democratic politician. Presidential Adviser and Envoy.
Hore-Belisha, Leslie	British Conservative politician. Secretary for War, 1937–40.
Hull, Cordell	US Democratic politician. Secretary of State, 1933–44.
Hurley, Patrick	Republican politician. Wartime Presidential Envoy.
Ismay, General Sir Hastings	Churchill's personal representative to Chiefs of Staff, and Chief Staff Officer. Head of War Cabinet Secretariat (Military).
Jacob, Lt. General Sir Ian	Member, War Cabinet Secretariat (Military). Deputy to Ismay.
Juin, General Alphonse	Vichy French Army C-in-C North Africa, later French Commander in Italy.
Jupiter	Proposed Allied landing in Northern Norway, 1942.

Kennedy, John F.	Democratic politician. US President 1961–3.
King, Admiral Ernest	US Chief of Naval Operations. Member, US Chiefs of Staff.
Knox, Colonel Frank	US Secretary for the Navy.
Laval, Pierre	Vichy French politician. Deputy Premier 1940. Premier, 1942–4. Executed post-war for treason.
Leahy, Admiral William	US Ambassador to Vichy, later Presidential Chief of Staff and Chairman, US Joint Chiefs of Staff.
Leclerc, General Jacques	Early adherent to Free French. Commander, 1st French Armoured Division.
Lindeman, Professor Frederick	British scientist and politician. Scientific adviser to Churchill.
Lloyd George, David	British Liberal Party Leader. Prime Minister, 1916–22.
Lyttleton, Oliver	British Conservative politician. Minister Resident, Middle East, later Minister of Production.
MacArthur, General Douglas	Allied C-in-C, South-West Pacific. Pre-war US Army Chief of Staff, postwar military governor of Japan.
Macmillan, Harold	British Conservative politician. Minister Resident, North Africa and Italy, 1943–5 (Post-war Premier).
Maisky, Ivan	Soviet Ambassador to Britain.
Mandel, Georges	French right-wing politician. Executed by Nazis.
Marshall, General George	US Army Chief of Staff. Member, US Chiefs of Staff (Post-war Secretary of State).
Massigli, René	Free French Commissioner for Foreign Affairs. Member, FNCL.
Micolajczyk, Stanislau	Premier, Polish London Government 1943–4 (Post-war Premier of Poland).
Molotov, Vacheslav	Soviet Foreign Minister.
Monnet, Jean	French public servant. Member FNCL (Post-war architect of European unity).
Montgomery, Field Marshal Sir Bernard	C-in-C, British Eighth Army, 1942–3. C-in-C 21st Army Group, 1944–5, NW Europe.
Morgan, Lt. General Sir Frederick	Chief of Staff to Supreme Commander (designate) 1943–4.

	Deputy Chief of Staff, SHAEF, 1944–5.
Morgenthau, Henry	US Secretary of the Treasury.
Mountbatten, Admiral Lord Louis	Chief of Combined Operations, 1941–3. Allied Supreme Commander, SEAC 1943–6.
Murphy, Robert	US diplomat. Presidential Representative, North Africa, and later Italy.
Muselier, Admiral Emile	Free French Naval Chief, 1940–43.
Nimitz, Admiral Chester	US/Allied Supreme Commander, Pacific Theatre.
Noguès, General Auguste	Vichy Resident-General of Morocco. Ousted by de Gaulle, 1943.
Overlord	Allied landings in Normandy, 1944.
Patton, General George	C-in-C, US 7th Army (Sicily) 1943. C-in-C US 3rd Army, 1944–5 (NW Europe).
Peabody, Endicott	Rector (Headmaster) and Founder, Groton College.
Peyrouton, Marcel	Vichy French Minister of Interior, 1940–41. Governor-General, Algeria, 1943.
Pétain, Marshal Philippe	Vichy Head of State, 1940–44.
Philip, André	Free French (Gaullist) Minister. Member, FNCL.
Pyrrhus	King of Epirus. Greek Commander against Roman Republic.
Reagan, Ronald	Post-war Governor of California. President of US 1981–9.
Reynaud, Paul	French Premier 1940. Imprisoned by the Germans.
Roosevelt, Eleanor	Wife of President Roosevelt.
Roosevelt, Brigadier Elliott	Second son of President Roosevelt.
Round-Up	Proposed Allied landings in NW France, 1943.
Shinwell, Emmanuel	British Labour politician. (Post-war minister).
Shingle	Allied landing at Anzio (Italy), 1944.
Sledgehammer	Proposed Allied landing in NW Europe, 1942.

Smith, Alfred — Democratic Party presidential candidate, 1928. Previously Governor, New York State.

Spears, Sir Edward — Churchill's Representative to Free French, 1940–2. Minister to Levant, 1942–4.

Stalin, Marshal Josef — Soviet Head of Government. General Secretary Communist Party of USSR.

Stark, Admiral Harold — Chief of Naval Operations, 1940–42. US Naval C-in-C, European Theatre, 1942–5.

Stettinius, Edward — US Secretary of State, 1945.

Stilwell, General Joseph — C-in-C, US Army, China. Chief of Staff to Chiang Kai-shek. Deputy to Mountbatten.

Stimson, Henry — US Secretary for War.

Taft, Robert — US Republican politician and a party leader in Senate.

Thatcher, Margaret — Post-war Conservative leader. Prime Minister, 1979–90.

Torch — Allied landings in French North Africa, 1942.

Truman, Harry — US Democratic Senator. Vice-President, 1945. President, 1945–53.

Truscott, Lt. General Lucien — US Corps Commander in Italy, later C-in-C US 5th Army.

Vansittart, Lord — Pre-war civil service head of British Foreign Office.

Voroshilov, Marshal Klimenti — Soviet Minister of Defence.

Wallace, Henry — US Vice-President, 1941–5.

Wavell, Field Marshal Sir Archibald — British C-in-C. Middle East, 1939–41 India 1941–3. Viceroy, India, 1943–7.

Wedemeyer, General — Deputy Chief of Staff, SEAC. Later Chief of Staff to Chiang.

Wellington, Field Marshall, Duke of — British and Allied Commander against Napoleon.

Welles, Sumner — US public servant. Assistant Secretary of State.

Weygand, Marshall Maxime — French C-in-C, 1940. Vichy Delegate-General to North Africa, 1940–42.

Wilson, General Sir Henry — British Middle East Commander, 1943. Later Supreme Commander, Mediterranean, 1944.

Wilson, Woodrow — US Democratic President, 1913–21.

Winterton, Earl — British Conservative politician.

Wood, Sir Kingsley   British Conservative politician.
                                      Chancellor of the Exchequer,
                                      1940–43.

Abbreviations
FNCL: French Committee for National Liberation.
SEAC: South-East Asia Command.
SHAEF: Supreme Headquarters, Allied Expeditionary Force, N. W. Europe.

Appendix B
US Ground Forces in the Mediterranean Theatre

In North Africa the Allied Forces had numerical superiority over the Axis, once the British Eighth Army had joined the British First Army and US II Corps, in February 1943. In Italy, however, there were roughly equal numbers (about twenty divisions) on each side. Since Britain was approaching the end of its manpower resources (especially after June 1944), the number of US divisions Marshall was willing to commit became of vital importance. The terrain in Italy favoured the defenders.

A. TUNISIA

Three US divisions initially, eventually four divisions. Large numbers of US troops who had landed in North Africa in November 1942 remained in Morocco and Algeria. They later saw service with the US Fifth Army in Italy from Salerno onwards. Number of British troops varied, but after February 1943 was normally more than twice the number of US troops.

B. SICILY

Initial landings: Four US divisions and five British.

C. ITALY

Salerno landings (under command US Fifth Army): Two British divisions, one US division (one US division as reserve).

Landings in South Italy (Reggio, Taranto, Bari): three British, one Canadian division. (Under command British Eighth Army).

In *December 1943*, US Fifth Army included five US divisions, three British divisions, one French division, and an Italian brigade.

In *January 1944*, Fifth Army included five US divisions, three and a half British divisions, two French divisions and Italian troops.

In *February 1944*, Fifth Army included two US Corps, one British, one New Zealand and one French Corps.

In *May 1944*, Fifth Army included seven US divisions, four French divisions and two British divisions.

Anzio landings (January 1944): Three and a half US divisions and two British divisions took part, under command US Fifth Army.

Note: British Eighth Army in Italy varied in size from seven to eleven divisions (including, at different times, two Canadian, one New Zealand, one Indian, one South African, and two Polish divisions).

D. EXTRACT FROM GENERAL M.W. CLARK, *CALCULATED RISK*, CHAPTER 12

The British Commonwealth paid the price, while other Allied Powers were still neutral, or while they were preparing themselves for action ... It also affected the way the War was fought after 1942. ... the British divisions were tired from months and even years of fighting, but few replacements were available ... [Sir Ronald Adam, British Adjutant-General] pointed out that the British were coming to the end of their manpower resources. ... he was breaking up divisions in the British Army at the rate of one division every two months, to use the men as replacements for other units committed to action.

Notes

All extracts from Churchill–Roosevelt correspondence are taken from Professor W. Kimball's comprehensive edition (Vol. I, Oct. 5, 1939–Nov. 14, 1942; Vol. II, Nov. 15, 1942–Feb. 29, 1944; Vol. III, Feb. 29, 1944–Apr. 11, 1945)

CHAPTER 1: UNEASY PARTNERS

1. In Churchill's case also, of course, his appeal to a wide spectrum of opinion was due to his association in American minds with the lone British stand in 1940, when the US was neutral.
2. Most striking of Churchill's subsequent setbacks (apart from those experienced during the war itself) was the electoral defeat of 1945 – a shock and an inexplicable mystery to most Americans.
3. Churchill had left the Conservative Party and joined the Liberals in 1904. In 1924 he had rejoined the Conservative Party. This chequered record was not forgotten by many orthodox Conservatives, who did not share Churchill's genial opinion that 'it is easy to rat, but it takes a good deal of ingenuity to re-rat'. Neville Chamberlain (Prime Minister 1937–40), in particular, always distrusted Churchill, as did many of Chamberlain's close associates – a distrust which was cordially (or rather uncordially) reciprocated. When Churchill became Prime Minister, he soon set about banishing the most prominent Chamberlainites to distant ambassadorships or to the political wilderness. Many lesser Chamberlainites remained in his government, but for the most part rigorously excluded from those offices which had to do with foreign or strategic policy. After Chamberlain's death in 1940, there were none of his disciples in the War Cabinet, except Kingsley Wood as Chancellor of the Exchequer.
4. Churchill's views on a future balance of power in Europe – between the Atlantic and the Urals – are dealt with in full in Chapters 4, 5, 6 and 7. They were anathema to Roosevelt.
5. (a) Like his son, Lord Randolph Churchill was never a good party man, and always liable, in the view of his more orthodox colleagues, to kick over the traces. His spectacular resignation from the Salisbury government in 1887 ended his political career; illness and an early death prevented a come-back. His marriage with Jennie Jerome, daughter of an American millionaire, introduced a vigorous Irish-American strain in the Churchill blood. Winston naturally made full use of the fact that he was half-American when addressing American audiences. Perhaps because of his ancestry he certainly seemed to

194

feel more at home in the United States, and with Americans, than many upper-class Englishmen. (b) Like Churchill, Montgomery's background was 'upper-class' – though unlike Churchill, not aristocratic. Montgomery's grandfather was Lieutenant-Governor of the Punjab, his father a colonial bishop. He had, in common with both Roosevelt and Churchill a boarding-school education (in England misnamed 'public schools', a term that most Americans, with good reason, find confusing).

6.   Churchill and Montgomery both reacted to some extent against some of their early boarding-school influences and values, though retaining a certain attachment to the 'old school'. Roosevelt, by contrast, retained a lifelong regard for Groton, and a lifelong friendship with its celebrated founder-headmaster, Endicott Peabody. 'You don't know how much I have depended on the Rector', he remarked, much later in life. It is fair to say that Groton moulded Roosevelt to a greater extent than Harrow moulded Churchill.

7.   (a) Roosevelt, an excellent yachtsman who loved the sea, was intensely proud of his connection with the Navy. The Navy Department and Woodrow Wilson were the important formative influences in his middle years (1912–20). The corresponding influences in Churchill's life at roughly the same age were the Army, then the Navy, and David Lloyd George. Churchill was an officer in the regular Army at the turn of the century, and, after leaving the Army for politics, became head of the Navy (First Lord of the Admiralty) in 1911. Both Wilson and Lloyd George, be it noted, were 'liberals' in social and economic terms. (b) Sixty years ago the governorship of a great state was thought an ideal preparation for the presidency. Since then, the American progress to first place on the world stage, and the consequent much greater importance of US foreign and military policy, has led some commentators to the view that the Senate or the Vice-Presidency may be a better stepping-stone. Whatever the pundits may say, however, it is clear that millions of ordinary Americans still think it a good idea to send to Washington a man previously uncontaminated by its environment.

8.   Roosevelt came to rely on Marshall to the point where he felt, in his own words, 'I could not sleep quietly with you [Marshall] out of the country'. This process is explored in Chapters 2 and 3.

9.   In the late thirties a conservative Supreme Court and the conservative wing of the Democratic party in the Senate had thwarted some important parts of Roosevelt's 'New Deal' legislation. Roosevelt's attempt to secure the election of more progressive senators, and to get a Bill through Congress to add more amenable judges to the Court both failed.

10. In 1941 Marshall and some leading members of Roosevelt's Cabinet became convinced that the US would have to enter the war. The only question was 'when?'

11. Churchill became Premier in May 1940, and immediately formed a national coalition government with the Conservative, Labour and Liberal parties. Labour leaders supported him loyally and guaranteed

the support of Labour in the Commons. Many Conservatives were at first less enthusiastic, but most rallied to him when he became Conservative Party Leader in late 1940.

12. Partly through necessity, partly through choice, Roosevelt and Churchill achieved probably the closest planning relationship between allies in history. Marshall was the moving force in this: the creation of the Combined Chiefs of Staff and the enforcement of the principle of a Supreme Allied Commander over all services and nationalities, in each theatre, were his instruments. It was hard for Churchill to swallow arrangements which put Britain in a subordinate position, but he did so.

13. Cordell Hull was Secretary of State 1933–44. Roosevelt retained him for so long because of his influence with Congress, a body traditionally distrustful of the State Department. But they were never close, and Roosevelt preferred to consult and rely on others – Hopkins, who was virtually an additional Secretary of State for long periods, Sumner Welles (Roosevelt's man in the State Department), Admiral Leahy (Chairman of the Joint Chiefs of Staff) and others.

CHAPTER 2: GRAND STRATEGY I

1. (a) Axis control of the southern European coast and the Libyan coastline exposed Allied convoys to air and submarine attack, as well as the threat, more putative than real, of the Italian navy. It made running of Mediterranean convoys in 1941 and 1942 virtually impossible. It was estimated that reopening the Mediterranean would save a million tons of Allied shipping. (b) Bradley, Patton and Truscott, as well as many lower-level commanders, all 'won their spurs' in Tunisia, gaining valuable experience for the future.

2. Rainbow, because the plan envisaged US participation in an Anglo-American alliance against an Axis alliance. Plan Dog, 'd' of a series of plans (a), (b), (c), (d).

3. King was crusty, tough (according to Roosevelt, he 'shaved with a blow-torch') and anti-British. He had unpleasant memories of dealings with the British in World War I. Dill's judgement that King 'was not a good co-operator' is not too unfair.

4. It is no reflection on Marshall to say that at this stage of the war he was as inexperienced in the problems of coalition warfare as he was unfamiliar with those of amphibious operations. He would have been first to admit it. To begin with, he tended to underestimate problems presented by a cross-Channel attack.

5. In his admirable study of Eisenhower as Supreme Commander, Professor S.E. Ambrose summarizes the case against Sledgehammer as (1) at worst it would be a complete disaster, and at best only establish a small permanent bridgehead; (2) it would not attract any German forces from the Russian front. Professor Ambrose appears to accept these arguments, as Eisenhower himself did in later years. He also

suggests that even in 1942 Marshall and Eisenhower were more concerned to stave off Gymnast than to launch Sledgehammer.

6. (a) At this period it did not seem improbable that German troops would break through in Caucasus and Egypt. In early 1942 also, a Japanese breakthrough into India did not seem unlikely. (b) Mountbatten was at this time C-in-C Combined Operations HQ, concerned with all landings, raids, etc. on enemy territory. His expertise in combined operations, and amphibious warfare was acknowledged. Eisenhower, indeed (probably with Marshall's approval), suggested he might command Sledgehammer.

7. Henry Stimson was previously Republican Secretary of State under Hoover. Knox, the Secretary of the Navy, was also a Republican.

8. The abandonment of Sledgehammer without any substitute would have meant, however, that Churchill would have had to persuade Roosevelt to 'welsh' on his promise to Molotov, which he might well have refused to do.

9. (a) 'Tunis by Christmas' was Churchill's initial objective, and hope. But this would probably have required landings at Bône and Philippeville – and Marshall was reluctant to go even as far east as Algiers. (b) A German invasion of Spain (Operation Felix) with the object of capturing Gibraltar and perhaps moving on to North Africa, was considered by the German on more than one occasion. Hitler, however, always finally decided that a neutral and friendly Spain was preferable to an occupied and hostile Spain. Goering thought this omission a major strategic blunder. (c) As to the consequences of Allied failure to land further east – a six months' campaign – though Churchill's hopes were dashed, US troops and generals gained wider experience than a short campaign would have provided. There was also a greater drain on Axis resources. (d) American leaders, such as Clark, found Anderson dour and uncooperative. Montgomery thought him second-rate. Nevertheless, it may be doubted if anyone else would have done better in early stages of campaign, in most unpromising circumstances.

10. Some military commentators consider a further contributory cause of the length of Tunisian campaign was Montgomery's alleged slowness in advancing across Libya to join hands with the Torch forces.

11. In September, Churchill had expressed to Roosevelt his hopes for control of all North Africa by the end of November 1942. This would have made Round-Up in 1943 possible.

12. British observers, including Mountbatten, thought Marshall's failure at Casablanca partly due to the fact that there was only a small US planning staff. As the British General Jacob put it, 'they left most of their clubs behind'.

13. There is not space here to deal adequately with the argument that the Italian Campaign had achieved its objects when Naples and the Foggia airfields had been captured, or at least after the fall of Rome, and should thereafter have been reduced to a purely defensive operation. The point should be made, however, that a prime object of this

campaign was to divert German resources from Overlord, which could best be achieved by keeping up the pressure in Italy.

14. (a) It was Oliver Harvey, private secretary to Eden, who claimed Churchill had 'sold the pass'. (b) Many years after war, Marshall said he had *offered* to resign once, and *threatened* to resign once, neither of these occasions being the one referred to here. At seventy-seven, however, Marshall's memory was not 100 per cent reliable. Possibly he implied or hinted at the possibility rather than making an outright threat. (F. Pogue, *Marshall Interviews*, pp. 203, 300, 477–8, 502–3.)

CHAPTER 3: GRAND STRATEGY II

1. For examples of the 'Balkan obsession' see (1) First Washington Conference Memos and Final Agreement quoted above, (2) Memos for Cairo Conference 1943, which emphasized support for Balkan resistance, Turkish entry into war; also resumption of Rhodes operations and possible bridgehead on Dalmatian coast. But cf. Churchill to Roosevelt, October 1943, 'I have never wished to send army into Balkans but only agents, supplies and commandos' – an assurance which was not believed.

2. (a) It would perhaps be fairer to say US carnage in the First World War was much less prolonged than the British: the US entered the war towards the end of 1917. (b) The value of Turkish entry was dubious, since the Turks were ill-equipped and would demand modern arms – a further drain on Allied resources. If a land campaign began, the Americans feared the 'suction effect' of such operations on US troops, whereas Germany could use Bulgarian troops which were not available against Russia (with whom Bulgaria was not at war).

3. See Ehrman, *British Official History of World War II*, vol. VII Appendix VI. However, although the British Chiefs produced no specific plan, this does not mean Churchill did not want a campaign. US fears were that encouragement of the Balkan Resistance would expand and grow into major campaign.

4. 'War is a continuation of policy by other means.' (Clausewitz).

5. (a) What is odd is that Roosevelt should have regarded weakening of British power *per se* as beneficial to the US – or alternatively that he did not fully realize loss of power must follow loss of Empire (which seems hardly conceivable). (b) Cato, a Roman politician, advocated total destruction of Carthage. Hence 'Carthaginian Peace' (see Chapter 7 on the Morgenthau Plan).

6. (a) It has been suggested by A. Verrier (*Assassination in Algiers*) that Roosevelt's motives for supporting Torch included a Machiavellian plan for permanent US domination of North Africa. This seems exaggerated (see Chapter 6). (b) See Chapter 5 for British attempts to limit Soviet influence, and for a further treatment: K. Sainsbury: *The Turning Point*, Chapter IV, W. Kimball, The Juggler, ch. 5. The

quotation of Roosevelt is from Elliott Roosevelt: *As He Saw It.* Of Marshall, from F. Pogue: *Ordeal and Hope.*

7. Brooke's 'feverish phrase' is, as his biographer, Sir David Fraser concedes (in a letter to the author) something of a mystery. One should not, however, deduce from it that Brooke wished a full-scale Balkan campaign.

8. See Appendix B for proportions of US and British troops in Italy, etc.

9. Burma operations would reopen land communications with China and facilitate movement of US supplies to Chiang Kai-shek – a boost to the Chinese, therefore.

10. A further sign of deteriorating relations was Roosevelt's refusal to visit the UK for a conference in 1944.

11. Churchill and the British Chiefs of Staff did secure postponement of Anvil by two months, mainly on the grounds that enough troops and assault shipping (especially tank landing-craft) were not available for Overlord, a *simultaneous* Anvil, *and* maintaining pressure in Italy. But Marshall and Roosevelt stuck firmly to their position that Anvil should not be abandoned completely.

12. 'Straight line is shortest distance' was also Marshall's view throughout strategic arguments. It must be conceded that Churchill preferred circuitous approaches to strategy.

13. Churchill–Roosevelt correspondence on Greece is dated 17 and 29 August, 1944.

14. Author's previous views are in *The North African Landings* (1976) and *The Turning Point* (1985). Some glosses on these views are given in Chapter 9.

15. (a) Montgomery might well have echoed the words of Wellington (another British general perennially short of manpower), 'we must husband our troops'. (b) In ancient times the Greek king Pyrrhus won many victories – but each victory left him weaker.

CHAPTER 4: A DIFFICULT ALLIANCE

1. Perhaps Roosevelt and Churchill sought by using a commonplace sort of nickname to reassure themselves that Stalin was after all a normal human being like others. They were trying, one feels, to domesticate the problem.

2. (a) Churchill's views on the Soviet alliance are well summed up in celebrated remark, 'if Hitler invaded Hell, I would make a favourable reference to the Devil in House of Commons'. (b) For losses in 1942 convoys and especially convoys PQ16–18, see Churchill, *Second World War*, Vol. IV, Chapter XV. This was the worst period. Two-thirds of the losses sustained in all Arctic convoys occurred in these three. (c) In March 1942 Churchill wrote to Roosevelt 'the principles of Atlantic Charter ought not to be construed to deny Russia frontiers she occupied when attacked'. Roosevelt on the other hand hoped the Sledgehammer proposal would 'take heat off Russia's [territorial]

demands' (Sherwood, *Hopkins Papers*, II, p. 533). Roosevelt in fact changed his mind and accepted Churchill's view on the frontier question within a year. (d) After World War I, Allied diplomats at Versailles drew a frontier line of eastern Poland, on the basis of available statistics. The line was named after then British Foreign Secretary, Lord Curzon.

3. In the event, Allied strategic decisions ensured no US/UK troops in Eastern Europe, except in Greece: and Roosevelt's intention was to withdraw *all* US troops from Western Europe in two years after the end of the war.

4. (a) Churchill's attitude to Russia is well summed up in a telex to the British Ambassador in Moscow, June 1943: 'No apology is called for from us' ... 'you should adopt robust attitude to further complaints' ... 'they stood by watching with indifference our [probable] obliteration' (Gilbert, *Road to Victory*, p. 432). (b) Soviet suspicion was prompted by German approaches for Italian armistice. See p. 84 and Gilbert, p. 1320.

5. 'Appeasement' was the term applied particularly to policy of Chamberlain Government 1937–9. But this policy was essentially a continuation of the previous line of the 1930s.

6. One revisionist historian (Resis) has gone so far as to suggest that Roosevelt's October 1944 message to Churchill and Stalin ('US is interested') indicated marked stiffening of attitude to USSR, and was in effect the beginning of the Cold War. This seems exaggerated, as Ross suggests (Deakin et al., eds, *British Political and Military Strategy in 1944*, Chapter V).

7. On supply, cf. Churchill to Hopkins September 1941, and to Stalin October 1941. (Churchill, III, pp. 416, 418). Churchill explained in a former message (and to Roosevelt) that supplying Russia would grievously affect British ability to maintain operations in Middle East, etc. In the latter message to Stalin occurs the phrase, 'We intend to run continuous cycle of convoys' – which makes Stalin's subsequent reproaches on "broken promises" (see p. 67) not entirely unreasonable.

8. On the convoys, Churchill was probably right in the short term. However, overall throughout war, Arctic convoys were a success – the main losses were in this period of 1942; on 'broken promises' see above, note 7.

9. (a) Stalin was very anxious in period of maximum danger (1941–3) to avoid provoking a Japanese attack on Russia. Not until the Moscow and Teheran conference (October–November 1943) would he promise to enter the Far East war, and then not till after German defeat. (b) Stalin's position as C-in-C was by no means a nominal one: in any case he was possibly reluctant to leave Russia in critical period for fear of internal coup. Roosevelt on other hand, had to sign bills from Congress 'in ten days' under US constitution. This difficulty was later got round. (c) Churchill pointed out, reasonably, to Stalin that the latter had refused a meeting when invited, so could not complain that he was not able to express his views.

10. Roosevelt to Churchill, 30 April, 1943, 'Russians and Poles must subordinate factional differences to common struggle', shows failure to grasp realities of Polish problem. Possibly Roosevelt realized this, for the message was not sent.

11. (a) Churchill's February message was a long memo on future world order, amongst other subjects, which Churchill called 'Morning Thoughts' – a title which provoked disrespectful comments in the Foreign Office. (b) In talks with Eden, Roosevelt again showed tendency to take Polish issue lightly – 'he did not foresee great difficulty' ... 'Poles might gain by agreeing to Curzon Line' ... Allies 'should decide on solution and Poles would have to accept'. Eden, *Reckoning*, pp. 372–3.

12. There seems no doubt that Davies conveyed an *à deux* invitation.

13. A large Axis air force (reinforced after Torch) was sent to Mediterranean: only a few German divisions were in North Africa until December 1942: number then increased. In Italy Germans employed about 20 divisions. In addition Germans were forced to keep divisions in Balkans, against possible invasion threat, but estimated numbers vary. Stalin at one point said only 13 divisions. In fact numbers seem to have varied between 15 and 25 at different times. Addition of divisions in Southern France, also against possible invasion, certainly brings the figure up to the 40 German divisions which Stalin admitted were diverted from Russian front. The Allied air offensive also kept million men employed who would otherwise have been available for the Russian front.

14. (a) In North Africa de Gaulle had been steadily ousting the US favourite, Giraud, from power (see Chapter 6) – much to Roosevelt's annoyance. (b) The US appreciation of Soviet power was first published quite early, in Sherwood, *Hopkins* papers, Vol. II, p. 744. The US of course also hoped for Russian assistance in the Far East war. It was not only post-war considerations which counted.

15. The Overlord commitment was actually 'by the end of May'. D-Day in the upshot was 6 June.

16. On the proposal that the USSR should attend CCS meetings, see cables 23 October, 11 November, 26 October 1943. The Russian representative (Voroshilov) attended one meeting of CCS at Teheran, but Russia did not become a regular member. For a US view on the Teheran Conference, see K. Eubank, *Summit at Teheran*, Morrow, New York, 1986.

17. The Warsaw uprising is discussed further in Chapter 5. On Soviet–US relations, see Hull, *Memoirs*, II, pp. 1200, 1400, 1436.

18. 'Get to Vienna', see Deakin et al., p. 60.

19. Romania, see Roosevelt–Churchill Correspondence, 10 June, 11, 23 June.

20. Alger Hiss, who was at Yalta, later said (in a lecture at the author's university) that Marshall, a man not given to overstatement, had also expressed great pleasure at the results achieved. Hiss's credibility is not 100 per cent but this rings true.

21. (a) On this period, see Churchill–Roosevelt correspondence, 8 March, 27, 31 May 1945. Professor Kimball thinks Churchill could not have hoped to do much for Poland by this stage, and attributes his concern to domestic politics, which is supported by the Roosevelt–Churchill correspondence. But Churchill's distress was quite genuine on wider grounds. (b) On Roosevelt's 'sharp reply', see Roosevelt–Churchill, 4 April 1945, and ff.
22. See Djilas '*Conversations*', (paperback edition) p. 61.
23. The Truman administration also swallowed many unpalatable draughts on Eastern Europe, in the end. Roosevelt might have done so more gracefully and with less harm to Soviet–US relations.

CHAPTER 5: THE UNSOLVABLE PROBLEM

1. At Yalta Stalin had said, with some justice, that the West could not expect him to be less good a Russian than Lord Curzon!
2. 'Postponement' was frequently used to describe Roosevelt's policy on a number of issues, but Churchill also favoured letting the dust settle on some issues, e.g Germany.
3. Perhaps tactically, Stalin reacted fiercely when Roosevelt appeared to link the government problem with frontiers. Harriman and Charles Bohlen (a Soviet expert) thought Roosevelt should have been tougher on Poland. (Harriman, *Special Envoy*, pp. 242–50. Bohlen, *Witness to History*, p. 128.)
4. Guarantees against aggression were offered by the Chamberlain government to these countries in 1939. Only through a Soviet alliance could they have been effectively honoured.
5. One of the mysteries about Roosevelt's attitudes was his apparent lack of concern for Poland – compared with, for example, Finland. Yet Polish independence was an important part of the Wilsonian canon, whereas Finland was an enemy state. For Roosevelt/Churchill views on Poland, see Sainsbury, *Turning Point*, pp. 104, 276.
6. (a) Roosevelt was no doubt influenced by wartime evidence of Croat–Serb conflict. (b) Presumably the Russians wished to exclude Bulgaria too, which like Romania had frontier with Russia. At Moscow, Molotov emphasized Russia's special interest in 'bordering states'. (c) That Molotov did not reject Eden's proposals out of hand *before* Moscow may have been influenced by fact US had not expressed views. Hull's cool reaction at Moscow may have encouraged outright rejection. (d) In my previous book, *The Turning Point*, I mentioned (p. 83) that 'the internecine feuds between the various races of Eastern Europe would make these objectives [federations] hard to attain', but did not develop this argument as fully as I should have done. Recent events in Eastern Europe, especially the break-up of the Yugoslav and Czechoslovak federations, have brought home to all of us, including the author, how fragile the foundations of such states may well have been. Professor Kimball has brought this point out fully in his recent book *The Juggler:*

Franklin Roosevelt as Wartime Statesman (p. 94). It is difficult to dissent from his view that such units might have proved 'confused and chaotic', though I do not think Eden and the Foreign Office fully realized this (as they should have done), or that it was their intention deliberately to create such states. I am still of the opinion that US support for the other elements in Eden's 'package' would have been valuable, if only to indicate to Stalin, at an earlier stage than was done, that the US *was* interested in the fate of these areas.

7. Roosevelt thought Flanders should be separated from south Belgium, which should join part of north France as new state of 'Wallonia'. Suggestion also indicates his cavalier attitude to France, and belief latter could be treated as conquered territory post-war, an idea not creditable to Roosevelt's heart or head.

8. (a) Eden's proposals not only ignored Eastern Europe's internecine feuds, but also the fact that there was no historic basis for democracy in that region, save in Czechoslovakia. All other Eastern European states had a tradition of dictatorships. (b) The Russians successfully blocked the Declaration on Liberated Territory in 1943, but Stalin accepted it at Yalta, when it was too late to do any good, or from his point of view, any harm. (c) At least one of Eden's biographers (Carlton) thinks he could have argued for Poland and Eastern Europe more forcefully, but Soviet opposition and US indifference hardly suggested this would have achieved much.

9. It is now generally conceded that Polish officers at Katyn were murdered by Russians, not Germans. However, the immediate importance was that it provided Stalin with the opportunity to break relations with the London Poles – 'they were unfriendly to USSR', (Churchill–Roosevelt, 27 April 1943, Roosevelt–Churchill, 26 April 1943).

10. Roosevelt had told Eden (March 1943) of his willingness to accept Russian demands, but evidently did not wish for discussion at this stage, (Roosevelt–Churchill, 30 April, not sent). (Eden, *Reckoning*, p. 373). Eden was surprised that Roosevelt now accepted the Russian demands he had previously objected to.

11. See A. Harriman, *Special Envoy* pp. 242–50, for his considered view. See also Eubank, pp. 357–66, 371–3 and Chapter 19.

12. (a) Stalin's reference to Czechoslovakia is doubly ironic. (b) One difficulty for London Poles was that leaders of the Polish Home Army (Resistance) were ultra-nationalistic. Concessions on frontiers would have affected morale and possibly loyalty to the London government. (c) See Churchill–Roosevelt, 21 March 1944, 1 April 1944 for objection to 'imposed' frontier changes.

13. (a) Churchill hoped a quick breakthrough to the Po valley might make possible an advance through the Ljubljana Gap in the eastern Alps into Yugoslavia – thence north to Vienna and Prague (see Chapter 3). (b) See Barker, *Churchill and Eden*, p. 281, on 'percentages agreement'.

14. (a) See Morgan, *F.D.R.*, p. 702, on Roosevelt's realism. (b) On 'spheres of influence', Roosevelt–Churchill correspondence, 10, 11,

12 June 1944. (Roosevelt – 'We must make it clear we are not establishing postwar spheres of influence') and 14 June 1944, etc., Jacob remarked, 'spheres of influence will always exist – so if you can limit the ones you don't like, so much the better'. (Deakin, et al., p. 52).

15. (a) Soviet armies halted outside Warsaw partly for military reasons (supplies, etc.), but political considerations may have also influenced decision. Stalin detested the Polish Home Army and labelled the rising 'an adventure'. Churchill–Roosevelt correspondence, 18, 20, 24, 25 August 1944. Minutes of Quebec Conference are in *Foreign Relations of the United States, 1944 (Quebec Conference)*. (b) On Greece, see Roosevelt's agreement to the dispatch of a British force, Correspondence, 26 August 1944. Having turned Churchill down on action to help the Warsaw Poles, Roosevelt perhaps felt disinclined to thwart him on this.

16. On 'percentages', see Churchill *War Memoirs*, Vol. VI, p. 198.

17. Deakin et al., *British Political and Military Strategy 1944*, Chapter 5.

18. Roosevelt–Churchill, 15 December 1944. Gilbert, *Road to Victory*, p. 1076.

19. Roosevelt–Churchill, 8, 10, 11, 12, 13 March 1945, etc., on later stages of Polish dispute.

20. Roosevelt did exert himself for Finland at Teheran, which may have modified Soviet policy; a similar concern for Poland would certainly have done no harm, though it might have made no difference in the long run.

CHAPTER 6: THE HEAVY CROSS OF LORRAINE

1. (a) One historian (G.D. Sheffield) attributes the celebrated 'heavy cross' remark to Spears. I have followed the more common attribution. It is possible, of course, that Churchill took up a witticism of Spears' and repeated it. (b) Reynaud and Mandel (a minister in his government who was Jewish) were imprisoned by the Germans, with Léon Blum and others. Weygand, the French C-in-C in 1940, and Noguès, preferred to serve Vichy. Noguès was Resident-General in Morocco. (c) Catroux was polished, diplomatic and rather 'slippery'. Lyttleton (Lord Chandos) thought him untrustworthy (letter to author, 27 April 1971).

2. De Gaulle was, of course aware of the damage Oran would do to the British and the Gaullist image in France.

3. (a) Historians differ on the legality of Vichy. Professor G. Warner, for example, thinks Pétain's succession to office constitutional, whatever one may think of subsequent actions (letter to author). However it was the moral authority of Vichy that de Gaulle denied, even more than its legality. (b) British economic warfare authorities were in fact not too happy about concessions to French North Africa. (c) Like Admiral Leahy, US ambassador to Vichy, Murphy was conservative (also a bit of

a snob), and rather suspicious of young resistance leaders, who were often left-wing, and sometimes Jewish. Murphy tended to feel the Vichy leaders were 'not so bad', as opposed to British dislike and distrust of them. Verrier, a critic of the whole Vichy policy, argues that Murphy achieved nothing of value to Torch. This is not the conclusion one necessarily draws from the detailed account of events in North Africa given by Funk (*Politics of Torch*) and others. Nor is it the author's conclusion. Murphy, and Americans generally, did however overestimate grossly Giraud's potential influence in North Africa.

4. (a) As to how far Pétain was a willing collaborator, it is difficult to judge exactly what went on in the mind of this vain, deeply conservative, often muddled old man. Perhaps he did not always know himself. (b) In relation to de Gaulle, it was of course the case, and quite naturally, that Roosevelt and the Americans preferred that a more pliant and pro-American leader than de Gaulle should take over in North Africa, after the successful Torch. There is no need to believe that Roosevelt had from the beginning a deep-seated plot to take over North Africa for good, though he came to hope US influence could continue post-war at least in the form of permanent US bases (and possibly British also). But Vichy policy and the 'Darlan expedient' were essentially opportunistic.

5. (a) British military authorities in the Dakar affair tended to make the Gaullists the scapegoats for their own mistakes. British security was itself not foolproof at this stage of war, however. (b) Support for Vichy *was* probably greater in 1940 and '41. Gaullist support and resistance generally became greater in 1942, and increased dramatically after Torch and the German occupation of Vichy unoccupied zone, in November 1942. (c) On de Gaulle's reaction to the Syrian armistice, Lyttleton to author, 27 April 1971. (d) In 1941 General Wavell, C-in-C Middle East, had to conduct campaigns in Egypt and Libya, Eritrea, Somalia, Syria and briefly in Iraq. British resources were very thinly stretched. Therefore it was important to bring the Syrian campaign to an end as soon as possible – which would be facilitated by handling the armistice negotiations with kid gloves. Catroux was present at the negotiations but did not sign the armistice.

6. (a) For Hull's views on St Pierre see *Memoirs*, II, p. 961. (b) The most celebrated instance of Churchill's views on the US and France was a de Gaulle–Churchill interchange, 4 June 1944, on the eve of the Normandy invasion. Accounts of their actual words and phrases differ, but all agree that Churchill said, in effect, that US friendship was more important than French, if forced to choose. Anthony Eden and Ernest Bevin (both present) indicated dissent from this as a *universal* rule of British policy. (De Gaulle, *Memoirs*, Vol. II, p. 227; Churchill, *Memoirs*, pp. 556–7; Eden, *Reckoning*, p. 453).

7. Muselier had a chequered career, which included suspicion by British of counter-intelligence activity, and several notable disagreements with de Gaulle.

8. (a) Roosevelt was unduly pessimistic about French recovery. France began to play a significant part in European affairs in 1946 and

economic recovery (with US help) was well under way by the early fifties. (b) For Churchill's views on France, see Churchill, VI, p. 309. The latter occasion was at Yalta, when Churchill expressed the view to Roosevelt and Stalin. Cf. Eden, *Reckoning*, pp. 397–8. (c) As a result of disagreements with Churchill over wording, Eden's memo was apparently not circulated. Yet Churchill's paper of the same date made essentially the same point. Eden implies that the former was temporarily unreasonable because of war strain. Cf. Eden, p. 347; Eden broadcast of the previous year.

9. Churchill–Roosevelt correspondence, 2, 4, 5 November 1942. Hull, II, p. 1192.

10. (a) There seems no real hard evidence for the view expressed by Verrier that Roosevelt's preference was *always* for working with Darlan. Indeed Verrier concedes this would be difficult to find. The Darlan deal was spur of the moment opportunism, prompted by the discovery that Giraud had little or no influence in North Africa. Press criticism naturally infuriated Hull, who attributed it to Gaullist manipulation of the Press. Roosevelt felt it necessary to bow to the storm, and described the use of Darlan as 'an expedient', which it was. Darlan complained that the Americans were treating him as a 'squeezed lemon'. (b) British intelligence groups in North Africa were in touch with Gaullist and other political groups, which included both left and right-wing factions. One of these, de la Chapelle, who was in fact a royalist, killed Darlan, but it could easily have been any one of a number of others. Verrier implies that the British and Gaullists were involved up to the neck in the affair, but does not explicitly say they organized the assassination. Probably the whole truth will never be known. One is reminded of President Kennedy's assassination. (c) Churchill and British were undoubtedly relieved by Darlan's death. Nevertheless, Churchill had gone along with the 'Darlan Expedient', and had told Eisenhower, in fact, to crawl to Darlan if thereby they could get the French Fleet. This, however, Darlan could not deliver. (Butcher, *Three Years with Eisenhower*, p. 251.) Churchill–Roosevelt correspondence, 11 November, 1942, 1 January 1943.

11. (a) Eden, *Reckoning*, pp. 386–7. Churchill, *Memoirs*, Vol. IV, p. 716. Not surprisingly, it was usually when in personal contact with Roosevelt that Churchill proposed to 'get tough' with de Gaulle. A previous occasion was at the time of the Casablanca Conference. (b) Churchill used the War Cabinet as an alibi on several occasions. In an amusing speech at the Teheran conference, Hopkins suggested that the War Cabinet exerted no real restriction on Churchill's power (Sainsbury, *Turning Point*, p. 266). For possible parallel on Morgenthau Plan, see p. 152 (c) Churchill–Roosevelt correspondence, 6 June 1943. On the new committee, Massigli, Philip and Catroux were committed Gaullists; only Georges and Monnet supported Giraud – and Monnet soon changed sides. The ratio of support was then exactly the opposite of Churchill's figures.

12. Correspondence 8 May, 17 June 1943. Churchill, *Memoirs*, V, pp. 157–9. De Gaulle had possibly a reasonable point when he argued that Giraud could not simultaneously hold joint political power with himself *and* sole military power. Roosevelt, who was (unlike Churchill) head of state *and* C-in-C of the armed forces, saw no objection, and in any case was adamant that de Gaulle should not share control of the French North African armies. De Gaulle won his point in the end.
13. Correspondence, 8 July 1943. (a) This reassurance to Roosevelt was prompted by pressure from the British Foreign Office and Eisenhower's HQ to recognize the French Committee as provisional government. Roosevelt sharply refused. Churchill also was exasperated by de Gaulle at this time, but above all anxious to maintain good relations with Roosevelt. See also Correspondence, 21, 22 July 1943, 3 August 1943. Churchill, *Memoirs*, V, Chapter X. (b) It is only fair to say that (as Professor Kersaudy points out) de Gaulle said, and probably believed, that British entry to the EC in 1963 would be inimical to French interests – possibly to European interests as well. One feels, however, that he was not exactly displeased to give the British a 'put-down'.
14. (a) For Syrian problem, see de Gaulle, *Memoirs* II, pp. 199-203, Churchill, *Memoirs*, V, pp. 164–5. (b) On Boisson, etc. Correspondence, 21, 22 December 1943; de Gaulle, *Memoirs*, p. 218. Roosevelt was very sensitive about Boisson and Noguès, since they had assisted Allies in North Africa and were US protegés. (c) On Eisenhower instructions, see Correspondence, 21 March 1944; Eisenhower, *Crusade in Europe*, p. 172. (d) Churchill's subservience to Roosevelt see Correspondence, 26, 27 May 1944. (e) On Churchill's meeting with de Gaulle, see note 6, and on 'currency question', Correspondence 9, 10 June 1944.
15. On the recognition question, Eisenhower's influence was a crucial factor.
16. (a) It is difficult to say how far Roosevelt's dislike was personal, and how far bound up with a clash between his view of the future of France and de Gaulle's. Roosevelt's plans for the future included retaining US bases in French North Africa, and he certainly would have preferred a more pliable and pro-American leader than de Gaulle. To this extent Verrier is right, though it is doubtful if Roosevelt had fully worked out all these plans *before* Torch (i.e. November 1942). Cf. note 10. Roosevelt certainly considered France not fit to rule her colonies, notably Indo-China. (b) If de Gaulle's relations with Roosevelt were conducted on 'a plane of unreason', the former's relations with Churchill alternated between periods of rational cooperation and (largely irrational) hostility and non-cooperation. Elsewhere I have compared them to a 'fever chart'. As Professor François Kersaudy has so well shown (*Churchill and de Gaulle*, 1981) Churchill's emotional temperament and de Gaulle's pride and suspicion were often a combustible mixture. De Gaulle's memoirs and Churchill's are often unsafe guides on their various disputes (e.g. Syria and the Lebanon).

CHAPTER 7: THE PROBLEM OF GERMANY

1. Sainsbury, p. 278. Eden, *Reckoning*, p. 370.
2. (a) Roosevelt sometimes referred to poor living standards of some of colonial peoples he had glimpsed on his travels. Did he, one wonders, ever think in terms of the living standards of Filipinos or Amerindians or Afro-Americans in terms of US stewardship? Perhaps. (b) At Teheran Roosevelt said to his son, 'Maybe the Russians will get strong in Europe. Whether that's bad depends on a whole lot of things'. (E. Roosevelt, *As He Saw It*, p. 186).
3. There were of course others in the UK besides Lindeman who argued for a 'peace of revenge'. Vansittart, pre-war head of Foreign Office was one, and this view was held by many of the British people. Attlee, Deputy Premier and Labour leader, had advocated a relatively harsh peace. The British Chiefs of Staff believed it would be to Britain's advantage to break Germany up, while the Foreign Office did not. (L. Woodward, *British Foreign Policy*, single volume, pp. 465–76).
4. On partition, Eden, *Reckoning*, p. 290.
5. On reparations, see Backer, *Decision to Divide Germany*, Chapters 3, 4, 5, 7.
6. (a) There appears to have been a marked difference on the possibility of separate Soviet–German peace between Washington's view and that of British Foreign Office in 1943 – and between some US and British historians today. See Sainsbury, pp. 40, 334. (b) In August 1939, the Soviet and Nazi Foreign Ministers had agreed on a third partition of Poland, and division of south-eastern Europe into spheres of interest, in the Molotov–Ribbentrop agreement.
7. For 'Fourteen Points', see H. Nicolson, *Peacemaking*, pp. 7–9, 29–34. French Premier Clemenceau remarked 'Le Bon Dieu was content with Ten!' It was Clemenceau also who dubbed Versailles: 'The Peace that passeth all understanding'.
8. (a) Churchill, *Memoirs*, IV, pp. 613–15, describes his surprise at Roosevelt's statement. (b) Churchill, Memoirs, V, p. 621 (Memo, 19 April 1944). To have said nothing on the subject of peace terms might have been best. (c) This February 1943 Memo was 'Morning Thoughts' (see note 11, Chapter 4).
9. (a) Eden, p. 379, on Washington visit. (b) State Department memo (H 24), see Backer, pp. 19–21. See also FRUS (1943) 24 July. Hull, *Memoirs*, pp. 1233–4, (see this also for Eden 'vacillation'). (c) Backer thinks Roosevelt was havering at this time but eventually came back to belief in partition. Roosevelt's habit of swinging backwards and forwards in discussion sometimes led his hearers to depart under a false impression of his views. The human failing of hearing what one wants to hear also applied perhaps to Hull.
10. (a) Teheran discussions, see Sainsbury, pp. 277–9, Moscow discussions, ibid., pp. 85–6. Churchill remarked that the President had 'said a mouthful'. (b) For EAC, ibid., pp. 69–72, 77–8, 86. See also, Eubank, pp. 285–6, 299–300, 314–6, 369–72.
11. Post-Teheran correspondence, see Churchill–Roosevelt, 2 and 6 January 1944.

12. EAC proposals, see Correspondence 29 February 1944, also Strang, *Home and Abroad*, pp. 209–12. Roosevelt and Hull always disliked and preferred to ignore the EAC, because it was London-based, this in spite of Hull's acceptance of it as the proper forum for discussion of various European problems (including German surrender terms) at Moscow Conference.

13. For State Department and Treasury Memos, July, September 1944, see Backer, pp. 25–6. Hull, I, pp. 1604–8. Welles, the main supporter of partition in the State Department, had resigned in 1943.

14. Morgan, *FDR*, p. 734. For Quebec discussions, see FRUS, 1944 (Quebec Conference), Hull, II, pp. 1602, 1610, 1614. The US system knows no principle of 'collective responsibility'. The Secretary of State is the President's principal adviser on foreign affairs, but presidents can seek advice where they wish.

15. (a) On the Morgenthau Plan, see Backer, p. 25, and his *Priming the German Economy, passim.* Hull, II, pp. 1207–8, 1602–22, Churchill, V, pp. 138, 209. Eden, pp. 475–6. FRUS (Quebec) for full discussion. (b) For US loan, see Gilbert, pp. 961–2, 964. The connection between this and acceptance of Morgenthau is fairly clear. Roosevelt seemed reluctant to commit himself until late in Conference. Gilbert implies that Roosevelt was not teasing, but sick, and unable to concentrate (p. 965): also, Roosevelt may not fully have realized Britain's financial plight. Whatever the reason, Churchill found it exasperating.

16. Sherwood, II, pp. 810, 824. Morgan, *F.D.R.*, pp. 735–6, 763. In spite of his *volte-face*, Roosevelt always hankered after the 'Morgenthau approach', and said so to Morgenthau the day before he died. (ibid., p. 763).

17. (a) Churchill told Stalin that the Morgenthau Plan was encountering opposition in the US (Woodward, pp. 474–5). (b) On Danubian Federation, see Churchill, VI, p. 210. (c) Roosevelt's *volte-face*, see Stettinius, *Roosevelt and the Russians*, p. 46. Backer, p. 32. Correspondence, 22, 24 November 1944. Eden, pp. 505, 516, on Germany.

18. Occupation Zones, see Correspondence, 7 February 1944, 23 February, 27 May 1944, 31 May 1944, 22 June 1944, 16 November 1944 ('A' and subsequent draft). Roosevelt eventually gave way but insisted on the US use of Bremen.

19. The quote is from J.R. Snell, *Meaning of Yalta.* Clemens, *Yalta* (pp. 281–2) states, rather misleadingly, 'they [the Big 3] agreed to the inclusion of the word dismemberment in the protocol, the terms of surrender', etc., ignoring the qualification, 'if they thought it necessary', which left future action in doubt.

20. Stettinius pp. 234–5. Full accounts of this and other discussions are in FRUS, 1945 (Yalta Conference).

21. (a) The War Department's directive to US occupying authorities in Germany (J.C.S. 1067) was influenced by Morgenthau's approach, and Roosevelt decided in favour of this directive, over State Department protests (see Backer, p. 40). (b) On the question of

Roosevelt and Churchill's influence, it could obviously be argued that the post-war future of Germany was essentially decided by (1) The position of Western and Soviet armies on VE Day and (2) Decisions on the occupation zonal boundaries. The two leaders by their decisions certainly influenced both of these outcomes. There is, however, a little more to it than that, and their decisions also determined the scale of Allied bombing; and Roosevelt's decisions influenced the beginning of dismantling of industry. Both of these 'cleared the decks' for remodernization of German industry under the Marshall Plan. Similarly Churchill's rearguard action against dismemberment – particularly radical dismemberment – *was* important. The ultimate division of Germany into two states and linking of West Germany with NATO was not too far from what British Chiefs of Staff had wanted, or from an important part of Churchill's wishes.

CHAPTER 8: THE GENERALISSIMO

1. There is no question of Roosevelt's dislike of European imperialism. He made no secret (to Churchill and others) of this. But it does not follow that throughout the war Roosevelt had a 'hidden agenda' to liquidate the British Empire; (as Morgan in his biography suggests). Quite frankly Roosevelt had more pressing problems on his mind most of the time. What is true is that Roosevelt (and the US Service Chiefs and US political leaders) did not wish to see American lives expended to restore the British Empire; and where he thought he had the power (as in relation to French North Africa and Indo-China) he was not averse to seeking to undermine colonial system. When the crunch came, however, at the end of the war, he did not try very hard to prevent colonial authority from being re-established.

2. (a) Chiang was not only a natural conservative, but dependent for support on equally conservative elements in Chinese society. The more liberal section of the intelligentsia were gradually alienated from his leadership: the peasantry also by his links with feudal landlords (whereas Chinese Communists had a land reform programme). (b) Stilwell was Army C-in-C US forces in China-Burma and Chief of Staff to Chiang Kai-shek, and later also Deputy to Mountbatten in SEAC. It was an impossible, even absurd combination of offices.

3. (a) Cf. Hull, pp. 1583, 1585, 1587 for US view on China. *Eden*, p. 377. (b) Stalin appears to have had no very high opinion of the Chinese Communists. According to Djilas (paperback edition, p. 141) he advised them to come to an agreement with Chiang. It was not really in Soviet interests to have a powerful China on its borders, and Stalin probably saw Chinese Communists, who were not at all

subservient to Moscow, and with whom relations had sometimes been strained, as potential rivals for leadership of the Communist world. A Sino-Soviet split should not have come as a surprise, except to those who regarded the post-war Communist bloc as solid and monolithic. (c) Churchill's views, see Churchill IV, pp. 505, 525, 837. The latter did not *always* remember to be tactful with Americans on this subject (see p. 172). Eden usually was (Eden, p. 376). Correspondence 3, 7 February 1942.

4. For SEAC, see Churchill–Roosevelt Correspondence, 19, 30 June, 3 July 1943. Churchill's first suggestion for SEAC 'Supremo' was Air Marshall Sholto Douglas, whom the Americans regarded as anti-American (he had indeed been somewhat critical of his US allies). Roosevelt suggested Cunningham, who got on well with Americans, or Montgomery (perhaps Americans already felt Montgomery should be removed from Europe). Finally they settled for Mountbatten.

5. (a) Churchill, IV, pp. 702–3. Churchill rather overlooked the fact that the Japanese had to fight against the same elements in Burma, and were no more used to them than were the British. (b) On Soviet promise to enter Far East War, see Sainsbury, pp. 111. Stalin repeated this promise at Teheran (ibid., p. 229).

6. (a) Correspondence, 7 January 1943, on the Burma campaign. Marshall always pushed for it, though Allied planners in 1943 already doubted its utility. (b) Roosevelt–Chiang meetings are fully recorded in FRUS, 1943, (Cairo and Teheran conferences); see also Sainsbury, Chapter VII; Eubank, pp. 128–31, 161–3, 169.

7. Cadogan, *Diaries*, p. 559. Churchill–Roosevelt Correspondence, 14 October 1943, 2 November 1943.

8. Churchill, V, p. 290, gives his impression of Chiang. Sainsbury, pp. 188–9, and ibid., pp. 260–1, and p. 321, for promises to Chiang and concessions to USSR. See also Eubank, pp. 129–31, 161–3, 169, 246, 323, 476.

9. Forty years after Yalta, journalists were still writing articles which accepted Yalta as the crucial venue for all important decisions, including those on the Far East.

10. Churchill–Roosevelt Correspondence, 10 March 1944. 'Bogged down in Burma'. (Churchill to British Chiefs), Gilbert, p. 884. To Roosevelt he wrote 'tied down' 10 August 1944). Churchill's more vigorous complaint was in a letter to his wife.

11. (a) For Hopkins letter, see Gilbert, p. 859. (b) On Germany, Sainsbury, p. 163. (c) On China, Morgan, p. 742, 753 (Wallace), 711 (Morgenthau). Cf. Thorne *Allies of a Kind*, pp. 427–33.

12. (a) Gilbert, p. 1183, (Churchill's 'slip'). (b) Stalin made two concessions to the Chinese. Dairen was to become a 'free port', unlike Port Arthur which was to be leased (that is under complete Soviet control): control of the Manchurian railway system would not be solely Russian, but would be shared with the Chinese. (c) For Churchill's remark, see Eden, pp. 513–14.

13. 'Long period of reform', see Thorne, p. 579.

CHAPTER 9: 'BY THEIR FRUITS YE SHALL KNOW THEM'

1. As I have indicated, I do not think Roosevelt's decision for Torch was mainly influenced by a sinister desire to take over North Africa after the war. Roosevelt was, however, certainly inclined to treat France and French possessions in a cavalier fashion.

2. (a) The abandonment of 'Europe First' enabled Admiral King to commandeer vital equipment, especially landing-craft, for Pacific operations in 1942–3. Without these craft amphibian operations like Overlord could not be carried out, at any rate not simultaneously with Mediterranean amphibious operations (Husky, Avalanche, Shingle, Anvil). (b) There were three possible outcomes of Sledgehammer, viz: (1) the worst case, complete failure: Britain and US would have lost valuable men and equipment, but, with Marshall behind it, Round-Up would probably still have taken place in 1943. (2) A permanent lodgement: The same would probably still have applied, viz: Round-Up in 1943. (3) Sledgehammer might have been abandoned: Round-Up in 1943 would have gone ahead.

3. (a) Tension between the USSR and the West crippled the enforcement powers of the UN Security Council from the beginning, and, in particular, the military sanctions provisions (Articles 42–47, UN Charter) have never been implemented to *enforce* decisions, except, with somewhat dubious legality, in the case of Korea, 1950–3, and more validly against Iraq, 1991. Small contingents to monitor truce and armistice agreements have been more common. Great Power vetoes have often succeeded in blocking even discussion by the Security Council. (b) Churchill always reacted explosively when the subject of 'trusteeship' came up. For a typical instance at Yalta, see Stettinius, pp. 210–11. As has been pointed out, Roosevelt did not in fact take effective steps to prevent restoration of the colonial system. Churchill's view that progress towards self-government must be correlated to the particular conditions of each colony was not wholly misguided, though he would probably have seen such progress, in the case of Africa, as being spread over a hundred years at least.

Select Bibliography

Alexander, Field Marshal Lord *Memoirs*, London, Cassell, 1962.

Ambrose, S.E. *The Supreme Commander*, London, Cassell, 1971.

Armstrong, A. *Unconditional Surrender*, Rutgers University Press, New Brunswick, 1961.

Arnold, H.H. *Global Mission*, New York, Harper, 1949.

Auty, P. and Cloggs, R. *British Policy towards Wartime Resistance in Yugoslavia and Greece*, London, Macmillan, 1975.

Avon, Earl of *The Reckoning*, London, Cassell, 1965.

Backer, J.H. *The Decision to Divide Germany*, Durham, NC, Duke University Press, 1978.

Barker, E. *British Policy in South-East Europe*, London, Macmillan, 1976.

——— *Churchill and Eden at War*, London, Macmillan, 1978.

Benes, E. *Memoirs*, London, Houghton, 1954.

Blum, J.M. *From the Morgenthau Diaries* (3 vols), Boston, Mass., Houghton, 1963–7.

Bohlen, C.E. *Witness to History*, London, Weidenfeld, 1973.

Bryant, Sir A. (ed.) *The Alanbrooke Diaries* (2 vols), London, Collins, 1957, and Fontana (pb), 1965.

Buhite, R.D. *Patrick Hurley and American Foreign Policy*, Ithaca, NY, Cornell University Press, 1973.

Burns, J.M. *Roosevelt, The Soldier of Freedom*, New York, Harcourt Brace, 1970.

Burridge, T.M. *Clement Attlee*, London, Jonathan Cape, 1986.

——— *British Labour and Hitler's War*, London, J.M. Dent, 1976.

Butcher, H. *My Three Years with Eisenhower*, London, Heinemann, 1946.

Calvocoressi, P. and Wint, G. *Total War*, London, Allen Lane, 1972.

Carlton, D. *Anthony Eden*, London, Allen Lane, 1982.

Ciechanowsky, J. *Defeat in Victory*, New York, Doubleday, 1947.

Charmley, J. *Churchill, the End of Glory*, London, Hodder, 1993.

Chiang Kai-shek, General *China's Destiny*, Ed. P. Jaafer, New York, 1947.

Churchill, W.S. *The Second World War* (6 vols), London, Cassell, 1948–54.

Clemens, D.S. *Yalta*, Oxford, OUP, 1970.

Clark, M.W., General *Calculated Risk*, Harper, New York, 1950 and London, Harrap, 1951; also Panther (pb), 1956.

Cunningham, Admiral Viscount *A Sailor's Odyssey*, London, Hutchinson, 1951.

Dallek, R. *Franklin Roosevelt and American Foreign Policy*, New York and London, OUP, 1979.

Deakin, F.W., Barker, E. and Chadwick, J. (eds) *British Political and Military Strategy in Central, Eastern and Southern Europe*, London, Macmillan, 1988.

Deane, J.R. *The Strange Alliance*, London, Murray, 1947.

de Gaulle, C. *War Memoirs* (3 vols), London, Weidenfeld, 1955–60.

Deutscher, I. *Stalin*, London, OUP, 1949, and Penguin (pb), 1951.

Dilks, D. (ed.). *The Diaries of Sir Alexander Cadogan*, London, Cassell, 1971.

Divine, R. *Roosevelt and World War II*, Baltimore, Md, Johns Hopkins, 1969.

Djilas, M. *Conversations with Stalin*, New York, Harcourt Brace, 1962, and London, Penguin (pb), 1951.

Edmonds, R. *The Big Three: Churchill, Roosevelt and Stalin*, London, Hamish Hamilton, 1991, and Penguin (pb) 1992.

Eisenhower, D.D. *Crusade in Europe*, New York, Doubleday, and London, Heinemann, 1948.

Eubank, K. *Summit at Teheran*, New York, Morrow, 1985.

Feis, H. *Churchill, Roosevelt, Stalin*, Princeton, NJ, Princeton University Press, 1957.

—— *The Road to Pearl Harbour*, Princeton, NJ, Princeton University Press, 1950.

Fischer, L. *The Road to Yalta: Soviet Foreign Relations, 1941–5*, New York, Harper, 1972.

Fraser, General Sir David, *Alanbrooke*, London, Collins, 1982.

Funk, A.L. *De Gaulle, The Crucial Years*, Kansas, Kansas State University Press, 1968.

—— *The Politics of Torch*, Kansas, Kansas State University Press, 1974.

Gaddis, J.L. *The United States and the Origins of the Cold War*, New York, Columbia, 1972.

Gilbert, M. *Their Finest Hour* (vol. VI of Churchill Biography), London.

—— *The Road to Victory* (vol. VII of Churchill Biography), London, Heinemann, 1986.

Giraud, General Henri, *Un Seul But, la Victoire*, Paris, Julliard, 1949.

Gladwyn, Lord *Memoirs*, London, Weidenfeld, 1972.

Greenfield, K.R. *American Strategy in World War II*, Baltimore, Md, Johns Hopkins, 1963.

—— *Command Decisions*, New York, Harcourt Brace, 1959.

Grigg, J. *1943: The Victory that Never Was*, London, Eyre Methuen, 1980.

Harriman, A. and Abel, E. *Special Envoy*, London, Hutchinson, 1976.

Harvey, J. (ed.) *The Diplomatic Diaries of Oliver Harvey*, London, Collins, 1970.

Herz, M.F. *The Beginnings of the Cold War*, New York and London, McGraw-Hill, 1969.

Higgins, T. *Winston Churchill and the Second Front*, New York, OUP, 1957.

Howard, Sir M. *The Mediterranean Strategy in World War II*, London, Weidenfeld, 1968.

Hull, Cordell *Memoirs* (2 vols), London, Hodder & Stoughton, 1948.

Ismay, General Lord *Memoirs*, London, Heinemann, 1960.

Kersaudy, F. *Churchill and de Gaulle*, London, Collins, 1981.

Kimball, W.F. *Churchill and Roosevelt: the Complete Correspondence* (3 vols) Princeton, NJ, Princeton University Press, 1984.

—— *Franklin D. Roosevelt and the World Crisis*, London, D.C. Heath, 1974.

—— *The Juggler: Franklin Roosevelt as War Statesman*, Princeton, NJ, Princeton University Press, 1992.

King, Fleet Admiral E.J., and Whitehill, W.M. *Fleet Admiral King*, New York, Norton, 1952.

Kucklick, B. *American Policy and the Division of Germany*, Ithaca, NY, Cornell University Press, 1972.

Langer, W.L. *Our Vichy Gamble*, New York, Knopf, 1947.

Leahy, Fleet Admiral W.D. *I Was There*, New York, McGraw-Hill, 1950.

Lewin, R. *Churchill as Warlord*, London, Batsford, 1973.

Lyttleton, O. (Lord Chandos) *The Chandos Memoirs*, London, Bodley Head, 1962.

Macmillan, H. *The Blast of War*, London, Macmillan, 1967.

Maisky, I. *Memoirs of a Soviet Ambassador*, London, Hutchinson, 1967.

Mastny, V. *Russia's Road to the Cold War*, New York, Columbia University Press, 1979.

McJimsey, V. *Harry Hopkins*, Cambridge, Mass., Harvard University Press, 1987.

McNeill, W.H. *America, Britain and Russia*, London, OUP, 1953.

Messer, R.L. *The End of an Alliance*, Chapel Hill, NC, North Carolina University Press, 1985.

Micolajczyk, S. *The Pattern of Soviet Domination*, London, Sampson Low, 1948 (published as *The Rape of Poland*, New York, McGraw-Hill, 1948).

Moore, R.J. *Churchill, Cripps and India*, London, OUP, 1979.

Moran, Lord *Winston Churchill, the Struggle for Survival*, London, Constable, 1966, and Sphere (pb), 1968.

Morgan, T. *F.D.R.*, New York, Simon & Schuster, and London, Constable, 1966.

Murphy, R. *Diplomat Among Warriors*, New York, Doubleday, and London, Collins, 1964.

North, R.C. *Moscow and the Chinese Communists*, Stanford, Ca., Stanford University Press, 1953.

Payne, R. *Chiang Kai Shek*, New York, Weybright & Tolley, 1969.

Pelling, H. *Winston Churchill*, London, Macmillan, 1974.

Pogue, F. *Ordeal and Hope*, New York, Viking, 1966.

——— *The Organiser of Victory*, New York, Viking, 1973.

Pratt, J.W. *Cordell Hull*, New York, Cooper Square, 1964.

Range, W. *Franklin D. Roosevelt's World Order*, Athens, Ga, Georgia University Press, 1959.

Richards, D. *Portal of Hungerford*, London, Heinemann, 1977.

Roosevelt, Eleanor *This I Remember*, New York, Harper, 1949.

Roosevelt, Elliot *As He Saw It*, New York, Duell, Sloan & Pearce, 1946.

Sainsbury, K.A.F. *The North African Landings: a Strategic Decision*, London, Davis Poynter, 1976.

——— *The Turning Point*, London, OUP, 1985.

Sherwood, R.S. *The White House Papers of Harry L. Hopkins* (2 vols), London, Eyre & Spottiswoode, 1948.

Slim, Field Marshal Lord *Defeat into Victory*, London, Cassell, (and pb), 1956.

Smith, Gaddis *American Diplomacy During the Second World War*, New York, Wiley, 1965.

Snell, J. (ed.) *The Meaning of Yalta*, Baton Rouge, La, Louisiana State University Press, 1956.

—— *Wartime Origins of the Dilemma over Germany,* New Orleans, La, Hauser, 1959.

Soviet Commission on Foreign Diplomatic Documents *Correspondence between the Chairman of the Council of Ministers of the U.S.S.R. and the Presidents of the U.S.A. and the Prime Ministers of Britain,* Moscow, Foreign Languages Publishing House, 1957.

Spector, R.H. *Eagle Against the Sun,* New York, Macmillan, 1984, and London, Viking, 1985.

Steele, R.W. *The First Offensive,* Bloomington, Ind., Indiana University Press, 1973.

Stettinius, E. *Roosevelt and the Russians,* London, Jonathan Cape, 1950.

Stimson, H.L and Bundy, McG. *On Active Service in Peace and War,* New York, Harper, 1947.

Stoler, M. *The Politics of the Second Front,* Westport, Conn., and London, Greenwood, 1977.

Strang, Lord *At Home and Abroad,* London, Deutsch, 1956.

Thompson, K.W. *Winston Churchill's World View,* Baton Rouge, La, Louisiana State University Press, 1983.

Thorne, C. *Allies of a Kind,* London, Hamish Hamilton, 1978.

Tsou, T. *America's Failure in China* (2 vols), Chicago, Chicago University Press, 1963.

Ulam, A.B. *Stalin,* New York, Viking, 1973.

Verrier, A. *Assassination in Algiers.* Macmillan, 1990.

Viorst, M. *Hostile Allies: F.D.R. and de Gaulle,* New York, Doubleday, 1975.

Warner, G. *Pierre Laval and the Eclipse of France,* London, Eyre & Spottiswood, 1968.

Werth, A. *Russia at War,* London, Barrie & Rockliffe, 1964, and Pan (pb), 1965.

Wheeler-Bennett, J. (eds) *Action This Day,* London, Macmillan, 1968.

Wheeler-Bennett, J. and Nicholls, A. *The Semblance of Peace,* London, Macmillan, 1972.

White, D.S. *Seeds of Discord,* Syracuse, NY, Syracuse University Press, 1964.

Wilmot, C. *The Struggle for Europe,* London, Collins, 1952.

Ziegler, P. *Mountbatten,* London, Collins, 1985, and Fontana (pb), 1986.

DOCUMENTS AND MORE DETAILED SOURCES

The military side of the war is covered in great detail in the multi-volume official Histories, published by Her Majesty's Stationery Office and the US Department of the Army respectively. The volumes on Grand Strategy in each series (including Leighton and Coakley on *Logistics and Strategy* in the US volumes) are of particular interest. US diplomatic documents on the war have been fully published in the *Foreign Relations of the United States* series, which includes special volumes on the various summit conferences. A selection of British military documents is given in the official histories, and of the diplomatic documents in Sir R. Woodward, *British Foreign Policy in the Second World War* (5 vols), but many remain unpublished.

British documents are mainly located in the Public Record Office, Kew Gardens, London. These include: (1) Prime Minister's papers (most importantly the PREM III–IV series): (2) War Cabinet Minutes and Memoranda (WM and WP series filed under CAB 65, 66, 68): (3) Defence Committee Minutes and Memoranda (D.O. series, filed under CAB 69): (4) British Chiefs of State Minutes and Memoranda (COS series, filed under CAB 79): (5) Records of War Conferences, filed under various CAB numbers: (6) Combined Chiefs of Staff Minutes and Memoranda (CCS series, filed under CAB 88).

Churchill's private papers and those of Attlee, Bevin, Halifax and Strang are at Churchill College, Cambridge; those of Cherwell (Lindeman) at Nuffield College, Oxford. The personal diaries of Brooke and Ismay are at King's College, London, and of Cunningham at the British Museum.

US military papers are mainly at Washington, under the control of the Department of the Army. These include Chief of Staff records (WDCSA series), War Department Operations Division (OPD series) and Joint Chiefs of Staff papers (JCS series). There are also the Marshall papers (George C. Marshall Library, Lexington, Virginia), the Stimson diary at Yale University, the Eisenhower papers (published in five vols by A.D. Chandler, Baltimore, 1970) and the Arnold, Knox and Leahy papers in the Library of Congress, Washington. Diplomatic papers include: (1) State Department papers (National Archives, Washington); (2) Hull papers (Library of Congress); (3) Roosevelt and Hopkins papers (Roosevelt Library, Hyde Park, New York State).

Index

Note: Roosevelt, Churchill, the US and Britain are referred to so frequently that they are not separately indexed.